A CONFEDERATE
BIOGRAPHY

A CONFEDERATE
BIOGRAPHY

THE CRUISE OF THE CSS *SHENANDOAH*

Dwight Sturtevant Hughes

NAVAL INSTITUTE PRESS

Annapolis, Maryland

Naval Institute Press
291 Wood Road
Annapolis, MD 21402

Library of Congress Cataloging-in-Publication Data

Hughes, Dwight Sturtevant, author.
  A Confederate biography : the cruise of the CSS Shenandoah / Dwight Sturtevant Hughes.
    pages cm
  Summary: "From October 1864 to November 1865, the officers of the CSS Shenandoah carried the Confederacy and the conflict of the Civil War around the globe through extreme weather, alien surroundings, and the people they encountered. Her officers were the descendants of Deep South plantation aristocracy and Old Dominion first families: a nephew of Robert E. Lee, a grandnephew of founder George Mason, and descendants of one of George Washington's generals and of an aid to Washington. One was even an uncle of a young Theodore Roosevelt and another was son-in-law to Raphael Semmes. Shenandoah's mission — commerce raiding (guerre de course) — was a central component of U.S. naval and maritime heritage, a profitable business, and a watery form of guerrilla warfare. These Americans stood in defense of their country as they understood it, pursuing a difficult and dangerous mission in which they succeeded spectacularly after it no longer mattered. This is a biography of a ship and a cruise, and a microcosm of the Confederate-American experience"— Provided by publisher.
  ISBN 978-1-61251-841-1 (hardback : alkaline paper) — ISBN 978-1-61251-842-8 (e-book) 1. Shenandoah (Cruiser) 2. United States—History—Civil War, 1861–1865—Naval operations, Confederate. 3. Confederate States of America. Navy—Officers—Biography. 4. Sailors—Confederate States of America—Biography. 5. Confederate States of America—History. 6. Voyages around the world—History—19th century. 7. Privateering—Bering Sea—History—19th century. 8. Bering Sea—History, Naval. 9. Ocean travel—History—19th century. I. Title.
  E599.S5H84 2015
  973.7'57—dc23

                                                                      2015029139

23 22 21 20 19 18 17 16 15   9 8 7 6 5 4 3 2 1
First printing

To my loving wife, Judi, the light of my life. She encouraged me to begin this book many years ago while I was undergoing cancer treatments and inspired me throughout.

If I take wings of the morning, and dwell in the uttermost parts of the sea;

Even there shall thy hand lead me, and thy right hand shall hold me.

———————————

Psalm 139:9–10 (KJV)

Contents

Cruise of the CSS *Shenandoah*   x

Plans of the CSS *Shenandoah*   xii

Preface   xvii

Introduction   1

1   "Otro *Alabama*"   6

2   "Do . . . the Greatest Injury"   14

3   "None but Fiends Could"   24

4   "Now Came the Trouble"   36

5   "Oh, It's a Grand Sight"   47

6   "Running Her Easting Down"   58

7   The Queen of the *Delphine*   69

8   End of the International Road   80

9   The War Down Under   91

10   Charley the Cook   102

11   "On the Bright Blue Sea"   113

12   "The Abomination of Isolation"   124

13   "Upon a Stone Altar"   135

14   The World on Fire   146

15   Invading the North   158

16   High Tide of the Confederacy   169

17   "The Darkest Day"   180

18   "A Feeling Approaching Panic"   191

19   "Having Done My Duty"   202

Epilogue   209

Notes   215

Selected Bibliography   225

Index   231

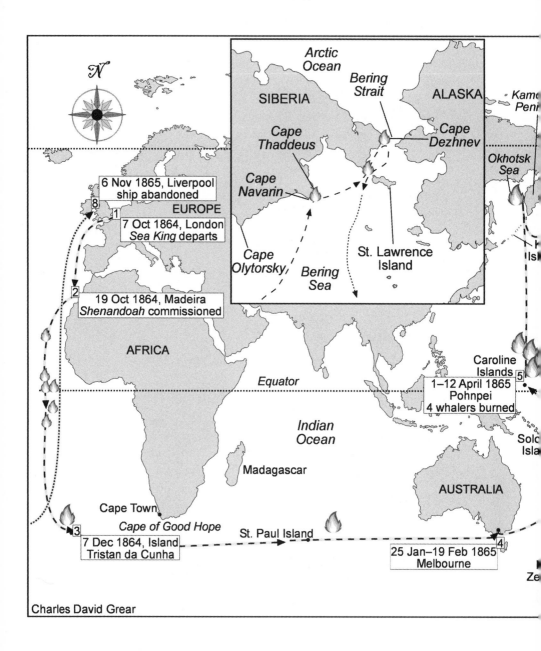

Cruise of the CSS *Shenandoah*
19 October 1864–6 November 1865

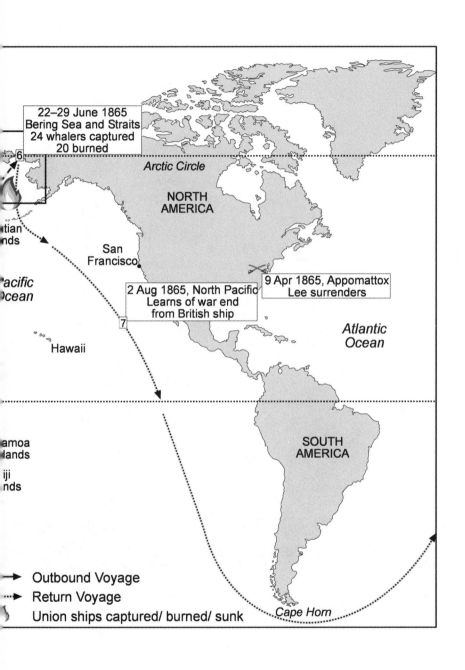

22–29 June 1865
Bering Sea and Straits
24 whalers captured
20 burned

6

Arctic Circle

NORTH
AMERICA

San
Francisco

2 Aug 1865, North Pacific
Learns of war end
from British ship

9 Apr 1865, Appomattox
Lee surrenders

tian
nds

acific
cean

7

Hawaii

Atlantic
Ocean

amoa
lands

iji
nds

SOUTH
AMERICA

→ Outbound Voyage
···► Return Voyage
Union ships captured/ burned/ sunk

Cape Horn

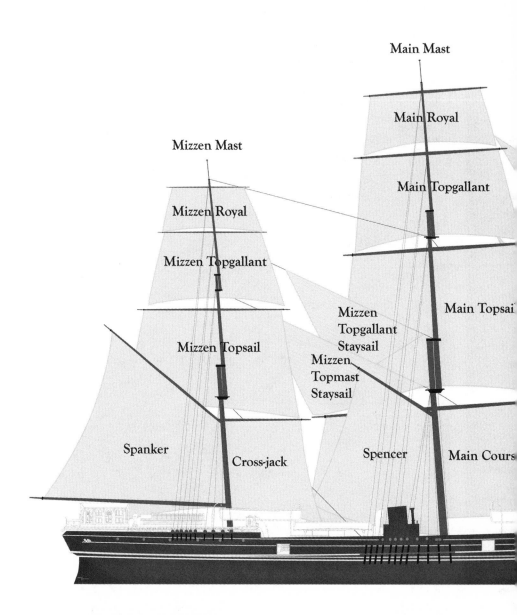

CSS *Shenandoah* Sail Plan
From Builder's Plans, National Maritime Museum, Greenwich
J. M. Caiella

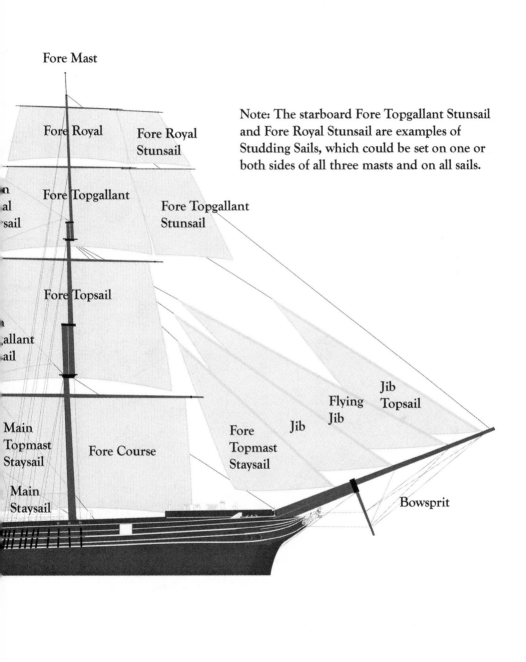

Fore Mast

Fore Royal

Fore Royal
Stunsail

Note: The starboard Fore Topgallant Stunsail
and Fore Royal Stunsail are examples of
Studding Sails, which could be set on one or
both sides of all three masts and on all sails.

Fore Topgallant

Fore Topgallant
Stunsail

Fore Topsail

n
al
sail

allant
ail

Main
Topmast
Staysail

Main
Staysail

Fore Course

Fore
Topmast
Staysail

Jib

Flying
Jib

Jib
Topsail

Bowsprit

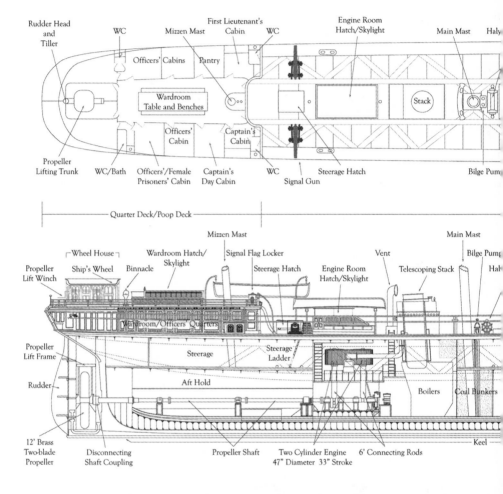

Rudder Head and Tiller — WC — Officers' Cabins — Mizzen Mast — First Lieutenant's Cabin — Pantry — WC — Engine Room Hatch/Skylight — Main Mast — Haly

Wardroom Table and Benches — Stack

Officers' Cabin — Captain's Cabin

Propeller Lifting Trunk — WC/Bath — Officers'/Female Prisoners' Cabin — Captain's Day Cabin — WC — Signal Gun — Steerage Hatch — Bilge Pum

Quarter Deck/Poop Deck

Wheel House — Wardroom Hatch/Skylight — Mizzen Mast — Signal Flag Locker — Vent — Main Mast — Bilge Pump

Propeller Lift Winch — Ship's Wheel — Binnacle — Steerage Hatch — Engine Room Hatch/Skylight — Telescoping Stack — Hal

Wardroom/Officers' Quarters

Propeller Lift Frame — Steerage — Steerage Ladder

Rudder — Aft Hold — Boilers — Coal Bunkers

12' Brass Two-blade Propeller — Disconnecting Shaft Coupling — Propeller Shaft — Two Cylinder Engine 47" Diameter 33" Stroke — 6' Connecting Rods — Keel

American Confederate Cruiser *Shenandoah* ex–*Sea King No. 42* Later the Sultan of Zanzibar's Yacht

The CSS *Shenandoah* was an auxiliary screw steamer with 200 horsepower vertical reciprocating engines by A&J Inglis and a design speed of nine knots.

From Builder's Plans, National Maritime Museum, Greenwich
J. M. Caiella

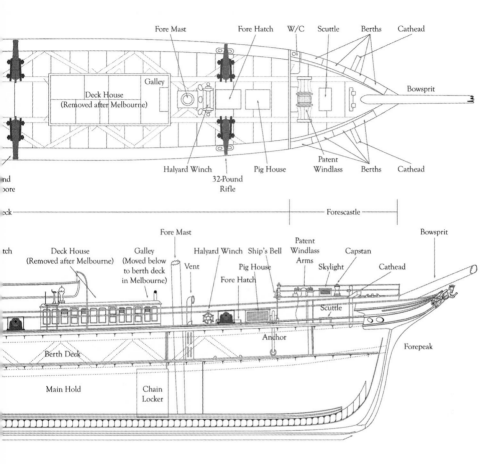

Fore Mast   Fore Hatch   W/C   Scuttle   Berths   Cathead

Galley

Deck House
(Removed after Melbourne)

Bowsprit

Halyard Winch   Pig House   Patent   Berths   Cathead
                              Windlass

32-Pound
Rifle

nd
oore

eck   Forescastle

tch   Deck House   Galley   Halyard Winch   Ship's Bell   Patent   Capstan   Bowsprit
       (Removed after Melbourne) (Moved below   Windlass
                          to berth deck   Vent   Pig House   Arms   Skylight   Cathead
                          in Melbourne)
                    Fore Mast   Fore Hatch

Fore Mast

Scuttle

Berth Deck   Anchor   Forepeak

Main Hold   Chain
                 Locker

Dimensions	
Length between perpendiculars	222' 7"
Extreme breadth	32' 8"
Depth of hold to top of floors	20' 6"
Tons burden	1,152
Gross tonnage	1,018
Registry tonnage	790

Preface

The officers of the CSS *Shenandoah*, along with those who sent them and those who confronted them, left an abundance of first-person accounts. This embarrassment of riches in primary sources generated a daunting, but rewarding, task of editing. And so, this tale can be told almost exclusively by those who lived it. The accounts are concentrated in four personal cruise journals, two memoirs, exhaustive official documentation of postwar claims against Great Britain for supporting Confederate commerce raiders, the ever-useful *Official Records of the Union and Confederate Navies*, and contemporary newspapers. Collectively, these sources provide virtually every contemporary word written by those involved in or concerned about the events described.

The author has attempted to edit, condense, collate, paraphrase, and quote their words into a consistent narrative, elucidating those events and times (as much as can be imagined) from their perspectives and leaving judgments to the reader. Most quotes derive from the four personal journals and the annotated log of the captain. Because these sources are chronological and organized by date, usually without page numbers, they are cited only the first time a quote from the writer is encountered. Unless otherwise noted, subsequent quotes from that writer are from the same source on or about the date in the context of the narrative.

Secondary sources contribute background and context not provided by direct participants. The author's personal training and experiences have proved helpful in clarifying the esoteric life at sea for those not familiar with it. His historical judgments beyond a love of the naval service, the sea, ships, and their history are, it is hoped, few and easily identified. The objective of this volume is to provide an entertaining and educational story not only for naval and maritime history enthusiasts but also for anyone who would enjoy a fresh perspective on the Civil War, even if they have never looked at it from across the water.

Introduction

Admiral Raphael Semmes, the foremost sailor of the Confederacy, introduced his *Memoirs of Service Afloat* with the following:

> The cruise of a ship is a biography. The ship becomes a personification. She not only "walks the waters like a thing of life," but she speaks in moving accents to those capable of interpreting her. But her interpreter must be a seaman, and not a landsman.

A ship is fundamentally a machine—an instrument of marine transportation, ocean commerce, and naval warfare. But to those who create it, to those who sail or encounter it, and indeed to one who studies the records a century and a half later, a ship is a great deal more. It is a highly sophisticated artifact of human ingenuity. It takes on vibrant life and distinct personality (traditionally female in a historically male profession). It engages the passions. A ship can be, therefore, a central character in a life story through which we view more clearly our ancestors, their epoch, and their momentous war. Of course, she is all of these things—and not just an inanimate object—only because of the men in her life and through their collective experiences in her company.

The officers of the Confederate States ship *Shenandoah* were a cross section of the South from Maryland, Virginia, North and South Carolina, Georgia, Mississippi, Louisiana, and Missouri. From 19 October 1864 to 6 November 1865, they carried the Confederacy and the conflict around the globe and to the ends of the earth through every extreme of sea and storm. Their observations looking back from the most remote and alien surroundings imaginable, along with the viewpoints of the people they encountered, provide a unique perspective of the war with elements both common to and differing from land-bound compatriots.

These officers included scions of the deep South plantation aristocracy and of Old Dominion first families: a nephew of Robert E. Lee; a grandnephew of founding father George Mason; descendants of men who served directly under George Washington in the Revolution; and a relative, by marriage, of Matthew Fontaine Maury. One officer was an uncle of a young Theodore Roosevelt and another the son-in-law of Raphael Semmes. The officer from Missouri, by contrast, was a middle-class Midwesterner and former drugstore clerk. All but two, the captain and the ship's surgeon, were under the age of twenty-five.

They considered themselves Americans, Southerners, rebels, warriors, and seamen embarking on what would be the voyage of their lives. They already had suffered three and a half years of bloody, discouraging conflict on board puny gunboats and lumbering ironclads up and down the interior waters of their fledgling country, frequently on the same vessels or in the same battles; a few were veterans of the CSS *Alabama*'s two-year cruise. They did not all fight for the same reasons but stood together in defense of their country as they understood it, pursuing a difficult mission in which they succeeded spectacularly after it no longer mattered.

Having sacrificed careers in the U.S. Navy that nurtured them, these men struggled to reproduce its essence in their new navy, one with few ships. Two of the five lieutenants had been deepwater sailors in the U.S. Navy and one in the merchant service. Four had attended the new Naval Academy at Annapolis, and two midshipmen had been appointed to the academy before secession changed their loyalties. Two of the lieutenants followed distinguished naval fathers who had served in Pacific exploring expeditions, in antislavery patrols on the coast of Africa, with Commodore Matthew C. Perry at the opening of Japan, and during the Mexican War. One of the fathers had been Naval Academy commandant of midshipmen; both fathers became senior officers in Confederate service.

Three heritages drove the men of *Shenandoah*. As grandsons of revolutionaries, they believed profoundly in liberty and democracy. They shared the atavistic social mores of the Southern gentleman class along with its timeless dedication to family, country, duty, and personal integrity. These characteristics were reinforced in their central identities as officers of the Confederate States navy, to which they applied the Southern martial tradition just as energetically as did their army brothers in arms.

The men they led, however, were a polyglot assemblage of international merchant sailors enlisted in foreign ports or from captured ships with enticements of gold and threats of confinement. They were of nearly every nation and color—including born-and-raised Yankees and several African Americans—representing that motley mixture of seafaring humanity operating within its own rigidly authoritarian and cramped society. In their professional roles, Confederate navy officers and seamen had more in common with Northern counterparts than with Southern comrades.

And all of them served *Shenandoah*—their mistress, their protector, their enabler. Having finally an opportunity to take the fight to the enemy in a fine blue-water ship, these Southerners endowed her with all the frustrated longing for victory, retribution, peace, and personal and professional honor. She was a magnificent ship, a reflection of a rich maritime heritage. The square-rigged sailing ship is among the oldest and the most complex creations of the human race, evolving slowly over millennia from fundamental concepts. For five centuries these vehicles dominated the oceans and enabled global civilization; they reached their most effective as well as their most esthetically pleasing expression in the clippers. Probably no other single technology had such far-reaching impact over so immense a span of time.

But in a few decades, natural elements of wood, hemp, and canvas would give way to forged and manufactured materials of iron and steel. The siren call of wind in the rigging was silenced by the thump of the engines and the roar of mechanical blowers; the fragrance of the sea was tainted by coal smoke. *Shenandoah* was a paradigm of dramatic transitions in the midst of the Industrial Revolution, and she presented stark contradictions: a valiant warship to Southerners, a hated pirate to Northerners. She was a swift and graceful tea clipper and a state-of-the-art steamer, an amalgam of wooden hull and iron frames, the epitome of the ancient art of tall ship construction, and a prime example of the new technology of the Machine Age. *Shenandoah* represented the quintessence of commercial sail while serving as one of history's most effective commerce destroyers. Nearly perfect for her mission, she was a new kind of warship, a prototype of cruisers to follow and an example for raiders stalking the oceans through the world wars.

The naval profession itself was undergoing wrenching transformations from the staid, inferior, wooden sailing Navy to (for a few years at least) the second largest and most powerful and technologically advanced fleet in the world. The old officer clique was small and inbred with its peculiar ethos— where family careers, intermarriage, and the most detached and esoteric of callings created a tight web of social kinship not unlike the Southern gentry. A generational clash arose between the orthodox antebellum Navy fettered by tradition and the professional officer corps emerging from the new Naval Academy, rapid technological advances, nineteenth-century social reforms, and the crucible of war. The academy represented a revolution in officer training, one that invoked intense dispute. This generational difference was manifest between the captain of *Shenandoah* and his young lieutenants.

Shenandoah's mission—commerce raiding or *guerre de course*—was a central component of U.S. Navy and maritime heritage, a profitable business, and a watery form of guerilla warfare in the spirit of John Mosby and Bedford Forrest with a bit of W. T. Sherman. To the consternation of Yankee shippers and ship owners, a few rebel cruisers virtually drove the American merchant marine from the sea and crippled the already declining whaling industry. As intended, they had considerable impact on home-front morale, boosting Confederate confidence while squeezing the Lincoln administration to achieve peace at the expense of Southern independence. But the strategic effectiveness of *guerre de course* during the Civil War remains questionable, and it was not considered even by its proponents to be the most professionally fulfilling or glorious of enterprises.

The Civil War also had repercussions far beyond familiar domestic battlefields and was, in turn, significantly influenced by faraway people and events. Navies by their nature operate in, are regulated by, and act upon the international arena in both war and peace—largely unobserved by most citizens. International affairs governed by complex and antiquated maritime law played a potentially decisive role in the conflict. The neutrality, or lack thereof, by major European powers was a central concern to both sides. As the most powerful maritime and imperial power, Great Britain wrestled with conflicting political forces that pushed the causes of both North and South. The fight across the Atlantic seriously endangered British trade, economy, and domestic stability; it threatened a disastrous third war with former colonies. *Shenandoah* and her sisters were smack in the middle of this diplomatic maelstrom and contributed to it.

Many Confederate warships and blockade runners, including *Alabama* and *Shenandoah*, were born in British yards, largely manned with British sailors— products presumably of lawful international commerce. But they generated intense controversy and deep hostility between Washington and London and Richmond. *Shenandoah*'s Captain James Waddell struggled with the uncomfortable roles of isolated diplomat and untutored international lawyer to represent a country not yet recognized; to acquire indispensable manpower, stores, and repairs in foreign ports; and to avoid international incidents.

Shenandoah's visit to the most remote and most British outpost of the empire throws these issues into relief, providing an outsider's view of the war. The citizenry of Melbourne, Australia (including a sizeable American expatriate community), were fascinated by the conflict and by their first and only rebel visitor. At the end of long and tenuous sea-lanes of communication, Australians reflected the politics, prejudices, and misperceptions of their homeland and were intensely concerned with issues of trade and commerce warfare. The people split into contentious political camps; one supported their Confederate guests while the other took up the Yankee banner—the antipodal manifestation of the struggle, or the war down under. The Confederates were feted as heroes by the former faction and nearly lost their ship to the latter, while the royal governor and bureaucracy muddled and vacillated. The British colony of Victoria had much in common with both the Confederacy and the United States and manifested some of their same differences.

Leaving Melbourne, *Shenandoah* sailed into the vast Pacific and at the paradisiacal island of Pohnpei captured and destroyed four more ships; the burning Yankee vessels illuminated alien surroundings, while in the South, Richmond went up in flames. This uniquely American conflagration flared simultaneously at both ends of the earth. Southern gentlemen enjoyed a tropical holiday, mingling with an exotic warrior society that was more like them than they knew. The history and customs of this land presented both intriguing parallels and stark contrasts with the Confederacy. As lonely rebels slept under tropic stars, guns fell silent at Appomattox, and with morale restored by rest, recreation, and destruction, *Shenandoah* sailed once more, leaving an enduring legacy in this faraway place.

While the Civil War struggled to conclusion and the nation began to bind its wounds, *Shenandoah* invaded the north, the deep cold of the Bering Sea. She fired the last gun of the conflict, set the Land of the Midnight Sun aglow with flaming Yankee whalers, almost became trapped by ice, and then headed back south. Off the coast of California, a passing British vessel delivered news of the end of the war—former Confederates were now pariahs, men without a country, profession, fortune, or future, presumably subject to imprisonment or hanging as pirates. Their fears amplified by great distance, these Southerners could only imagine homes destroyed, families destitute and starving, menfolk imprisoned, dead, or executed.

On 6 November 1865, seven months after Lee's surrender, *Shenandoah* limped into Liverpool. Captain Waddell lowered the last Confederate banner without defeat or surrender and abandoned his tired vessel to the British. He and his officers went ashore to reconstitute their lives. This volume is, as Admiral Semmes describes, a biography of a cruise and a microcosm of the Confederate-American experience.

Chapter 1

"Otro *Alabama*"

The British steamship *Laurel* lay placidly under the stars at the island roadstead of Funchal, Madeira, in the North Atlantic, four hundred miles west of Casablanca. Orders were given that there would be no communication with the shore except as necessary with Portuguese officials and for purchase of fuel. The captain reported a cargo of merchandise for Bermuda and Matamoras, twenty-nine passengers who were noted as Poles volunteering in the Confederate army, and a crew of forty men. *Laurel* had been coaled and made ready for sea; her papers at the customhouse were cleared for imminent departure. But the crewmen were ignorant of their true mission. After days of enforced idleness in harbor, the passengers milled impatiently about the moonlit deck as a lookout stood at the masthead with instructions to report immediately all approaching vessels.

During the midnight to 4 a.m. watch on 18 October 1864, a ship-rigged vessel came in sight, steaming slowly and displaying recognition lights. Passing ships regularly identified themselves so that their safety and progress could be recorded by national consulates and by Lloyd's of London representatives. Captain Frederick Marryat's codebook listed the names and types of English and American merchant vessels, as well as lights and flags to signal the ports of departure and destination. But this particular visitor turned and cruised by the harbor mouth a second and then a third time. The shadows on deck stirred and, watching intently from the rail, one of them murmured, "That's her!"[1]

As daylight came and the sun rose full of fire, the strange ship appeared once more with flags flying from her mastheads, displaying the identification number of *Laurel*, to which *Laurel* responded with the same. Boiler fires had been kindled and steam was up. The anchor chain was hove in to short stay. A cry arose from surrounding shore boats: "Otro *Alabama!*"—"Another *Alabama!*" One of *Laurel*'s passengers recalled the scene: "The vessel's quiet swing to a single anchor only increased our restlessness to follow the black steamer, whose symmetrical outlines the bright light played fairly upon and made her appear to be the very object for which we had left Liverpool." The writer was James Iredell Waddell, a North Carolinian lawyer's son who, despite civilian attire, was a lieutenant in the Confederate States navy. He carried orders to assume command of a new rebel raider and to continue depredations on Union commerce so effectively advanced by the CSS *Alabama*, a vessel now resting silently on the bottom of the English Channel after her fiery clash the previous June with the USS *Kearsarge*.

At ten o'clock *Laurel* steamed out to rendezvous. The day was fine, the atmosphere clear and bright; a stiff southwest wind rolled the little ship like a tub in heavy seas. As they approached, Lieutenant Waddell could see three words in large white letters across the stern of the vessel: *Sea King—London*. Other passengers scanned the newcomer with spyglasses, rendered opinions, and seemed delighted with her looks. Some faults were found, but for a merchant ship, most thought she was remarkably well fitted for their purposes. "For my own part," recorded Midshipman John Mason in his personal journal, "being no judge of such matters, I was like the little boy the cart ran over, I had not a word to say. . . . One thing however pleased me very much. She was a full rigged ship & as I looked at her three tall masts & her yards & rigging, I thought what a fine opportunity I would have of learning seamanship & I made up my mind to make the most of it."[2]

The two ships sought refuge in the lee of a nearby volcanic rock called Las Desertas, providing calm water, deep holding ground, and isolation from suspicious authorities. *Sea King's* anchor plunged to the bottom as *Laurel* made fast alongside. Ship's Surgeon Dr. Charles E. Lining, a South Carolinian, also kept a journal: "I immediately went on board to take a glance of what is to be my home for many, many months. I found her a splendid, roomy ship, with a fine wardroom, but nearly entirely void of furniture etc."[3]

Sea King carried a large quantity of provisions and seven hundred tons of coal, much more than the bunkers could stow; bagged piles of the dirty fuel occupied parts of the cavernous hold and berth deck. *Laurel's* holds were crammed with equipment, supplies, and bales of clothing to convert a peaceful merchant ship into a deadly commerce destroyer and to sustain her on a long cruise. There was no time to lose. Despite all efforts at secrecy, those in Madeira with memories of that renowned vessel understood that the stranger was "otro *Alabama*." And as *Laurel* waited in Madeira harbor, U.S. consul Robert Bayman had been alerted to *Laurel's* purpose and had been watching. He badgered authorities to detain her for purported violations of international law—claiming she was just another rebel pirate—and sent out reports and calls for assistance on every departing ship. An American man-of-war could appear any time.

Fires were kept in *Sea King's* boilers with steam up, the anchor cable ready to slip at a moment's notice. *Laurel's* passengers—Confederate navy officers, warrant officers, and petty officers—shifted their personal gear to *Sea King*. Tackles were erected and purchases rigged to the main yardarm as crews of both ships began transferring cargo, a demanding task normally accomplished in port. "Being thus shorthanded & thinking it no time to stand on our dignity," noted Midshipman Mason, "all of us, the officers, went to work with a will. . . ." They removed coats and vests, rolled up sleeves, and began breaking out cases from *Laurel* and hoisting them on board *Sea King*. Men and officers kept hard at it until midnight, taking time for only meals and a break for grog. Mason turned in that night "tired to death with sore hands & exhausted body." If this sort of life lasted much longer, he thought, they would all become expert sailors; it would be good for their health.

In the fourth year of bloody, frustrating conflict, these warriors of the sea finally could do what they did best: take the fight to the enemy in a fine blue-water ship, a rare opportunity in the Confederate States navy. They were more cynical than when the struggle began but not disillusioned; morale and expectations were high.

A fishing boat with five Portuguese came alongside. Waddell bought some fish, invited the fishermen on board, plied them with liquor, employed them in the work, and detained them overnight so they could not spread word in Funchal of the cargo transfer. Work continued at daylight as the wind shifted and the vessels ground dangerously against each other. Captain John F. Ramsay of *Laurel* presented Dr. Lining with a table, camp stool, and mattress for his cabin, which were much appreciated. Crates with guns, gun carriages and fittings, powder, shot, and shell, along with stores of all kinds were swung across.

The transfer was completed by 2 p.m., but no guns were mounted, no breeching or tackle bolts driven, no gunports cut, no powder magazine or shell room provided; all had been hurriedly piled in a lumbering, confused mass. Lieutenant William Whittle, second in command to James Waddell, recalled, "Every particle of work, of bringing order out of chaos and providing for efficiently putting everything in a condition for service, and of converting this ship into an armed cruiser at sea, amidst wind and storm, if encountered, stared us in the face."[4]

Sea King, commanded by Captain Peter Suther Corbett, was, like *Laurel*, a registered British merchantman. Corbett executed written authority from the owners to sell the vessel outside British jurisdiction for not less that £45,000. Lieutenant Waddell assumed ownership in the name of the Confederacy. "I felt I had a good and fast ship under my feet," he recalled, "but there was a vast deal of work in as well as outside of her to be done, and to accomplish all that a crew was necessary."

Sailors of both ships were called aft on the main deck where Captain Corbett informed them that *Sea King* had been sold and now would become a Confederate cruiser: "As you are all young men, I advise you to join her, as you will make a fine thing of it." Waddell emerged from his cabin and mounted the ladder to the quarterdeck in gray uniform with sword and pistol, the gold stripes of a lieutenant on his sleeves. He was over six feet and two hundred pounds with broad shoulders and thick, dark hair. Corbett introduced Waddell as the new captain without mentioning his name. One of the *Laurel* passengers—another disguised Confederate—told the sailors on deck that Waddell was Captain Raphael Semmes, former commander of *Alabama*. This alarming bit of Confederate disinformation would echo halfway around the globe.[5]

Waddell was forty years old with over twenty years in the U.S. Navy, having mastered the skills of the mariner across many oceans. Upon resigning to join the Confederacy, he had declared that he owned no property in the seceded states and was not hostile to the Constitution. He venerated the U.S. flag and only desired "to hazard life and limb in its defense against some foreign foe." He wished it to be understood that "no doctrine of the right of secession, no wish for disunion of the States impel me, but simply because my home is the home of my people in the South, and I cannot bear arms against it or them."[6]

But this was his first command and Waddell remembered feeling completely alone. The challenges were greater than any he had faced; his abilities were untested, and the trials ahead unknown. He stood at the quarterdeck rail above the gathered sailors that sunny October afternoon with only sea, sky, and rocks as witness. He blandly informed them that the vessel was the property of the Confederate States with the name *Shenandoah*. Any who joined would receive kind treatment and good wages. He read his commission, turned, and walked into the cabin. "For all the effect it had, [Waddell] might have spoken to the winds," recalled another of his officers, Lieutenant John Grimball. Over a hundred sailors were needed to sail the ship and man the guns, but just twenty-three signed on and most of those shipped for only six months.[7]

Two years earlier, August 1862, the new CSS *Alabama* rendezvoused with her stores ship near the island of Terceira in the Azores for the same purposes. Captain Semmes was equally concerned then: "I could not know how many of them would engage with me. . . . No creature can be more whimsical than a sailor, until you have bound him past recall, unless indeed it be a woman." With officers in full uniform and crew neatly dressed, Semmes mounted a gun carriage as his clerk solemnly read the commission and orders from the secretary of the navy. At a wave of his hand, the British flag dropped and the Confederate banner appeared at the peak. The commissioning pennant of a man-of-war streamed from the main royal masthead; a gun roared out in salute. The air was rent by cheers from officers and men as the band played "Dixie," "that soul-stirring national anthem of the new-born government."[8]

They would be fighting, Semmes told them, "the battles of the oppressed against the oppressor, and this consideration alone should be enough to nerve the arm of every generous sailor." However, he would not expect foreign sailors to understand the rights or wrongs of nations, and so he explained the individual advantages: adventure, new ports, and money. "Like a skillful Secretary of the Treasury, I put the budget to them in the very best aspect." Payment in gold, double ordinary wages, and prize money would be theirs. Semmes recruited eighty of ninety men from the two ships and felt very much relieved.[9]

Captain Waddell hoped to repeat this performance but didn't carry it off, for the *Alabama* had looked like a man-of-war, built and configured specifically as a cruiser. Semmes had his guns mounted, provisions stowed, and ship in order. His decks had not presented the discouraging and chaotic appearance of *Shenandoah*. Midshipman Mason was conscious of these precedents, having brought with him a copy of Semmes's first memoir, *The Cruise of the Alabama and the Sumter*, published in London a few months earlier. *Alabama*'s captain would become an admiral and leading naval hero of the Confederacy, and Mason would quickly conclude that Waddell was not cut from the same cloth.

Commander James Bulloch, Confederate naval agent in England, had supervised the design and building of *Alabama* and sent her to sea. He purchased and fitted out *Sea King* and *Laurel* and did everything possible to provide a full complement of men. As explained in his instructions to Waddell, Bulloch engaged an unusually large crew for *Laurel* including only young and, as far as possible, unmarried men "whose spirit of adventure and lack of home cares would, it was thought, naturally incline them to a roving cruise." He authorized an enlistment bounty and wages above normal rates, promising that the navy department would supply whatever Waddell chose to expend. "As seamen, so far as our service is concerned, are merchantable articles with a market value, you must either pay the price demanded or dispense with their services, which would cause the abandonment of your cruise."[10]

The experienced warrant and petty officers that Bulloch provided and Waddell brought with him were mostly English and Irish, having never set foot on American soil, although several were *Alabama* veterans. Boatswain Harwood was an old Liverpool salt, a Royal Navy pensioner and member of the Royal Naval Reserves; he had been of particular assistance to Semmes in enlisting his crew. Bulloch requested that Captain Ramsay of *Laurel* and Captain Corbett of *Sea King* encourage their men to join. Both were Confederate sympathizers, and Ramsay was a commissioned lieutenant in the Confederate navy as well as licensed British merchant master.

Liquor flowed as the officers struggled to convince sailors to sign on. One seaman reported that a bucket of gold sovereigns appeared: "The officers took up handfuls to tempt the men on deck." They were promised the best of living conditions, provisions out of ships captured, and prize money at the end of the war. Waddell told them that his orders were to simply destroy federal commerce; the vessel was not made to fight, and he intended to run away unless in a very urgent case. The Confederates anticipated that at least fifty men would sign on, which would prove sufficient until reinforcements could be enlisted from captured ships. They got less than half that.[11]

Midshipman Mason faulted Commander Bulloch as well as British and American officials for making it difficult to recruit sailors. "The men got frightened at the looks of things, did not like the way they had been deceived, in short got the old devil into them." Some were "considerably riled." *Sea King* quartermaster John Ellison, another member of the Royal Naval Reserves, had never earned a shilling in America in his life and did not wish to fight for it. England was his country and he was not ashamed to own it. Pointing to his reserves cap, Ellison stated: "If I were to desert from this, you cannot place any confidence in me."[12]

Captain Corbett was said to be the worse for drink, upsetting his former crewmen even further by refusing to immediately pay three months' wages for breach of contract as entitled by British law. And the political climate in England had changed, reflecting a marked loss of both sympathy for the Confederacy and confidence in Southern victory. Laws forbidding the Queen's subjects to take service in a foreign navy, a crime punishable by fine or imprisonment, were being more stringently enforced. So, despite all inducements, most of the sailors insisted on returning with *Laurel*.

Captain Corbett and Captain Ramsay advised Waddell not to continue with so small a crew. It was too dangerous. Waddell conferred with his new first lieutenant, suggesting that they proceed south to Tenerife in the Canary Islands and communicate with Commander Bulloch to have a crew sent to them. But Lieutenant Whittle differed with his captain, as he would in the future. He knew each of the lieutenants personally; they were all "to the manor born." He recalled the sad fate of the CSS *Rappahannock*, which a year before had gone into Calais for repairs and been held inactive ever since by stubborn French officials and Union blockaders. Repeating such a course, he counseled, would bring ignominious failure. "Don't confer, sir, with those who are not going with us. Call your young officers together and learn from their assurances what they can and will do." Waddell did convene a conference and the sentiment was unanimous: take the ocean. "Let those who hear the sequel judge the wisdom of the decision," Whittle wrote years later.[13]

The captain of a ship of war was regarded as supreme in all things. He remained aloof and normally did not share details of the mission, much less request conferences with his officers on fundamental strategic decisions. Only

Captain Waddell and First Lieutenant Whittle had been told where they were bound and for what purposes. In contrast to Waddell's apparent indecision and lack of resolve, Bulloch would later note, the junior officers demonstrated that "pluck and that ingrained *verve* and aptitude of the sea which is characteristic of the Anglo-Saxon race."[14]

Dr. Lining saw no chance of recruiting men in any port within many a long mile, and he did not wish to risk being detained or blockaded. They had plenty to eat—the ship was well provisioned—but nothing else. The wardroom was bare of furniture; staterooms had perhaps a washstand and a shelf but no lockers, no drawers, most of them not even bunks, not a chair apiece; and no storerooms existed for boatswain, sail, or gunnery supplies. But the holds were large and the wardroom and berth deck were spacious. They began striking everything below, putting it anywhere to clear the decks.

Just then, a vessel with the look of a warship appeared over the horizon bearing down upon them under topsails. They were armed only with swords and pistols, Enfield rifles, and two small saluting and signaling cannon. The big guns remained in crates disguised as "machinery." "I, for one," wrote Lining, "thought our cruise would be but a short one." Hands were ordered to the anchor windlass as engineers rushed to generate steam. *Laurel* raised her anchor and bore away for the strange sail to lead her away, if possible, should she prove a Yankee. It was a gallant action on Captain Ramsay's part, noted the doctor: "[I] began to think the anchor would never come in, & that my arms & shoulders would break first, but we worked away." Suddenly the stranger sheered away setting English colors. *Laurel* returned and stood by while *Shenandoah* finally got under way. It was about three o'clock in the afternoon, the weather rough with heavy swell running.

Letters home were hurriedly prepared. Captain Waddell wrote final dispatches including a note to Liverpool expressing doubts that he would accomplish all that was expected. Bulloch would recall this letter as "somewhat desponding." The mail was sent across and *Laurel* was off under steam for Tenerife where she was to coal, proceed to Nassau, and then try running the blockade. Captain Ramsay and crew gave three cheers as *Laurel* passed, and they were returned with a will, wrote Midshipman Mason: "[We will] never . . . see her again, most probably, for we are bound on a cruise, which will last until the end of the war, provided, of course, we are not sunk in the meantime." Mason superintended crewmen on the forecastle securing the anchor for sea under the eye of a lieutenant. It was his first watch on *Shenandoah* but "it was not the last, I'm happy to say."[15]

A little before sundown the Confederate flag was raised—unnoticed, wrote Lining, by all except himself and the officer on deck. "We with our small crew, willing, however, to suffer & do all we could . . . started off on our cruise, our only trust being in a just God, and in our cause." Having discharged the Portuguese fishermen (who were nearly swamped astern by the screw wake), *Shenandoah* stood clear of the land to the southwest. About 9 p.m., the engine was stopped, boiler fires banked, and topsails set. The doctor went to bed directly after supper, more tired, he thought, than ever in his life. The Confederate ensign flying at the peak was the second national pattern with the familiar battle flag for the canton and a pure white field.

Captain Waddell's thoughts that evening of 19 October 1864 were not recorded. In a postwar report to posterity, he sounded more confident (and more poetic) than he undoubtedly felt at the time:

> And the little adventurer entered upon her new career, throwing out to the breeze the flag of the South, and demanded a place upon that vast ocean of water without fear or favor. That flag unfolded itself gracefully to the freshening breeze, and declared the majesty of the country it represented amid the cheers of a handful of brave-hearted men, and she dashed upon her native element as if more than equal to the contest, cheered on by acclamations from *Laurel*, which was steaming away for the land we love, to tell the tale to those who would rejoice that another Confederate cruiser was afloat.

At almost the same moment and an ocean away, as autumn blazed the Shenandoah Valley in Virginia, General Philip Sheridan routed Confederates under Jubal Early at the Battle of Cedar Creek, a bloody ending to the Second Valley Campaign. This beautiful breadbasket of the South was securely in Union hands. Grant had instructed Sheridan that the valley be made such a waste that, to fly over it, a crow would have to carry rations. By spring Sheridan's troops would denude the area of crops, livestock, and farm buildings; residents would be starving. The very day that lost one Shenandoah to the Confederacy saw the birth of another. The new warship honored the place, recalled Lieutenant Whittle, "where the brave Stonewall Jackson always so discomfited the enemy. The burning there of homes over defenseless women and children made the selection of the name not inappropriate for a cruiser, which was to lead a torchlight procession around the world and into every ocean."[16]

For these Southerners, the ship symbolized the future in their determination to emulate her famous sisters and to achieve retribution, victory, and peace. The cruise would be the subject of history "successful or not," concluded Lieutenant Grimball. But the CSS *Shenandoah* was not a man-of-war yet—dangerously undermanned, guns not mounted, chaos on deck and below, an untested foreign crew, vulnerable to both the enemy and the weather, she sallied forth into the Atlantic with more hope than substance.

Chapter 2

"Do . . . the Greatest Injury"

Fifteen months before *Shenandoah*'s commissioning—18 August 1863—a
notice appeared in the *North British Daily Mail*: "Messrs. A. Stephen &
Sons launched from their new shipbuilding shed at Kelvinhaugh, another of
their wood and iron ships." The *Sea King* was described as a fine screw steamship of about 1,200 tons, certified class A1 at Lloyd's of London. She was the
first clipper ship with iron frames and wooden planking (called a *composite*
ship), and also the first steamer specially constructed to compete with "the
fastest ships in the trade direct from China to London, in bringing home the
first teas of the season." Confederate commander James Bulloch and Lieutenant Robert Carter had been searching the north bank of the River Clyde for a
steamer to purchase when they noticed *Sea King* in the bustle of fitting out for
her first commercial voyage. She appeared to be just what they were looking
for, but they got only a quick look. *Sea King* also caught the attention of retired
police detective Matthew Maguire working for the energetic American consul
in Liverpool, Thomas H. Dudley. He reported her as a potential rebel raider
needing close observation.[1]

Georgian James Dunwoody Bulloch was forty years old, a former U.S. Navy
officer, merchant master, and businessman with extensive experience, formidable organizing talents, and fierce determination. He served as chief
purchasing agent in England for the Confederate navy department from his
headquarters in the pro-Southern shipping and shipbuilding city of Liverpool,
where, a contemporary opined, more Confederate flags flew than in Richmond. Bulloch's half brother, Irvine Stephens Bulloch, was sailing master on
Shenandoah. (The Bullochs' sister, Martha, married Theodore Roosevelt Sr.
and bore the future president.)

Reporting directly to Confederate secretary of the navy Stephen Mallory,
James Bulloch accomplished more than any other Confederate on foreign soil.
Against persistent Union espionage and intense diplomatic pressure, he
launched the most successful raiders—*Alabama*, *Florida*, and *Shenandoah*—
along with blockade runners crammed with hundreds of tons of arms and
equipment. He contracted the Laird Shipyards to build two iron-hulled steam
warships, each with an iron beak—the "Laird rams." Bulloch had been slated

to command *Alabama* but reluctantly relinquished the position upon request of Mallory, who considered him indispensable in his current position. U.S. minister to Great Britain Charles Francis Adams wrote that Bulloch and associates were more effectively directing hostile operations than if they had been in Richmond. "In other words, so far as the naval branch of warfare is concerned, the real bureau was fixed at Liverpool." But Mallory, an experienced maritime lawyer from Key West, Florida, played a vital role as arguably the most effective of Jefferson Davis' cabinet officers. Mallory served before the war as U.S. senator and chairman of the Committee on Naval Affairs where he was a vigorous proponent of naval modernization. Davis, whose talents and interests lay almost exclusively in military affairs, left the navy to Mallory.[2]

Early in 1861 Raphael Semmes had advised a prominent Southerner, "If you are warred upon at all, it will be by a commercial people, whose ability to do you harm will consist chiefly in ships, and shipping. It is at ships and shipping, therefore, that you must strike. . . . Private cupidity will always furnish the means for this description of warfare." It would be required, maintained Semmes, only to place licensed privateers under sufficient legal constraint to prevent degeneration into abuse and piracy. Even New England ships and New England capital would serve the Confederacy for profit. Privateering would be analogous to the militia system on land.[3]

The Confederate congress duly authorized privateers, and in response President Lincoln threatened to license his own but did not carry it out. There were virtually no Southern merchant ships on the seas to capture, and Lincoln needed every available vessel to blockade their harbors. A few rebel privateers made it to sea in 1861 with short-lived success. Europeans denied both sides permission to bring captured vessels into neutral ports for adjudication and sale, while the blockade increasingly restricted Southern harbors. For the first time in three hundred years, the business was not profitable.[4]

Mallory was an innovator, as demonstrated in his adoption of ironclad warships and torpedoes (mines). So, he determined to buy or build vessels configured solely for commerce destruction and fund them from the treasury. *Florida* and *Alabama* had been prototypes, built from the keel up and magnificently suited for the purpose. But starting with Raphael Semmes' little *Sumter* in 1861, most Confederate raiders had been civilian ships converted, armed, and commissioned as warships—a practice not prevalent since the emergence of the big-gun warship centuries before. Now the advantages of fast sail were merged, in a single vessel of relatively low cost, with steam propulsion and minimum armament against a vast merchant fleet almost exclusively under sail and virtually unarmed—an overwhelming tactical superiority.

On 18 July 1864 Mallory wrote from Richmond to Bulloch: "The loss of *Alabama* was announced in the Federal papers with all the manifestations of universal joy which usually usher the news of great national victories, showing that the calculating enemy fully understood and appreciated the importance of her destruction. You must supply her place, if possible." A month earlier, Lieutenant Whittle and Lieutenant Grimball had been in Cherbourg as *Alabama* prepared for battle. They offered their services but were turned down; it would have been a violation of French neutrality to take on new men. Along with thousands of others, the future *Shenandoah* officers watched from the bluffs as guns of the USS *Kearsarge* destroyed and sank *Alabama*.[5]

Secretary Mallory desired an iron ship of from 600 to 1,200 tons, with powerful engines and room for one or two guns. It should be fast under steam and sail but "unpretending to man-of-war airs and graces." It might be built for commercial purposes such as the fruit or opium trade or as a yacht. The vessel must carry supplies—especially ordnance stores—for a global cruise. There would be no access to home ports; the ability to refit, resupply, and recruit in foreign harbors could be restricted by international law and politics. As Bulloch had noted, "[The] flag was tolerated only, not recognized." Concluded Mallory, "You will regard it but as a suggestion and as evidence of my anxiety to get cruisers to sea, rather than as a direction. Perhaps you can do better. Do not wait for instructions, but do the best you can under the circumstances."[6]

For once Bulloch had ample funds after being required by British authorities—motivated by vociferous Union threats of war—to sell the Laird rams to the Royal Navy rather than see them delivered to Confederate service. This was a grievous setback and one of his most severe disappointments; he was determined to put the proceeds to good use but had few options. The British Foreign Enlistment Act, prohibiting belligerents from acquiring war vessels within the realm for a conflict in which Great Britain was neutral, was being evermore strictly enforced. He no longer could have a warship built as he had *Florida*, *Alabama*, and the rams; the British would demand proof of ownership by a neutral state. A surreptitious warship purchase would require intermediaries and bribes and probably would deliver a cast-off product. "The necessities of our position greatly narrowed the field for selection, and it was only through a fortunate chance that a suitable vessel was found," wrote Bulloch.[7]

Bulloch's assistant, Lieutenant Robert Carter, was a scion of the Virginia clan from Shirley Plantation on the James River and an occasional courier between Liverpool and Richmond. He departed on a blockade runner, penetrated the Union cordon at Wilmington, and reported to Richmond where he described *Sea King* to the navy secretary as a potential cruiser. Carter then proposed a mission for her: penetration of the far Pacific where no Confederate had yet sailed and where strategic opportunity awaited. He knew this because he had been there.

The Navy played an expansive role in the nation's burgeoning overseas commerce during the first half of the century. The U.S. Exploring Expedition of 1838–42 to the Pacific and Antarctic had been a phenomenal scientific and surveying success. In 1852 Congress appropriated funds for additional surveying expeditions of the China Seas, North Pacific Ocean, and Bering Strait. The value of the Pacific whale fishery was their primary justification; under pressure from industry leaders, Congress wished to encourage the lucrative trade. Americans dominated the world market and the economic return was immense. Then U.S. Navy Lieutenant Carter served with the expeditions, as did his friend Lieutenant John Mercer Brooke. Beginning shortly after Commodore Perry pried open the reclusive Japanese nation in 1854 to March 1860, they collected a wealth of scientific, commercial, and nautical information, including several dozen charts. Brooke became a Confederate navy commander, scientist, engineer, and adviser to Mallory.[8]

Lieutenant Carter and Commander Brooke, reunited shipmates from the Pacific, teamed up to convince Mallory of the need for a cruise against the Union whaling fleet—the secretary required little prodding. Just the previous February, Bulloch had written, "there really seems nothing for our ships to do now upon the open sea." In an Atlantic cruise of several months, the CSS *Tuscaloosa* encountered one American vessel that carried neutral cargo and was released on bond. *Alabama* had sighted few enemy ships in the West Indies, heretofore rich in Yankee traffic. A French captain observed no American ships at the Guano Islands off Peru in 1864, whereas in 1863 there had been seventy or eighty standing by for this profitable cargo. The American consul at Hong Kong told his Liverpool counterpart that the brief presence of *Alabama* in the area had made it virtually impossible for Northern vessels to find freight in Asian ports.[9]

Only one in a hundred Yankee vessels sailing in foreign trade actually was taken, but the major impact had been psychological—the real damage done by fear of capture. Marine insurance rates soared. Eight Confederate warships destroyed over 100,000 tons of Union shipping worth $17 million, but drove another 800,000 tons into foreign ownership with British and others eagerly buying them. Many that remained were too old or rotting to be of interest. This was called "the flight from the flag." The war brought maritime New England's golden age to a close, mostly to the benefit of the British who were delighted at this humbling of their only serious rival in ocean trade. It was a blow from which the U.S. merchant service never fully recovered.[10]

By March 1864 Bulloch no longer felt justified in commissioning cruisers, but Mallory had other ideas. The Yankee coasting trades, fisheries, and California routes had suffered little. He wanted to place raiders simultaneously on the New England coast and fishing banks, in the South Atlantic, in the East and West Indies, and in the Pacific. This ambitious scheme "would have a decided tendency to turn the trading mind of New England to thoughts of peace. I am exceedingly anxious to do this." On 10 August, after conferring with Carter and Brooke, Mallory again wrote to Bulloch concerning the enemy's vulnerability: "His commerce constitutes one of his reliable sources of national wealth no less than one of his best schools for seamen, and we must strike it, if possible. . . . A blow at the whalemen is a blow at New England exclusively, and by keeping in distant seas where steamers rarely go and coal is unattainable they might make a very successful cruise."[11]

The North Pacific and Arctic represented the pinnacle of American whaling. From 1835 to 1860 there were seldom fewer than four hundred vessels in the Pacific annually; the number diminished steadily thereafter. Whale oil lost market to new and inexpensive kerosene in the nation's lamps. Businessmen turned to the burgeoning industries of the Machine Age, while potential sailors turned their backs on the sea and looked westward to the opening frontier. Already feeling the pinch, wealthy New England whaling magnates, like their merchant marine counterparts, would be in no mood to lose more ships and cargo because some damned rebel was loose in the Pacific. Whale oil still was a critical lubricant in the cogs of the Union's industrial war machine.[12]

In late summer 1864, Northerners were pessimistic about victory. Union desertions surged and the government was deep in debt. Bloodbaths at the Wilderness, Spotsylvania, and Cold Harbor, and stalemate in the trenches around Petersburg brought a chorus of condemnation down on the president and General Grant. Pressure to negotiate peace was intense. Lincoln despaired of winning reelection in November against the antiwar candidacy of Democrat George McClellan. The previous strategy—cruisers proceeding randomly along regular trading routes and taking any Yankees found there—clearly was no longer productive or practical. The Confederate navy needed a rapid, decisive, and punishing blow against vulnerable but concentrated high-value targets.

As described by Carter, Mallory believed *Sea King* would make a splendid cruiser. She was an auxiliary steamer, a clipper ship with a steam engine to assist in calms and contrary winds. The engine could drive comfortably at nine knots with an estimated 200 horsepower; to reduce drag under sail the propeller could be disconnected and lifted clear of the water and the telescoping smokestack lowered. These vessels were not commercially successful and only a few were built. Steam still could not compete with fast sail on long ocean voyages carrying high-value cargo. Occasional quicker passages did not compensate for added expense and loss of capacity for engines, coal, and engineering crewmen. For commerce raiding, however, the combination was perfect.

Under sail or steam, *Sea King* could overtake almost any victim and outrun any enemy.[13]

Mallory enclosed a memorandum in which Brooke laid out a detailed plan based on his Pacific explorations: Passing the Cape of Good Hope by 1 January 1865, a new cruiser would reach Sydney in forty days with twenty days for delays there. Leaving Australia on 1 March, she would proceed through whaling grounds around New Zealand and the Caroline group, touching at Ascension (Pohnpei) Island and, allowing another thirty days for delays, would reach the Ladrones (Mariana) Islands by 1 June. She could visit the Bonin Islands, Sea of Japan, Sea of Okhotsk, and North Pacific and be in position about 15 September north of Oahu to intercept the whaling fleet bound there with products of their summer cruise. Ship and mission were coming together. Carter set off for England with Mallory's instructions.[14]

Meanwhile, *Sea King* returned from her maiden voyage. She had stopped at New Zealand under government charter to debark troops for the Maori War. From there she sailed to Sydney, then to Shanghai in twenty-three days, on to Woosang, Hong Kong, and Swatow; and with a full cargo of tea, she made fast passage back to London in seventy-nine days, "beating the clipper ships, as anticipated." She made 330 miles in one twenty-four-hour period. Bulloch wasted no time, writing to Mallory on 10 September 1864, "I have now the satisfaction to inform you of the purchase of a fine composite ship."[15]

Bulloch would have preferred to superintend preparations in person, but ubiquitous Union spies required him to trust intermediaries. A British owner, register, and customhouse clearance were needed as cover, but it was difficult to find a trustworthy citizen willing to front for the ship and prepare her for the voyage while meeting requirements of law. Bulloch convinced an English friend and Southern sympathizer, Richard Wright, to purchase the vessel in his own name at a cost of £35,500, and, without remuneration, to provide power-of-attorney to sell her after leaving London. Wright was a wealthy Liverpool merchant and father-in-law to Charles K. Prioleau, managing partner of Fraser, Trenholm and Co., European financial agents for the Confederacy and primary conduit for Southern funds in Europe. The transaction was executed so skillfully that painstaking review of documents by U.S. agents could find no grounds for complaint. A secret condition of the purchase was that the ship, once commissioned, would not fire a gun before British register documents were returned to England and canceled, insulating Mr. Wright from liability.

Lieutenant Carter returned to Liverpool on 28 September and was delighted to find *Sea King* already in hand. When informed of the mission, Bulloch consulted Commander Matthew Fontaine Maury, obtaining from him a set of charts containing migration paths of the great whales to augment the Brooke memo.

Maury, world-famous scientist and "Pathfinder of the Sea," had conducted the first systematic study of the oceans as a U.S. Navy lieutenant and superintendent of the National Observatory in Washington. His most famous work, *The Physical Geography of the Sea* (1856), compiled study results and charts, generating a revolution in ocean trade. With this information, mariners more effectively plotted courses maximizing good and minimizing poor wind and sea conditions, which contributed significantly to the success of the clippers. Maury charts—created to aid the whaling industry—would now be used to help destroy it.

Bulloch had *Sea King* moved to London by a roundabout route resembling preparations for a trading venture, ostensibly to Asia. He stowed 800 tons of coal but added nothing of a warlike nature. Any alteration of internal arrangements or addition of equipment not consistent with a mercantile purpose and not required for the voyage would cause inquiry by Yankee agents and British authorities. He engaged the services of Captain Corbett, acquired a crew, and prepared papers for ownership transfer beyond British jurisdiction. He purchased *Laurel*—a new 269-ton iron screw steamer built for Liverpool-to-Ireland packet service—and advertised through an agent for a voyage to Matamoras via Havana and Nassau.

He appointed Captain Ramsay and loaded *Laurel* with crated and disguised cannon, munitions, small arms, equipment, and stores for a fifteen-month cruise. False bills of lading included ten tons of "machinery." He quietly gathered *Alabama* veterans and other Confederate naval personnel from around the city. Their baggage was crated up and loaded as freight; passenger tickets were issued under assumed names. At about nine o'clock in the evening, a tug came to the wharf and inconspicuously loaded the men for transfer to *Laurel* at anchor. One was accompanied by his wife, who was to see him off so that onlookers would believe they were on a short excursion.

This strategy worked with *Florida* and *Alabama*, but shipyards and docks now were under extremely close surveillance. U.S. consuls had established a secret system of inspecting ships loading for foreign voyages. U.S. minister Adams informed the secretary of state for foreign affairs that British subjects were actively engaged in fitting out a vessel to resume the dirty work of *Alabama*. Secretary of State William H. Seward warned that the British government would be held accountable for depredations of a new cruiser. If customs officials could be persuaded that the Foreign Enlistment Act was being violated, the ship would be seized. Bulloch noted that *Sea King* was perhaps the only vessel of her type and class in Great Britain. Her "comely proportions and peculiarities of structure" and fitness for conversion to a cruiser were manifest. "I felt confident that the spies of the United States Consul would soon draw his attention to her, and that she would be keenly and suspiciously watched."[16]

Bulloch prepared instructions for Lieutenant Whittle: He was to meet secretly with Richard Wright and Captain Corbett at a London hotel for consultation and would sail in *Sea King* to Madeira under the name McDonald. Corbett would not exchange signals with passing ships or at least not show official identification, and upon arrival he would hoist the recognition signal for *Laurel* rather than his own; she would respond with same. It was critical that *Sea King's* movements not be reported. Whittle was to acquaint himself with the ship's sailing qualities, observe the crew, inspect internal arrangements, learn stowage of provisions and stores, pick out positions for magazine and shell rooms, and discuss alterations with Corbett. Corbett remained legal commander, and for reasons of policy as well as courtesy, Whittle was to express all wishes as requests. When they joined *Laurel*, Whittle would report to Lieutenant Waddell and thereafter act under his instructions. "Relying upon your discretion and judgment, and earnestly wishing you a successful voyage, I am, respectfully, your obedient servant, James D. Bulloch."[17]

Commodore Samuel Barron, commander of Confederate naval forces in Europe, appointed Waddell as commanding officer. Bulloch issued him instructions for a cruise "in the far-distant Pacific, into the seas and among the islands frequented by the great American whaling fleet." In light of vast distances to be covered, difficulties of transforming a merchant vessel to a warship at sea, and isolation from aid and comfort of their countrymen, continued Bulloch, "a letter of specific instructions would be wholly superfluous." He then proceeded to do just that, expounding "purely advisory" remarks of over 3,500 words concerning the rendezvous, conversion, and coordination with both Captain Corbett and Captain Ramsay. He commented on navigation based on examination of Pacific Ocean charts and advice from Carter and Brooke. Every precaution was to be observed to prevent the direction or intent of the voyage being known in Europe. When *Laurel* reached Nassau, everything would be exposed, but by then *Shenandoah* would be beyond interference. "In moments of doubt, when unlooked-for obstacles and apparent troubles are found in your path, that happy inspiration which rarely fails the right-minded officer, who is earnestly intent upon his duty, will come to your aid, and you will thus intuitively perceive the most judicious course of action."[18]

Bulloch instructed Waddell to strike southward from Madeira using the northeast trade winds, cross the equator through the Doldrums applying the engine as necessary, and make the southeast trades in a favorable position to weather the Brazil coast. Avoiding the vicinity of Cape Town, Waddell was to continue well south into the steady southwest winds of the higher latitudes and by 1 January pass the Cape of Good Hope at 45° south. There the cruise would properly begin. Due to unknown sources of supply in the Pacific, Waddell should husband coal, acquiring what he could at Sydney or Melbourne and among the islands through which he passed. Brooke's memo would guide him from there. By the time Waddell reached the position north of Oahu, continued Bulloch, the ship probably would need repairs. If she were still sound, Waddell could proceed to Valparaiso for news. If she were no longer fit for service, he should sell her, preferably in South America or Asia, and release the crew.[19]

Waddell should avoid returning to Europe, where "[*Shenandoah*'s] presence might give rise to harassing questions and complications." He was provided with ample cruising funds but would draw supplies from prizes. He carried £2,000 in gold, £2,000 in marginal credits on the Bank of Liverpool, and a letter of credit from Messrs. Fraser, Trenholm & Co. for £1,000 to use at Sydney or Melbourne. Bulloch would write privately and forward letters via Manila to Waddell at the island of Guam in the Ladrones Islands, but official documents could not be trusted by that route. Waddell should direct progress reports from wherever possible to Fraser, Trenholm & Co. of Liverpool; Bulloch would forward them to the navy department. "I can think of nothing else worthy of special remark. You have a fine-spirited body of young men under your command, and may reasonably expect to perform good and efficient service. I earnestly wish you Godspeed. I am, respectfully, your obedient servant, James D. Bulloch, Commander, C. S. Navy."[20]

Commodore Barron added his cautions: Waddell was to remember that many American ships had been sold to the British, were now under protection of a neutral flag, and could not be harmed. He must observe strictest regard for neutral rights, lose no opportunity to cultivate friendly relations with naval and merchant services, and place "the true character of the contest in which we are engaged in its proper light." Waddell must not hesitate to assume responsibility whenever the interests of his country demanded it. He was above all "to do the enemy's property the greatest injury in the shortest time." The maintenance of strict naval discipline would be essential to success; he must enjoin this principle upon the officers and "enforce its rigid observance, always tempering justice with humane and kind treatment."[21]

Despite efforts of Union officials, *Sea King* glided unchallenged down the Thames and slipped into the English Channel on the morning of 8 October 1864. *Laurel* cleared Liverpool that night. "The entire expedition is far away at sea," reported Bulloch to Secretary Mallory, beyond interference by any U.S. authority in Europe. Minister Adams had stationed the USS *Niagara* off the mouth of the Thames and the USS *Sacramento* in the English Channel, but they had no instructions concerning *Sea King* if they saw her. On the 12th, Commodore Thomas T. Craven of *Niagara* received a letter from the Liverpool legation with intelligence that *Laurel* had sailed, undoubtedly in support of a new rebel pirate. Captain Semmes was said to have sailed in her with eight officers and about one hundred men, forty of whom were formerly of *Ala-bama*. The consul recommended that she be taken wherever found. Craven immediately raised anchor and proceeded to the Channel Islands to make a thorough but fruitless search. Similar alerts were forwarded to consuls in Paris, Brussels, and Lisbon, from which word was passed to the Madeira consulate.[22]

Bulloch again wrote to Mallory six weeks later. He was proud of the accomplishment given the difficulties but did not think it wise to attempt a similar adventure until excitement over this one had "somewhat subsided." However, if the war continued until the next summer (of 1865), he was convinced that "a formidable naval expedition can be fitted out." On the same day Bulloch wrote this letter, Mallory penned one to him—not having received reports from Liverpool, the secretary was anxious. Northern newspapers had already head-lined the departure of *Sea King*, speaking of her as a new Confederate raider. Mallory expressed concerns for the safety of men, ship, and mission. "I trust that it has been in your power to carry out what I have long had so much at heart. The success of this measure would be such an effective blow upon a vital interest as would be felt throughout New England."[23]

Chapter 3

"None but Fiends Could"

Soon after leaving Madeira, Lieutenant Whittle opened his personal cruise journal and started daily entries with *Shenandoah*'s position, progress, course, and weather, adding his thoughts and observations. "Thank God we have a fine set of men and officers, and although we have an immense deal to contend with, all are industrious and alive to the emergency." On the other hand, "never I suppose did a ship go to sea so miserably prepared." They were afloat in a vessel constructed for peaceful pursuits that was to be transformed in midocean into an active cruiser carrying a battery for which she was not constructed and with no hope of defense or friendly port for shelter.[1]

Midshipman Mason found it difficult to maintain his journal or to read or study while everyone from the first lieutenant on down worked about the deck making sail, taking it in, stowing the hold, and doing everything else that was needed. Back in the spring of 1861, John Thomson Mason of Virginia had been planning to take up his appointment to the Naval Academy, but instead joined the 17th Virginia Volunteer Infantry Regiment, fought at First Manassas, and then transferred to the new navy. (He was a distant nephew of founding father George Mason and cousin to James Murray Mason, Confederate commissioner in England and victim of the *Trent* Affair.)[2]

The midshipman intended to record every detail of the last few weeks, which he considered the most eventful of his young life, but he was at a loss where to commence with a description of "confusion worse confounded." The junior officers' quarters in the steerage were uncomfortable—full of rope, iron bread tanks and "all sorts of stuff that smelt bad." But they strung their hammocks and made the most of it. The first task was to discover what they had and where it was. Cargo invoices from *Laurel* were worthless; many pieces of equipment were missing. To locate the smallest item required extensive searching, and before stowing anything in the hold men had to sort out and restow what already was there. The running gear, used to manage the yards and sails, was so worn it became necessary to rig all new lines. John O'Shea, the ship's carpenter, hurt his foot badly and had no trained assistants. The bulwarks required reinforcement to absorb gun recoil and gun ports were to be cut. Several officer cabins had no berths while buckets were used as washbasins.

Officers worked aft while crewmen worked forward, shifting coal from the fore hold and berth deck to bunkers so men could sling hammocks and clearing the spar deck for mounting the battery. Clean mattresses were issued. The royal yards—the highest on each mast—were sent up and crossed, quite an undertaking as spars, sails, and rigging were scattered all over the ship. In the absence of a magazine, gun powder was stored under a tarp in the captain's day cabin and then moved to the small space in the steerage underneath his cabin. It was like cutting down a mountain to put things in order, recalled Lieutenant Grimball, "but there was always so much good humor prevailing that not until after we finished our task could we fully appreciate what we had gone through."

Despite heavy swells, the big guns were lifted from their crates, swayed up by the halyard winches and tackles from the masthead, and mounted in carriages: two Whitworth 32-pound rifles and four 8-inch, 68-pound smoothbores. Warrant Officer John L. Guy, ship's gunner, attempted to assemble the gear; there was plenty of rope for the gun tackles, but no suitable blocks and without them the battery was useless. He cut gun ports anyway. "At a distance *Shenandoah* presented quite a warlike appearance with guns looking out on each side," noted Lieutenant Francis Chew in his personal journal, but if a Yankee man-of-war should appear, they would have to "depend on their heels."[3]

Furniture in the captain's cabin consisted of one broken, plush velvet-bottomed armchair—no berth, no bureau, no clothing lockers, no washstand, pitcher, or basin. A half-worn carpet, which reeked of dogs or something worse, covered the deck. "It was the most cheerless and offensive spot I had ever occupied," recalled Waddell. A problem with the engines was corrected in a few hours, but left the captain uneasy about their condition. "It would be too great a labor to enumerate the variety of work which was done . . . and those who have undertaken the work on a wide and friendless ocean can only appreciate the anxieties accompanying such an expedition."

Waddell ran *Shenandoah* away from the rendezvous, seeking invisibility, lighter winds, and smoother seas. With only four men per watch, sail handling was difficult. No one knew the lead of the ropes, and whenever a brace or a sheet was to be hauled, crewmen wasted minutes just finding the right one. The few coal heavers quickly became exhausted in the stifling boiler room. The captain used the engine during daylight as work continued, then after darkness put the vessel under easy sail while most men rested. "The wind was free; my course was to southward, and as the breeze freshened after night the ship made nearly as much per hour under sail as she did during the day under steam."

Waddell had promised to wait six weeks before capturing a Yankee, but after a few days, he worried that the heavy work and chaos would dishearten the crew and discourage potential recruits. Applying a common term for sailors, he noted: "Work is not congenial to Jack's nature; he is essentially a loafer." The captain decided to take the first enemy vessel encountered. Dr. Lining continued his journal: "I never saw any set of men work better or harder than ours, for the officers set them the example & were always foremost in all work. . . . I am sleeping my mattress right on the deck, not very comfortably." They sighted ships from neutral nations, but did not speak to them. Whittle thought a great deal was being accomplished under the circumstances, and the men seemed—with one exception—in good spirits. He would trust in God's aid for the future. "No indeed I never shall regret the advice I gave [to Waddell], which advice, I flatter myself, kept us at sea." They sighted the first Yankee sail that afternoon but much to their disgust were unable to come up with her before sundown and lost her in the night.

The exception to the mood of cheerfulness was the captain. Waddell himself recalled being somber and withdrawn, weighed down with problems and possible emergencies: "I have no doubt I very often appeared to those with me an unsocial and peculiar man." He appreciated encouraging remarks from the officers that were intended to lighten his mood, but they had no effect. Command was a new experience. The lieutenants were accountable for the ship only during a four-hour watch as officer of the deck, but the outcome of so vast an enterprise depended on his judgment alone. Success would be shared by everyone, but who would share failure? "The former has friends; what has the latter!" He was responsible to a nation struggling for its very existence.

The ship was not his only concern: "The novel character of my political position embarrassed me more than the feeble condition of my command, and that was fraught with painful apprehensions enough." As a seaman Waddell had experience and a compass to guide him; he could manage a vessel in stormy weather, he knew from boyhood the dangers of the sea and was well prepared for fighting. But warship captains served as lonely ambassadors in faraway places with no communications to home. Promptly and without counsel, he would have to resolve complex questions of international law "over which lawyers quarreled with all their books." Waddell brought with him the fundamental principles of law in Blackstone along with Sir Robert Phillimore's *Commentaries on International Law.* "Most of my leisure hours were devoted to Phillimore, and I found him a good friend, but requiring [intense] study."

International relations for the Confederacy were fraught with opportunity and danger, as were the complex and antiquated rules governing activities of a commerce-destroying cruiser. Early in the war, Confederate leaders had anticipated national recognition and support from prospective European allies, particularly Great Britain; however, this hope was essentially dead by 1864. But even then, any false diplomatic step could bring dire consequences for command and country. Waddell had been cautioned accordingly (as had his predecessors) and was determined to persevere. "My admirable instructions and the instincts of honor and patriotism that animated every Southern gentleman who bore arms in the South buoyed me up with hope," he later wrote; but at the time it appeared that his anxiety predominated.

While the captain ruminated, the first lieutenant carried on managing daily operations and maintenance, supervising junior lieutenants and warrant officers in getting the ship in order. Interaction between the two *Shenandoah* senior officers was prickly from the beginning. Whittle's journal leaves the impression of competence and dedication, combined with a somewhat self-absorbed and brittle sense of honor, typical of young men of his class and time. He seldom discusses Waddell except to disagree with him and pointedly assumes all burdens of ship management. Waddell, on the other hand, mentions the first lieutenant only once in his postwar notes, writing with faint praise that Whittle was "always active and intelligent in the discharge of his peculiar duties."

The problem was not just the age spread (twenty-three to forty)—there was a professional generation gap. When Waddell was sent to the new Naval School at Annapolis in 1847—just the second year of its operation—he had already had six years of active service afloat. He and others like him found themselves among raw cadets in a staid academic environment being taught from books what they believed they already knew from experience. Nevertheless, Waddell demonstrated marked proficiency in mathematics and navigation in the examination for passed midshipman. He met and married Ann Sellman Inglehart, the daughter of an Annapolis businessman, and then went back to sea through the turbulent 1850s. It was a period of crisis in Navy leadership and discipline characterized by the abolition of flogging and a bungled attempt to reform the moribund officer seniority system. In the small, inbred service of the time, Waddell shared the mutual suspicion and distrust that were rife among fellow officers.

In his memoirs, Waddell declared that the place to teach the profession of the sea was at sea on ships, even though he made Annapolis his home with Ann and served two tours as instructor at the school. The second tour, during which his daughter Annie was born, was as assistant professor of navigation and assistant commandant. (With her father away in Confederate service in spring 1863, Annie would die of scarlet fever and diphtheria.) Waddell believed he had become an officer the hard way and the right way—a slow, tedious progression through the ranks, which gave enormous prestige to promotion. He doubted the practicality of classroom learning. Attitudes like these among hidebound careerists held back establishment of the Naval Academy until forty years after the founding of West Point. In Waddell's mind, his *Shenandoah* officers did not represent the spectrum of age and experience he was accustomed to seeing in the U.S. Navy. He could not relax for a minute, which exacerbated a sense of isolation and the weight of his responsibilities.[4]

William Conway Whittle Jr., however, entered training at Annapolis in 1854 with no prior experience. In 1840 he had been born to a prominent Norfolk, Virginia, naval family that was, like Waddell's, of Irish descent. Whittle's father had a distinguished career in the U.S. Navy and would become one of the few ranked captains in the Confederate navy. By 1850 the Naval School had been reorganized and renamed the Naval Academy with standards nearly comparable to those of West Point, increasing the professionalism and respectability of a Navy career. Whittle was regarded as an outstanding student and most promising officer, graduating in 1858 with his friend and future shipmate, John Grimball (George Dewey of Spanish-American War fame was another classmate). He served two years at sea in the U.S. Navy before the war. These young men were the new navy; they took their schooling proudly, as would every class that followed; and not a few of them, like Whittle, brought that pride to the Confederate navy.

In 1861–62 Whittle served as acting lieutenant in the CSS *Nashville*, one of the first merchant ships refitted for commerce raiding. She set vital precedents in international law as the first Confederate ship of war to fly the flag in British waters and the first to make a capture in North Atlantic shipping lanes. Warmly received in Southampton, *Nashville* secured belligerent status for Confederate warships in the face of vociferous Union protests and proved the safety of British ports. Based on his experience in both navies, Whittle came to believe that he was just as qualified to command *Shenandoah*, a feeling reinforced by Waddell's apparent hesitance. His commander seemed to represent the past, to underappreciate his subordinates, and to be ill equipped for challenges of present and future.[5]

In his journal, Charles Lining would contribute observations from the sidelines, many critical of the captain. In August 1858 Lining had sailed as assistant surgeon with the sloop of war USS *Cyane* around the tip of South America to the Pacific, returning in late 1860. The long cruise of the unhappy *Cyane* was a microcosm of stresses afflicting the officer corps at midcentury. The doctor witnessed close at hand a great deal of drunkenness, lack of discipline, and feuding among officers, which upon their return resulted in numerous courts of inquiry; nearly every officer was court-martialed, including the captain. Much of the dissension could be traced to dissatisfaction over prospects for promotion.[6]

That experience would color Lining's perceptions during this voyage. His medical duties were not demanding; he had no direct role in the operations of the ship and he was often bored. At thirty years of age, Lining was between the lieutenants and the captain. Because of his professional and social status and his position outside the chain of command, young officers could turn to him to vent frustrations or ask advice. At least some of them—notably First Lieutenant Whittle—talked to him openly of their differences with the captain. The doctor participated actively in these discussions, took sides, and offered opinions that had nothing to do with medicine.

One issue concerned the capabilities of the four watchstanding lieutenants. In order of seniority, they were John Grimball of South Carolina; Sidney Smith Lee Jr., another Virginian; Francis Thornton Chew of Missouri; and Dabney Minor Scales from Mississippi—all under the age of twenty-five. Grimball and Lee had the experience to stand as officer of the deck, supervising the highly specialized and frequently dangerous business of sailing a large, deepwater ship. Grimball was the privileged son of a wealthy Charleston planter, state senator, and signer of the South Carolina secession proclamation. He graduated from the Naval Academy with Whittle in 1858 and served afloat in the U.S. Navy before the war.[7]

Sidney Smith Lee Jr. was the nephew of Robert E. Lee, brother of Confederate general and future Virginia governor Fitzhugh Lee, and great-grandson of George Mason, one of the founding fathers (and also cousin to Midshipman Mason). Like the senior Whittle, Lee's father served the U.S. Navy for many years before becoming a ranked captain for the South. His son did not immediately choose a Navy career but went to sea and gained considerable experience in the prewar merchant service. These officers were supported by the experienced and capable sailing master Irvine Bulloch, warrant officer in charge of navigation (and younger half brother to Commander James Bulloch). Irvine Bulloch had served in *Alabama* and was credited with firing the last shot as she began to go under.

Francis Chew was an anomaly: a middle-class Midwesterner and a pharmacy clerk from Richmond, Missouri, who joined the U.S. Navy over the objections of his widowed mother after reading a novel about Matthew C. Perry's expedition to Japan. "It was beautifully and profusely illustrated, my head was completely turned and I concluded that the Navy was just the place for me. Drugs lost all their charms; ships, sailors, officers in their showy uniforms, filled my mind with new thoughts and an earnest longing for the sea." Through acquaintance with a judge, Chew secured appointment to the Naval Academy, entering in 1859; Dabney Scales, the son of a Mississippi planter, also entered the Naval Academy in 1859—in spring 1861 both resigned without graduating to join the Confederate navy.

All of these men had significant wartime experience on ironclads and shallow-water steam gunboats: In the fall of 1861, Chew and Scales served in the "mosquito fleet" at the loss of Port Royal Sound, South Carolina; Chew observed the fall of Fort Pulaski two months later; Waddell had been on one of the Confederacy's doomed ironclads at the Battle of New Orleans in April 1862, while Whittle, Lee, and Chew were together on another; that same month on the Mississippi, Dr. Lining witnessed the fall of Island Number Ten and New Madrid, Missouri. A few weeks later, Waddell supervised the big guns at Drewry's Bluff on the James River when they turned back the Union fleet threatening Richmond.

Grimball and Scales had close calls on the bloody gun deck of the ironclad CSS *Arkansas* in July 1862 when she charged guns blazing through Admiral Farragut's fleet above Vicksburg. And in April 1863, Chew was on board the ironclad CSS *Palmetto State* as they stopped a Union waterborne attack on Charleston. Scales and Lee reported to the ironclad CSS *Atlanta* in Savannah, which in June 1863 ran aground after a short fight and was captured by Union monitors. By the summer of 1863, future *Shenandoah* lieutenants all had been dispatched to Europe awaiting orders as part of a Confederate fleet that never was. Chew and Scales, however, had never been to sea, which made Waddell particularly uncomfortable. Whittle, who felt perfectly capable of mentoring his junior colleagues, would become incensed when the captain's nervousness on the subject impugned his competence.

Now in the isolated and confined embrace of a ship so far from home, these men were settling into a web of formal and informal relationships that would define the effectiveness of the command—its ability to meet the enemy and the weather and not only to survive but to prevail in the mission. Meanwhile, work continued apace: the sailmaker prepared and fitted canvas hoods for the hatches, while engineers distilled freshwater—one of the revolutionary advantages of steam on long voyages. They could produce five hundred gallons a day, but this required a significant expenditure of coal. The captain instructed that the name *Sea King* be erased from the stern. Lining observed the Island of Palmas in the Canaries from fifty miles off and saw flying fish for the first time, a sign that they were approaching the tropics. He had worked harder than ever in his life; it had been a difficult time, but not an unhappy one.

Another vessel appeared, clearly Yankee built, which, when stopped and questioned, proved to be under British registry and could not be detained. "Better luck next time," wrote Whittle, who was subject to his own melancholy, in what would become a typical journal entry: "Notwithstanding my being so busy, I have time to feel blue, as I can't get my usual letters from my own dear ones. Oh! how much would I give to know how they are. I leave them and all to God. We have so much to be thankful for." With occasional heavy rain and violent squalls of wind, waves crashed against the sides; decks and hull seams leaked like sieves, admitting a fine spray into berth deck and cabin.

The captain was, however, impressed with his new command as they met and passed other ships. "*Shenandoah* was unquestionably a fast vessel, and I felt assured it would be a difficult matter to find her superior under canvas." Three times the Confederates dipped their ensign in salute to passing English vessels, which responded in turn—a sign of respect and friendship between nations (now as then); coming from representatives of the most powerful nation on earth, it was particularly gratifying. Waddell noted, "Our prospects brightened as she worked her way toward the line [equator] through light and variable winds, sunshine, and rain."

On 28 October 1864, due south of the Azores and west of Dakar in the afternoon, a vessel broke the horizon ahead. Experienced sailors could guess a ship's nationality from the contours of sails, masts and spars, and lines of hull. U.S. vessels—widely recognized as among the best—generally carried taller and narrower rigs with cotton sails in place of the grayer flax canvas preferred by Europeans. Raphael Semmes described similar encounters, praising the "whitest of cotton sails, glistening in the . . . sun," "well-turned, *flaring* bows," "grace and beauty of hull," and "long, tapering spars" on which American ship-builders and masters prided themselves. For some lookouts, it was almost a matter of instinct and a glance of a minute or two: this vessel was a Yankee.[8]

Shenandoah gained rapidly on the ship, closing to seven miles as dusk fell. Waddell reduced sail and regained contact at dawn, but the quarry had worked its way to windward. He ordered boilers fired, had the propeller lowered, took in royals and topgallants, and approached under steam. About 1 p.m., he raised English colors. The stranger replied with the U.S. flag or "the old gridiron" as Lieutenant Chew called it: "Then joy could have been seen depicted on each face. We were all desirous of seeing a ship destroyed at sea and especially when that destruction touches a Yankee pocket." The Confederate flag replaced the English; the bark of the signal gun echoed across the water and, as required by international law, the vessel hove to for inspection.

Waddell lowered a boat and armed the crew under the direction of sailing master Bulloch. They were received at the gangway by the captain in his shirt sleeves, an informality Midshipman Mason considered to be "true Yankee style." She was the bark *Alina* of Searsport, Maine, on her maiden voyage to Buenos Aires from Newport, Wales, with a cargo of railroad iron. Bulloch examined the ship's papers, sent *Alina*'s captain and first mate to *Shenandoah*, lowered the U.S. flag, and waited impatiently for orders.

Lining observed from across the water, "I never saw greater excitement than was on board our ship when the Yankee flag came down, which showed us we had the first prize to *Shenandoah*." Whittle was delighted to see the "emblem of tyranny" thus humbled. In accordance with his understanding of international law, Waddell assembled a board of officers in the wardroom as prize court. He sat as judge at the head with First Lieutenant Whittle and *Alina*'s master, Captain Everett Staples, to his left. Paymaster and captain's clerk

Breedlove Smith was on Waddell's right, other officers filling the table. Whittle put the prisoner under oath and interrogated him concerning the vessel's ownership, tonnage, and cargo.

The cargo of railroad iron was owned by an English firm, as specified on the bill of lading. Although *Alina* was a U.S. registered vessel, she had been loaded at a neutral port in Wales and was bound for another neutral port, Buenos Aires, with a cargo presumably owned by citizens of a neutral nation. The prize should have been bonded and released; they could not destroy the enemy ship without sacrificing neutral cargo. (A bond was formal written assurance that, in lieu of capture or destruction, the vessel's owners would pay ransom equal to the value of ship and cargo. It would have been legal international debt had the Confederacy achieved independence.)

Here again, Raphael Semmes blazed the way. (In addition to his naval career, Semmes was an experienced lawyer and student of international law who first held prize courts on board *Sumter* in 1861 and again on *Alabama*.) He claimed to have never condemned a ship or cargo "without the most careful, and thorough examination of her papers, and giving to the testimony the best efforts of my judgment." However, to justify destruction of ship and cargo, Semmes was at least as punctilious in finding ambiguity or inconsistency in the paperwork—efforts for which his enemies vociferously branded him a pirate.[9]

Yankee masters, in turn, applied every stratagem to avoid loss by hiding behind nebulous provisions of the law and false documents. One favorite trick was to have an official in a local British consulate certify the cargo belonged to one of their citizens, whether true or not. Upon examination of these certificates, Semmes pronounced them fraudulent and burned the ship. "The New York merchant is a pretty sharp fellow, in the matter of shaving paper, getting up false invoices, and 'doing' the custom-house; but the laws of nations . . . rather muddled his brain." Semmes preserved records of the "Confederate States Admiralty Court" on *Alabama* to justify these decisions.[10]

Unfortunately for Captain Staples of *Alina* (named for his daughter), Waddell followed Semmes' example. In this case, the cargo owner had not sworn before a magistrate that the iron was his property and that he was an Englishman; there was no seal and notary signature to that effect. The lack of this legal detail sealed the fate of the vessel. Waddell officially condemned her as a prize of the Confederate States of America. Upon hearing this, recorded Lieutenant Chew, the Yankee's lips trembled. He remained silent for a time, then said, "[Captain], if you burn my ship you will make me a beggar. I have been going to sea for twenty three years. All my profits of these years of toil and danger are invested in that vessel." Waddell replied, "It is a sad duty, but it is one I owe my government and my people. Think of the property destroyed, the orphans and widows made by the Yankee army." With this, the hearing ended; the captain rose from the table and all followed.

Alina crewmen gathered personal property and were rowed over to *Shenandoah*. Lining boarded the prize: "Such a scene of indiscriminate plundering commenced as I never saw before or expect to again." Grimball noted that she was brand new, in good order, and of good quality, "the prettiest barque I ever saw." Everything that possibly could be of use was seized and put into boats. Waddell admitted that there were no people who understood the equipment of vessels so well as Yankee shipwrights. They carried off a variety of blocks, including ones suitable for the gun tackles, along with line and cotton canvas for sailmaking. Cabin doors were taken down, drawers from under bunks taken out, and furniture removed. Officers fitted themselves out with basins, pitchers, mess crockery, knives, and forks. Waddell obtained a spring-bottomed mattress. Chronometers and sextants were seized. The doctor recovered a store of canned meats for the wardroom as well as flour, bread, and other items.

They had not been working long when another vessel was sighted, possibly a Union warship, coming down from windward, "in which case the joke would be turned against us," wrote Chew, now in charge on board the prize. Or maybe it was another Yankee merchantman. The captain wished to be ready in either case—chase or run. Chew received instructions to send over only valuable articles and to sink *Alina* immediately. The carpenter knocked a hole below the waterline and bored holes in the bottom with an auger. Boats scuttled back and were hoisted on board. *Shenandoah* steamed off, all attention focused on the strange sail.

The newcomer turned out to be a neutral vessel, so they turned back and saw *Alina* settling in the water. Mason stood on the poop watching, an entirely new spectacle for him. She was a beautiful little thing, he wrote, as neat as a pin. Yards were square, all sails set and sheeted home including royals and flying jib. At every pitch the doomed vessel seemed not to rise as much as before. At about 5 p.m., the sea reached deck level and swept over the stern. She pitched heavily once more and then reared up like a warhorse; thrust her bowsprit to the heavens; and, accompanied by a crescendo of cracking and tearing of rigging and sails, snapping lines, crashing masts, and tumbling and rumbling cargo, slipped straight out of sight, swallowed in an instant by the sea. As the bow went under, an enormous jet of water erupted into the air followed for some time by loose gear—hatch covers, blocks, spars, and flotsam—bursting the surface to splash among a boiling mass of wreckage.

"It was a grand and peculiar sight," recorded Chew. "I was saddened at the thought of being in duty bound to such work. I felt very sorry for them even after thinking of the hellish work of the Yankees at home, of the tears they have wrung from once happy, beaming eyes. No, none of us took pleasure in it. None but fiends could." Whittle described it as grand and awful: "You might go to sea for many a day and would not see a vessel sink. . . . She was in this position [like] a man going down for the first time and struggling to prevent it." Lining wrote, "It was a beautiful, yet to me a melancholy sight, to see her go down, even though she was an enemy's property. It is our duty to do it, & stern necessity alone makes it right."

Alina's captain watched to the last. The doctor could not help feeling sorry for him although he regretted it later: "[Captain Staples] was a black hearted rascal & will do us all the injury in his power. He showed a mean spirit during all his stay on board, for he was a real down-east Yankee."

A sailor learns to love a ship as something almost animate, recalled Master's Mate Cornelius E. Hunt: "To see one deserted in mid-ocean by her guardians and slowly settling in the unfathomable waters is like standing beside a death-bed to watch a soul sinking into the ocean of eternity. But I was fated to have a large experience in this direction ere the *Shenandoah* and I finally parted company."[11]

The manner of destroying a vessel depended on her cargo, wrote Waddell; if it were heavily freighted like *Alina*, it would be better to scuttle. She would sink rapidly and disappear as a whole, leaving a few pieces of deck and bulkheads floating over the great abyss. More frequently it would be necessary to burn the ship, which was better than abandoning it disabled and a danger to navigation. But fire leaves a small portion of the keel and floor timbers afloat as a hazard; red glare in the sky could alarm Yankees within thirty miles; and a warship might be attracted or prospective prizes frightened off.

Under more favorable circumstances, captured ships could be sailed to a home or neutral port for adjudication by admiralty court. Each vessel would be formally condemned and sold with proceeds distributed to captain, officers, and crew. A ship could even be repurchased by original owners. However, Union blockaders restricted access to Southern harbors and neutral ones were closed to them. This was another of the Confederacy's grievances with the British, who, concerned about appearing neutral, had prohibited both belligerents from bringing prizes to any port under their jurisdiction—a policy that in practice favored the North. When other nations followed suit, Confederates had no recourse but to sink or burn, concluding that Yankee howls about brutal rebel cruiser captains causing such maritime destruction should have been directed at the British government.

Chew evaluated the bill of lading and valued the ship and cargo at $95,000. The estimate was recorded in the ship's log for the navy department to use in distributing prize money at the end of the war. "A long look ahead I must confess, yet we all hope to receive someday a reward for our present work." For his part, Whittle considered it a good day's effort notwithstanding the demoralizing nature of the work: "God grant that we may have many just such prizes." He gave the order to splice the main brace, serving out an extra ration of grog.

Whittle did not care for Captain Staples either: "Oh how I do hate the whole [Yankee] race—and still, I can't help from treating him kindly." Without conscious irony and true to their heritage, these Southerners expected of their captives the same gentlemanly respect, courtesy, and calm resignation to the fortunes of war that they would expect of themselves. A few prisoners would earn respect for genteel behavior, but the Southerners' scorn for most of them was hidden under a veil of hospitality, which probably helped them feel better about visiting destruction on helpless merchant vessels.[12]

Chapter 4

"Now Came the Trouble"

Alina's Captain Staples and two mates, paroled and promising not to interfere with operations, remained free of restraint. Lieutenant Chew penned a portrait of Staples as "a splendid specimen of the 'down easter.'"; he was "cute and unprincipled." When speaking, he would look at you, grin, squint one of his eyes, and then everything he says, he "calculates" or "guesses." The vessel was built, Staples told Chew, after his own "idey." But he was a good seaman, and *Alina* was a splendid specimen of naval architecture. Nine crewmembers, "all strong, fine looking fellows" according to Chew, were confined in irons. One volunteered to enlist and was directed to encourage the rest to do likewise. After a few days' confinement, all joined except one Yankee; they did not want him anyway. Midshipman Mason noted with contempt that the rejected Northerner was a protégé of *Alina*'s captain and had made his first trip to sea only to avoid conscription. New men included Germans, French, Dutch, and one Swede—all of whom could speak little English—and a native of Madras who had taken the name William Bruce and settled in New York as a naturalized citizen. Ship's complement increased to twenty-nine sailors.[1]

Captain Waddell sensed a marked difference in morale following the capture. Work pressed heavily on the men but there were more of them, "and the cry of 'Sail ho' was always greeted with manifestations of pleasure." The sailors collected in the gangways after working hours and gave themselves up to dancing, jumping, singing, or spinning yarns. "Jack is easily entertained and simple in his credulity," Waddell noted. "The course was still southward through the bright rays of a hot sun, popping out from behind a cloud which had just wept itself away, to dry our jackets."

Sunday, 30 October, was a well-earned day of rest. "We have done nothing all day, and unless it is absolutely necessary we will always observe the Sabbath," wrote First Lieutenant Whittle. But Monday was back to work; it would take three months to get the ship in order—what *Alabama* had accomplished in two weeks. "An Executive Officer under such trying circumstances has an immense deal to do. I thank god that I have the health, strength and will to accomplish all." As the ship approached equatorial calms, conditions worsened with warming temperatures and heavy rain. A squall hit without warning in predawn darkness, heeling her over dangerously, but *Shenandoah* reacted more easily than Whittle had thought a vessel her size would. He took a close reef in the topsails and a single reef in the foresail, which rendered the ship more comfortable.

Rain offered welcome opportunity to fill casks and to wash clothes in freshwater. Crewmen were allowed one fresh gallon per day for drinking and personal use. They usually bathed and did their washing in salt water, which tended to leave garments stiff, crusty, and abrasive; but, noted Waddell, seamen believed rainwater to be much wetter than salt water and that one never takes cold from exposure in salt water. With the shortage of stewards, the gentlemen were required to do their own washing, and Whittle had a good laugh at the efforts of Lieutenant Grimball and Dr. Lining. The doctor was not feeling well—the ship was damp and disagreeable—and he did not enjoy scrubbing in the rain "like a washer woman." He could not get it right and had to turn the task over to one of the sailors. Later captures would provide additional personnel, relieving officers of these undignified duties.

Greeted one morning by a nice little breeze, the captain ordered the propeller raised and all plain sail set. "She spreads a great deal of canvas," wrote Whittle. "The ship is very much more comfortable under sail than steam, and I am always glad to see her going steadily with her wings spread. I have been very busy all day. My hands are full, and every one comes to me for everything." He rigged new forebraces, new main topsail halyards, and a main brace using all the captured rope from *Alina*. Additional such work would await another prize.

On 5 November, one week after the first prize and 7° north of the equator, *Shenandoah* took her second, overhauling the 168-ton schooner *Charter Oak* with the usual routine, first showing the English flag and when the victim responded with the Stars and Stripes, firing a blank charge, raising the Confederate banner, sending an armed boat, and retrieving the captain, mates, and ship's papers for a hearing. *Charter Oak* was bound from Boston to San Francisco with a hundred tons of coal, lumber, furniture, and preserved fruits, meats, and vegetables—"in fact almost everything that we wanted," recalled Grimball. Master's Mate Hunt thought that rounding the stormy Cape Horn at the foot of South America in this tiny ship was "a noteworthy instance of Yankee perseverance and daring."[2]

"Now came the trouble," wrote Whittle: women were on board. Grimball wondered, "What in the world could we do with them? Where could they sleep?" The captain was unsure whether to destroy *Charter Oak* and thus burden *Shenandoah* with two females and a child or to bond the captured vessel and let her go, so he left the decision to the first lieutenant. Another example of tentative leadership, thought Whittle. "I concluded that whatever be the difficulties we should burn her—and it was decided upon."

Charter Oak captain Samuel J. Gillman whined that his earnings of four years were invested and he would be made a pauper, and then—to the considerable amusement of his captors—he said, "Well sir, if you are going to destroy my schooner, for God's sake save the preserved meats and vegetables." They assured him the stores would receive due attention, asking only where they were stowed. Gillman was rowed back to his doomed ship and fetched his wife, widowed sister-in-law, Mrs. Gage, and her four-year-old son, Frank, along with personal effects.

Despite the inconvenience, the presence of females brought forth the captors' Southern gentility, perhaps enhanced by the knowledge they were about to destroy the family's property and means of livelihood. So every courtesy was extended, with Waddell providing the first example. When Gillman was asked, under oath, if he possessed private or public funds, he admitted having about $200. Whittle advised his captain not to take the money, reminding him that it might be all Gillman had. Nevertheless, Waddell ordered the prisoner to give over his cash and then turned and ostentatiously presented it to Mrs. Gillman on behalf of the Confederacy with the stipulation that she not give any of it to her husband, to which she readily agreed.

It was mere pretense, recalled Waddell, driven by compassion for ladies who would be landed he knew not where. "The thought of inflicting unnecessary severity on a female made my heart shrink within." The captain symbolically discommoded the (male) enemy without making war on a woman; his honor was intact on both counts. The Gillmans were thunderstruck and grateful. Whittle relegated one of his lieutenants to the steerage and assigned the ladies to the starboard aft wardroom cabin, where, he believed, they would be much more comfortable than they had been in the tiny schooner. According to Waddell, Gillman later acknowledged the kindness in a New York newspaper; if so, it would have been a singular instance in the North of positive press for rebel raiders.

Chew had not expected to capture ladies—a novel experience—but he was pleased at the development, hoping their presence would lend charm to a roving life. He was, however, disappointed; the women were not at all attractive, although the boy was bright eyed and interesting and he seemed delighted at the change from a dirty little schooner to a large, fine ship. Chew wrote, "Innocent child, he knew but the kisses and caresses of a mother!" Mason was not impressed either: "These women certainly were the most stupid I ever saw." They could not converse and came to meals in the most remarkable gowns. Lining noted that Mrs. Gilman was a plain woman of about thirty, while her sister was a buxom widow with perfectly auburn hair, a rare thing in his mind. And the women made themselves quite at home.

Shenandoah lay near the prize while everything possible was removed. To Lining's regret, they never found the preserved fruits but did retrieve vegetables, including two thousand pounds of canned tomatoes, and six hundred pounds of canned lobster. Mason thought the lobster was excellent and the furniture, though difficult to transfer, was welcome—chairs, tables, bureaus, and sofas. He would like to have fitted out his Confederate friends with some nice pieces that were ultimately thrown overboard or burned along with farm implements such as ploughs and harrows. The edibles were divided among the messes fore and aft. The tomatoes lasted six months.

Charter Oak would not sink as *Alina* had with her cargo of iron, so the new victim was prepared for burning. Combustibles such as tar, pitch, and turpentine were scattered throughout. Bulkheads were torn down and piled up in cabins and forecastle, hatches opened, yards counterbraced and halyards let go so sails hung loosely. Fire taken from galley and cooking stove was deposited in the hold and about the deck. The captors waited nearby in the boat and watched as flames spread quickly, enveloping the vessel. It took a long time to burn. By the end of the war, thought Whittle, they would all know how to make good fires, but how horrible it would be if anyone were still on board. "It is to me a pitiful sight to see a fine vessel wantonly destroyed but I hope to witness an immense number of painful sights of the same kind, and I trust that *Shenandoah* may be able to continue her present work until our foolish and inhuman foes sue for peace."

The ladies settled into their quarters and were accepted into the wardroom mess along with Captain Gillman. Mrs. Gage was the widow of a federal army sergeant killed at Harpers Ferry; Whittle was surprised that she did not seem to hate her captors. The captain and two mates were paroled while *Charter Oak* crewmen were confined in single irons in the forecastle. The first lieutenant asserted his gallantry further by personally assisting the master-at-arms making and arranging beds in the starboard cabin. The prisoners seemed pleased, especially the ladies. "I am astonished at myself," wrote Whittle, "when I consider how stud[i]edly cruel [the Yankees] are to our dear women." After hoisting boats and propeller, they made all plain sail as the burning wreck fell astern. Whittle saw both masts topple and watched the glow hanging in the sky long past midnight.

On Sunday morning according to timeless routine, the crew mustered and the captain read the Articles of War. "Today at dinner," Whittle wrote, "I did a thing which has rendered me very unhappy in as much as it is very dangerous." While eating a slice of rhubarb pie he swallowed a piece of the glass bottle in which the fruit had been preserved. The cook had broken the neck off the bottle instead of drawing the cork. Dr. Lining worried that the glass could cause internal bleeding and be life threatening, so he prescribed three strong emetics to induce vomiting. Although anxious, Whittle put his life in God's hands.

The four mates of *Alina* and *Charter Oak* refused to clean out the forecastle where they slept and so were clapped in irons with paroles withdrawn. The first lieutenant had his first disciplinary cases among the crew and was determined to make an example of him: Fireman George Sylvester had been insubordinate, refusing to take a turn at cooking for his mess. He was put in irons, and triced up (suspended from the rigging by the wrists with his toes barely touching the deck). When Sylvester complained, he was gagged and after an hour, begged to be let down. Whittle told him he should be ashamed of himself.

Discipline was absolutely necessary to the happiness of the men and to survival of all on board, recorded the first lieutenant; this was not tyranny but a "thorough governing." Whittle would examine closely all reports and give the accused the advantage of doubt, but judging him guilty would respond promptly and decisively. "I hate to punish men but it must be done. You must either rule them or they will rule you. . . . When the men once see you determined and firm they will be better, happier and better conducted."

An English seaman named Thomas Hall gave particular grief. When a quarrel with a French sailor came to blows, the first lieutenant put them both in irons embracing each other around an iron stanchion, hands secured to a beam over their heads. Their first impulse was to laugh, but they quickly concluded the joke was on them and politely asked to be let down. Whittle considered Hall to be smart and energetic with the makings of a good sailor, but the seaman continued to get into fights and was punished several times. "I was determined to conquer him, and I kept him up eight hours more and I found him as subdued as a lamb. He gave me his word that I would never have any more trouble with him." Seaman Hall did not keep his word.

Methods of disciplinary punishment were more a matter of tradition and captain's prerogative than formal regulation. Whittle thought that tricing had "a most wonderful effect," although a Melbourne newspaper would later characterize it as "cruel and barbarous" and "a species of crucifixion." If problems stemmed from abuse of alcohol, as they often did, Whittle would stop the grog ration. Imprisonment in irons was not helpful since it just gave the crewman a break from work and burdened the other men. One option Whittle did not have was flogging; the ancient practice had been abolished in the U.S. Navy in 1850 after much resistance from officers and veteran sailors and was never adopted in the Confederate navy.[3]

The first lieutenant also had to manage prisoners. Security in a confined environment required restraint and isolation with occasional punishments for bad behavior. Prisoners could not be housed on the berth deck with the crew, many of whom were former captives themselves. So the forecastle was the only space available—a cramped environment and particularly uncomfortable in high seas, which also housed sheep, chickens, and pigs. But *Shenandoah* would be chronically undermanned; the first priority was to recruit them. "When they first came off," wrote Lieutenant Grimball, "they generally refused to ship, but we kept them in irons so long that, as is the case with all sailors, it makes little difference to them what side of the fence they are on, in preference to being in 'limbo' they joined *Shenandoah*. We have a splendid crew the majority being *young men* of all nations." Whittle counted on crewmen employing "rough persuasion in the dark" to convince newcomers to join.

Shenandoah next captured the bark *D. Godfrey*, captained by Samuel Halleck, thirty days from Boston to Valparaiso. She was an old vessel with a valuable assorted cargo including tobacco and prime beef; however, most of it was underneath forty thousand feet of pine lumber and would have taken too long to move. A few hundred feet of rope and good plank, well suited for building a magazine in the hold, were confiscated.

Cabin and pantry bulkheads were knocked down by a few blows of the carpenter's hatchet and thrown in a pile on the deck. A match was applied and in fifteen minutes flames burst through the skylights. "Darkness had settled around us when the rigging and sails took fire," recalled Hunt, "but every rope could be seen as distinctly as upon a painted canvas, as the flames made their way from the deck, and writhed upward like fiery serpents. Soon the yards came thundering down by the run as the lifts and halyards yielded to the devouring element, the standing rigging parted like blazing flax, and the spars simultaneously went by the board and left the hulk wrapped from stem to stern in one fierce blaze, like a floating, fiery furnace."[4]

Whittle was amused at the female prisoners who appeared to be quite in love with *Shenandoah*, enjoying a capture as much as he and his fellow Confederates; the little boy gave three cheers for Jeff Davis every day. The men of *D. Godfrey* did not seem sorry to see the old ship go—apparently Halleck had planned to sell her in Valparaiso anyway—and to the first lieutenant's joy, five of the six sailors (three English, one Yankee, one from St. Johns, New Brunswick) along with a black steward signed the shipping papers. "They are all good, young men and the darkey is the very man I want for ship's cook." Whittle was proud of the crew; they had behaved well in this demoralizing work: "When in the world's history was a parallel ever known[?]" A board of officers appointed to assess the prizes fixed the value of *Charter Oak* at $15,000 and *D. Godfrey* at $36,000.

The new black crewmember was John Williams, a freedman of Boston. He would desert in Melbourne and, in an affidavit for the U.S. consul, swear that

Captain Waddell had urged him to join, saying that "colored people" were the cause of the war, and it would go better for him if he signed on or be hard on him if he did not. Waddell (according to Williams) said he wanted all colored persons he could get and offered a berth as a coal trimmer for six months with a month's advance pay. Williams agreed to work but initially refused to join because he was a loyal citizen who had served the U.S. Navy. He claimed to have discharge papers from the USS *Minnesota* and also to have been on board the USS *Congress* when she was sunk by the CSS *Virginia* in Hampton Roads on the day before her battle with *Monitor*. *Shenandoah's* shipping articles show that Williams signed on as a landsman at a salary of $15.58 per month, the position and pay offered to those with no seamanship experience. Along with his shipmates, Williams made his mark on the day *D. Godfrey* was captured, so whatever the degree of his resistance, it did not last long. The others signed on as seamen at $29.10 per month.[5]

The naval service was accustomed throughout its history to men of all shades, at sea in its own world—its authoritarian structures customized through centuries to the unique needs of that shipboard life and hardly less strict than slavery. The Union Navy, also desperate for men, had been far ahead of the U.S. Army in quietly enlisting hundreds of freedmen and "contrabands." In both navies, to place one group into a separate category based on race would have disrupted efficiency and discipline. In general, and far more so than on land, men were accepted for their skills and performance regardless of color. It was a matter of teamwork and often of survival. Waddell would have enlisted blacks as seamen or even petty officers and paid them accordingly had they possessed the experience; he could not afford to do otherwise and would have seen no inconsistency in the notion. At least three of them would be enlisted from prizes as landsmen or ordinary seamen.

On 8 November, Lining noted the one-month anniversary of their boarding *Laurel* at Liverpool and that "a good many things have taken place since that!" He was delighted with the "Hindostanee" steward from *Alina*, William Bruce, who was quite dark but spoke English perfectly. The officers' messes finally were set up as custom dictated with commissioned officers in the wardroom, midshipmen and warrants in the steerage, and petty officers in a designated portion of the berth deck. The warrant officers—not of the gentleman class and "some very disagreeable people" according to the doctor—had been dining in the wardroom until other spaces were cleared away.

The first lieutenant had a portion of the large deckhouse knocked away, providing additional space for working the two 8-inch guns forward, although he hoped he would never have occasion to use them, considering *Shenandoah's* mixed crew of merchant sailors untrained in such work. With his armament finally in position and most running rigging renewed, Whittle was anxious for action: "Nothing gives me more pleasure than to do as much harm as I can in a legitimate way to our inhuman foes. . . . But how often do I think of my dear home and country. Oh how they are all suffering. . . . Will we ever meet again? God grant that we may, and in the meantime I invoke the protection of god on [them]."

The next day, they encountered the Danish brig *Anna Jane* bound from New York to Rio de Janeiro. Waddell wished to relieve the crowding and so convinced the vessel's captain to receive some of his prisoners. Captains, mates, and one seaman each from the late barks *Alina* and *D. Godfrey* were sent as passengers, along with a barrel of beef and a barrel of bread for their use and a captured chronometer for the captain's trouble. The ladies of *Charter Oak* did not seem displeased that they were not included. Whittle opined that they were better treated and more content on *Shenandoah* than at any time in their lives. "It is a perfect farce to call them prisoners." As Captain Staples and his mates departed, they demonstrated regular Yankee character, thought the first lieutenant, by not expressing gratitude for kindness received or even saying goodbye. "What a miserable set of villains our enemies are. I hate them more than ever the more I see of them." Whittle had opposed the decision to release prisoners because it would spread word of *Shenandoah*'s location and activity. Lining also thought it important to keep her movements unknown so the enemy could not surmise their destination.

It was "another glorious day in our legitimate calling," wrote Whittle on 10 November. He awakened early to the news that there was a brigantine close on the weather bow. She hoisted the "detestable Yankee rag" and after the second gun threw her head yards aback and hove to. Chew rowed across with an armed boat. She was *Susan* of New York, Captain Hansen, with coal from Cardiff, Wales, to Rio Grande de Sul, Brazil. Lining thought her the funniest looking craft he had ever seen: she leaked badly and sat low in the water with a paddle wheel something like a steamboat's on the lee side, which connected to a pump and discharged water as she moved along.

Once again, despite alleged English ownership of the cargo, the vessel was condemned because the bill of lading had not been notarized. Lieutenant Chew brought her under the lee of *Shenandoah* for transfer of provisions, a set of cabin drawers, and a mess table for the steerage. They also brought across some dogs, one of which was made a pet for the men. With holes cut in the side below the waterline and others bored through the bottom, she went down by the head in about half an hour. The Yankee captain seemed rather glad to be rid of the old thing. Values were estimated at $5,000 for the vessel and $436 for the cargo. "Quite a small amount yet small favors are thankfully received," concluded Chew. Whittle wished she had been a fine clipper.

Captain Hansen of *Susan*, a German, desired to sign on *Shenandoah* but felt honor-bound to return to New York and report the capture of his ship; the insurance company might refuse to recognize the owners' claim on presumption that he had turned traitor and given up the vessel voluntarily. Three English crewmen signed on immediately, and Whittle expected that another would soon. That day, he tacked the ship three times and each time she went round beautifully. "I never saw a vessel work better." The crew could complete the complex and critical evolution of tacking with efficiency and they could man the guns, but the first lieutenant still wanted sixty more men. He had them holystone the decks and reeve new topsail braces and topgallant gear. The remaining prisoners preferred standing duty to being in irons, so Whittle divided them into two watches. "I am always very tired at night but manage to sleep very well."

Shenandoah cruised the Atlantic narrows between the bulges of Africa and Brazil—previous hunting grounds of *Sumter*, *Florida*, and *Alabama*—where prevailing winds funnel trade into busy shipping lanes to and from Cape Horn and the Cape of Good Hope. They passed through the belt of calms and variable winds north of the equator—the Doldrums—and through a "gate" between 28° and 32° west longitude, which to most mariners provided the best of the light airs.

On a gray afternoon, they were buffeting about in heavy southerly winds and squalls when a large ship was spotted to windward. Whittle clewed up sails and steamed to intercept as they chased her into a dreary dusk. By midnight nearly all hands were on lookout, even the two female prisoners who hoped to see a big catch. Suddenly a towering shadow emerged from the gloom passing close aboard. Whittle barked an order and a blast of noise and flame erupted from the signal gun. "What ship?" hailed the first lieutenant. The response was shredded by the wind, but she hove to while an armed boat with Lieutenant Lee in charge wallowed across. She was *Kate Prince*, Captain Henry Libby of Portsmouth, New Hampshire, and another Yankee carrying coal to Bahia, Brazil; but this time the papers were in order with a properly notarized oath naming Liverpool cargo owners.

Once again Whittle disagreed with his captain: the Cardiff coal was of little value compared to the vessel, he thought, whose loss would be felt dearly by the enemy—they should destroy ship and cargo and afterward compensate the owners for the coal. Nevertheless, Whittle was ordered to bond the prize, transfer all prisoners, and send them on their way. "[The captives] were all exceedingly grateful for our kindness particularly the women who I am quite certain, would have preferred to have stayed." The little boy said he liked rebels and did not want to go. As soon as the ladies were informed, recorded Chew, "there was a great hurrying to & fro, looking after band boxes, bundling up hooped skirts, in a word collecting those thousand things which always accompany women."

The first lieutenant was glad to be rid of the females and fervently desired never again to be thus burdened (a hope to be dashed in the Indian Ocean). He superintended the passenger transfer in torrential rain and by 5 a.m. was heartily tired. Captain Libby sent over two barrels of Irish potatoes for their use. Lining, like Whittle, believed that Waddell was making a mistake in releasing the vessel: "However, the deed is done, & there is no use of talking about it." *Kate Prince* was bonded for $40,000.

That afternoon, they overhauled another vessel and fired a gun. She hoisted the flag of Buenos Aires but so closely resembled a Yankee that Waddell decided to investigate. The Baltimore-built clipper bark *Adelaide*, formerly *Adelaide Pendergrast*, was bound from New York to Rio with a cargo of flour. The papers were ambiguous, so Captain James P. Williams of Matthews County, Virginia, and his mate were brought over to testify. "And now took place the most curious concatenation of circumstances, making the greatest 'mess' I have ever known," wrote Lining.

Who owned the cargo? Who owned the ship? And where was she legally registered? At first, Captain Williams swore *Adelaide* had been sold to parties in Buenos Aires and was therefore neutral, but he could produce no bill of sale. The first mate testified that the sale was a pretense to fool federal authorities; the vessel was still owned by Mr. Pendergrast of Baltimore, an earnest Southerner with two sons in the rebel army. Then Williams admitted the lie and begged Waddell not to burn the ship—he was a young man just married with all of his meager savings invested in her, and the owner would be heartbroken at the loss. *Adelaide*, named for Mrs. Pendergrast, was not insured for a single cent.

On paper, the cargo was shipped by Mr. Pendergrast but owned by a New York firm. "The case was very much mixed up and there was evidently foul play somewhere," concluded Whittle. Waddell decided that any vessel shipping Yankee flour from New York warranted destruction even if the owner was a Southerner. Several hours were occupied transferring stores and removing crew and passengers with their baggage to *Shenandoah*. The doctor found good larder for the mess—hams and preserved fruits. Lieutenant Chew and his men broke out the skylights on *Adelaide* to provide draft, capsized cans of kerosene, and piled combustibles in the foreword hold; they upset a barrel of tar amid the flour.

Meanwhile personal letters discovered in the captain's cabin revealed that the paperwork showing cargo ownership by the New York firm was fake, intended to avoid interference by Yankee authorities; the flour, like the ship, belonged to Mr. Pendergrast of Baltimore. Waddell concluded that he could not burn the vessel and sent orders across to Chew, catching him just before he lit the match. Whittle was truly sorry for the incident but put the blame on the prevarication or ignorance of Captain Williams. Everything possible was done to return what had been taken and to restore the damage, although much had been lost or destroyed. *Adelaide* was perfectly seaworthy, however. Williams took the ship back joyfully. He was provided a barrel of sugar and some lamp oil to replace what they had poured all over his decks.

To further allay federal suspicions, Waddell bonded the "enemy" cargo while recognizing the bogus sale of the vessel, acknowledging it to be under a neutral flag. It was nearly dark as they parted ways. Whittle vowed to explain the situation to Mr. Pendergrast if ever given the chance and sent along a letter to his dear Pattie. "There is no telling how long it will be before she gets it, but I am pretty certain that it will be received some day or other. Oh! How much would I not give just to know that my darlings are well. My thoughts are constantly of them. I console myself very often by reading over and over again the letters to me. Letters full of affection and love."

————

That same day in London—12 November 1864—correspondence arrived on the West Africa mail packet *Calabar* from Tenerife along with Captain Corbett, formerly of *Sea King*, and twenty-some of his crewmen. The British consul at Tenerife wrote the secretary of state for foreign affairs reporting the arrival and subsequent departure of *Laurel*, leaving Corbett and his sailors behind. *Sea King*, they stated, had been wrecked off the Desertas. But Corbett aroused suspicion by his prevarication and suspicious behavior, so the consul obtained affidavits from four sailors who, among other details, confirmed that they had been instructed to say their ship had foundered. Corbett was placed in custody under suspicion of violating the Foreign Enlistment Act by recruiting British sailors for a foreign navy. Corbett also fully briefed Commander Bulloch in Liverpool.[6]

Calabar also delivered a letter from the U.S. consul at Tenerife to U.S. minister Adams with a full report from the same sources. Adams' secretary thought the British consul had covered up; he must have known that *Sea King* had been sold to rebels and was about to cruise under Semmes. Word was passed to Secretary of State Seward in Washington and to the Navy. The U.S. consul in Liverpool recalled *Sea King* as an excellent sailer and "altogether a fine vessel for the business of privateering," which he assumed was now burning and destroying American vessels.[7]

Chapter 5

"Oh, It's a Grand Sight"

On 13 November 1864, the Sabbath was interrupted by the schooner *Lizzie M. Stacey*, Captain William Archer, from Boston to Honolulu. She was 143 tons with seven sailors and officers—a fine little vessel that First Lieutenant Whittle would like to have captained himself as a cruiser, had there been crewmen to spare: "This is a nice piece of Sunday's work." *Stacey* carried assorted stores for *Shenandoah*'s ultimate target, American whalers in the Pacific, and was apparently the third vessel dispatched for this purpose by unlucky owners. Their first two had been reported missing off Cape Horn. The prize was valued at $15,000.

At about 6:30 p.m., *Stacey* was fired and burning furiously to leeward when she caught a gust and forged suddenly ahead, almost ramming *Shenandoah*. Whittle shouted orders and men jumped. Lee braces and sheets were cast off, the great wheel spun, weather braces hauled. The huge hull and massive yards swung. Sails thrashed and boomed as the wind jammed them back against the masts and the bow passed through the eye of the wind; sails filled again. She pivoted on her heel like a giant ballerina and settled on the opposite tack pulling away from the flaming wreck. Such movements would appear elegant and stately to an observer but would be slow-motion disaster if *Shenandoah* came into contact with the fire. Dry wood decks caulked with pitch, canvas sails, hemp and manila lines shushed with tar would go up in a heartbeat.

The first lieutenant was delighted when a Baltimore African American from *Stacey*, Charles Hopkins, signed on as ordinary seaman; a Swedish sailor named Hansen joined; and a Scotsman named Strachen shipped as coal passer. (Hopkins had parted company with John Williams, the cook from *D. Godfrey*, at a New York boardinghouse only a few weeks earlier; they were quite surprised at seeing each other.) *Shenandoah* now had forty-three men—double the original number—and twenty-four officers. Whittle was able to work the crew a normal "watch and watch" schedule—four hours on and four hours off with half relieving the other day and night. This was more efficient than working all hands all day and getting by with a small deck watch at night. They still could not handle all lines for taking in all sails quickly, but they could manage the few sails set in heavy weather. Whittle worried that these men chose to enlist only for six months at the end of which they could demand their pay and leave, but he was confident he would acquire more recruits and do his best to enlist them for the duration of the cruise.[1]

Shenandoah crossed zero degrees latitude shortly before noon on 15 November. "The usual ceremonies attendant upon that event on board a man-of-war were not neglected," recalled Master's Mate Hunt. In ceremonies descended from ancient attempts to propitiate gods of sea and wind (and still a Navy custom), vessels passing the equator would receive a visit from "his aquatic Godship Neptune," who holds court there, suffering no ship to pass until he has satisfied himself that those who have not previously crossed the line are properly initiated. "We had a number of novices among officers and men, and consequently the event was anticipated with even more than ordinary interest."[2]

Festivities were postponed until after dark to heighten the fun. Two ward-room stewards—William Bruce and James—were so affected that Dr. Lining had to reassure them Neptune would do them no harm. It was eight bells (8 p.m.) when a rough voice over the bows hailed the ship: "Heave to. I want to come on board." A fantastical figure ascended the side dressed in an oilskin coat and wearing a wig of Manila yarn. He was accompanied by two other grotesqueries representing his majesty's wife and his official barber, with a bucket of slush and a three-foot razor manufactured from an iron hoop. Neptune, holding a speaking trumpet under his arm and a trident in his right hand, stepped on deck with all the dignity his position warranted. "What ship is this?" he demanded. "The Confederate cruiser *Shenandoah*," replied the officer of the deck, touching his hat.[3]

In dim lantern light and wavering shadows, Neptune required that all who had never entered the kingdom be brought before him immediately. Those who had passed the ordeal were appointed as "police" and dispersed in search of initiates. "They were scented out, and dragged before the Ocean Deity, where they were solemnly lathered from the slush-bucket, and shaved with the iron hoop, according to immemorial usage," continued Hunt. The shaving over, a hose from the seawater pump was turned on them, filling eyes and face and wetting them through and through.[4]

The party worked its way through the uninitiated officers. Lieutenant Chew broke for his cabin, but after a few minutes of friendly resistance walked quietly up to the chair, followed by Midshipman Browne and Midshipman Mason. They knew not to answer any questions and kept their mouths shut. Then came Assistant Surgeon Francis J. McNulty. When the barber asked him where he was from, McNulty replied politely and took a mouthful of shaving slush. Blood flaring, McNulty let out a roar and knocked the barber sprawling as a stream of water hit his face, much to the amusement of all hands. Mr. Cobb, one of the engineers, thought it damned foolishness and had to be carried by force to the chair and held there for his dunking. Lieutenant Lee and Sailing Master Bulloch dragged Lieutenant Grimball up, after which Grimball himself collared the first lieutenant who pulled off his coat to the undershirt and suffered the ordeal. "It was rare sport," thought Whittle, "but I am very glad that it comes but once." Lining thought it was good recreation and a break in monotony.

Neptune strode aft and informed the captain that everything had been attended to, that he would bid him good-bye and wish him a good voyage. Waddell ordered all hands to splice the main brace, in which Neptune, his wife, and barber participated before departure. Boatswain's Mate Warren played Neptune; Master-at-Arms Reid was Mrs. Neptune; and Mr. Guy, the gunner, was his barber. The shaving soap was a "most wonderful mixture" of soap, grease, molasses, and stewed apples. *Shenandoah* crossed the line about six hundred miles northeast of Cape San Roque, the eastern tip of Brazil.

Days returned to routine and boredom and hard work. "Fairly in the trades bowling along most pleasantly," noted Lining. "Nothing in sight except the English ship we passed last night, which is now nearly hull down astern." A few days later, while enjoying a splendid breeze, he wrote, "We find, that whenever *night* comes on, and she is going her nine or ten knots, the skipper begins to get uneasy, can't sleep, gets fidgety, & then takes in sail. So tonight about 9 p.m. he had the royals taken in & brailed up the spanker." With few men and two inexperienced watchstanding lieutenants, Waddell was not taking chances, but the doctor believed he was too cautious.

Whittle was feeling wretched, his sickness ascribed to either the piece of bottle glass he might have swallowed or to excessive tobacco. He assumed the glass, if there, would prove fatal. "I trust that I may be better tomorrow for the anxiety makes me miserable." He improved the next day and, deciding that tobacco was the problem, determined to stop both chewing and smoking by giving all supplies to his mess mates. This was not his first attempt at quitting, but being so busy now, he hoped temptation would be blunted. It is not clear that the normally compressed Whittle was successful in this particular exercise at self-control. Waddell continued tightening discipline by issuing written orders, the first of which required officers to be in uniform on deck: black or blue trousers were allowed, but gray coats or jackets were to be worn with caps; slouch hats were forbidden. Lining could no longer wear his floppy broad-brimmed hat in the hot sun so he drew some flannel from ship's supplies and "went to tailoring" to make a cool tropic jacket.

———

In Liverpool, U.S. consul Dudley obtained depositions from former *Sea King* sailors and prepared a report for Minister Adams in London, which Adams promptly forwarded to Foreign Secretary John Russell, belaboring in exquisite detail that the two ships *Laurel* and *Sea King* flew the English flag and that owners, captains, crew, arms, ammunition—"everything down to the coal in the hold"—were English. "It seems to me that nothing is wanting to stamp this as an English transaction from beginning to end and the vessel now called the Shenandoah as an English piratical craft," without regard to the colors she may display when in chase of a peaceful merchantman or whaler "or when she lights up the ocean with her fire." According to the sailors, wooden cases containing up to three and a half tons of guns and carriages, shot and shell, had been transferred along with sixty barrels of powder. Crates broke open revealing contents. It had taken four of them to carry an iron safe into the captain's cabin; by the rattling sound, the safe must have contained money. Consul Dudley still believed that Raphael Semmes commanded the new cruiser.[5]

With poop awning spread and a nice regular trade wind, it was quite pleasant on deck as Whittle mustered the crew at quarters and held regular Sunday inspection. The men looked good now that uniforms had been made up, he wrote, "but grey will never stand the sea air." Uniforms were scarce; Confederate officers frequently resorted to U.S. Navy articles while sailors wore anything at hand. Whittle's uniform, new when the cruise began, now appeared as if it had been worn for a year. "Oh! no the old blue was the best, and I think the only color which will stand." (One veteran recalled: "Who ever heard of a gray sailor, no matter what nationality he served.")

Lining reported a "most curious display of waterworks" from the smokestack steam pipe as an overfilled boiler suddenly shot steam as high as the topgallant sail. One morning four sail were in sight, which to their disappointment proved to be Dutch, Spanish, and English. To conceal their identities, the officer of the deck informed the English ship that *Shenandoah* was the HMS *Hesper* on a cruise.[6]

Waddell ordered all midshipmen to maintain a training journal. They were to go back to the beginning of the cruise and work out the ship's position each day by dead reckoning, using courses steered and distances made good as recorded in the log, and then continue this practice daily, along with computation of current latitude and longitude by altitudes of sun and stars. The captain and first lieutenant reviewed the results regularly. These duties along with normal watches kept Mason busy and put him behind in his journal, but he expected to have time for reading and even for studying German in addition to his French. He and Midshipman Browne practiced with two French sailors employed to look out for their hammocks and wash clothes.

Kate Prince arrived in Bahia, Brazil, on 23 November with her load of prisoners. Captain Libby provided a detailed report to the local American consul, but this first definite word of *Shenandoah*'s location and activities would take more than four weeks to reach Minister Adams in London.[7]

Dr. Lining's brief journal entries through a typical week reflect generally cooling but variable conditions and the numbing routine of a ship at sea with wind, wave, and weather at the center of existence. Thursday, 24 November, they were still going along with a spanking breeze. On Friday, breezes were light but fair from the north with a warmer, hazy atmosphere and the heaviest dew he had ever seen at sea. Saturday morning saw little wind but was raining and quite cool; before night a balmy south wind brought a good blow. Lining got out a blanket and was glad to keep to the wardroom or cabin along with companions not on watch.

Sunday, 27 November, was like other days except the call to quarters, inspection by officers of divisions, and absence of routine work. Weather was cool and pleasant but with a heavy swell, which made it rather uncomfortable. Monday was blowing quite sharply with a high sea running. "Our ship is behaving remarkably well, comparatively dry, & rolling very little." The doctor sighted his first albatross, indicating they were getting pretty far south, and he read some Dickens. On Tuesday his eyes were inflamed so he could not read or write. "What is left to a poor cove in such circumstances at sea, but to go to bed? So I acted accordingly." It was, again, a rainy, squally day with "nothing of interest going on."

If the doctor wasn't busy, the crew was: hauling on braces and sheets, adjusting sails to wind and course, reefing and shaking out reefs, setting and taking in sail, along with never-ending cleaning, maintenance, and overhaul. Whittle remained optimistic and was feeling better about the condition of the ship. He continued renewing the running gear, exchanging old, stretchable hemp for new manila line taken from prizes. Crewmen broke out and restowed paymaster's and boatswain's stores in new storerooms in the deckhouse. The work progressed slowly but surely. "All these are heavy jobs, but thank God, the heaviest of our work is over."

One morning in the midwatch (midnight to 4 a.m.), Whittle was aroused by a great noise on deck. He rushed out in slippers to see that they were about to collide with a bark on the opposite tack. He gave the order hard aport to pass right under her stern. It was a close call, just the sort of event Waddell feared with junior lieutenants on duty. Lieutenant Scales had been officer of the deck, but, wrote Whittle, despite his lack of experience, Scales was watchful and attentive and would make an excellent officer. Later that day, they hauled fires and blew water out of the boilers to enable Chief Engineer Eugene Matthew O'Brien to clean them—a filthy and disagreeable task that Whittle suspected had not been done since the ship was built. Whittle was getting bored—the work was tedious and he wanted another capture.

The next day, strong winds modulated to a good breeze; sail was made to royals and flying jib, but it was foggy and damp. They sighted a great deal of plankton in thick red streaks and spots on the water, indicating the presence of whales and therefore of Yankee whalers. The first lieutenant was fascinated with this "whale food." He had a bucketful brought on board and found the water alive with little red insects that looked like lobster or shrimp. "They say that the whales eat this, but some say that they do not." (They do.) *Shenandoah* approached the remote South Atlantic island of Tristan da Cunha, a good whaling ground. Lining joined Lee and Grimball in the latter's cabin that evening and had a long talk—a "gas"—about the war and their opinions of various Southern generals, a discussion that probably included Lee's uncle, R. E. Lee.

Fog and overcast limited visibility on 4 December at 37° south. A large double-topsail-yard ship—obviously of Yankee origin—loomed through the mist but when challenged, raised an Italian flag. Like so many others, she had been sold and was now *Dea del Mare* from Genoa to Rangoon for cargo. To confuse pursuers, *Shenandoah* officers removed caps and coats and dressed in blue as much as possible. The Italians were told they were the USS *DeSoto* on a cruise after Confederate raiders. Two other vague shapes ghosted along in the distance; as they cautiously approached under plain sail, Whittle became suspicious. One was a long, low bark-rigged vessel carrying a great deal of sail and what could have been a lowered smokestack abaft the main mast—perhaps a gunboat, maybe a Union one. They would keep a safe distance. With a splendid breeze and smooth sea, he noted, "it would have taken a wonderful vessel to catch us." As the breeze freshened, they hauled up close to the wind with royals set. "She went hour after hour ten knots, and I never was in a vessel, which could compare to her." *Shenandoah* passed every vessel in sight.

That afternoon, Tristan da Cunha Island shimmered indistinctly far to port, pricking the hazy gray-blue boundary where sky met sea. Then the mist rolled through again as the wind went down and the helmsman spotted another sail on the lee beam. At 5:45 p.m. they steamed down and found her hove to under double-reefed topsails. Up went the English flag; the stranger raised the Union banner. "This gave us great joy," noted Whittle, "as it is just three weeks since our last." She was a whaler with a bloody carcass wallowing alongside, black smoke billowing in the still air, and light flickering in brick furnaces as crewmen sliced chunks of blubber and boiled them down to oil in huge caldrons. "The odor from a whaling ship is horribly offensive," wrote Waddell, "but it is not worse than that of the green hide vessels from South America, which can be smelt fifty miles in a favorable wind." He would conclude, however, that the space below decks in a whaler where baleen, or whale bone (a cartilaginous filter-feeder system in the whale's mouth similar to bristles), was stowed stunk beyond his ability to describe it.[8]

Dusk descended as Sailing Master Bulloch rowed over with an armed crew, unceremoniously put a stop to the work, and took charge. Captain Charles Worth, his mates, and crew from the New Bedford bark *Edward* were brought back. They were four months out and ten days on the South Atlantic ground, during which they had taken only the one whale. Bulloch was instructed to show lights through a night of heavy rain and fog so the two ships could stay in company. *Shenandoah* lay by for two days as her boats, augmented by five whaleboats manned with prisoners, scuttled back and forth ferrying mounds of stores and supplies. The weather was perfect, smooth and misty, so a vessel could pass quite near without seeing anything. They took 50 barrels of beef, 49 of pork, 46 of flour, 2 of black fish oil, 1 of hams, 2 half barrels of sand; 6,000 pounds of bread, 1,200 of soap, 600 of coffee, 400 of butter, 1 of pickles; and a large quantity of manila rope. "Now anyone who would not be content with this is very unreasonable," concluded Whittle. "We have more than enough provisions to last us our cruise." Whaling ships stocked up for voyages lasting years, with months between port visits.

Navigation instruments and charts were seized along with harpoons and a shell gun that fired a long explosive spike to kill the whale after he had been harpooned and exhausted. "The [whaler captain] was the best specimen of a man we have yet captured," noted Chew. "As his profession would indicate, he was a brave, determined man, [who] met his misfortune with manly courage. I had some respect for him & sympathized with him in his distress." About 6 p.m. Whittle and his crew fired *Edward* fore and aft and returned to *Shenandoah*. They hoisted boats and stood off toward Tristan da Cunha. Most of the whalemen were Portuguese and, according to Whittle, so cowardly that they could not be induced to enlist. Only an Englishman, Seaman Francis Tuft, joined *Shenandoah* and was rated as a cooper.

All prisoners except the captain and one mate were put in irons, bringing the prisoner count to twenty-eight—too many to run loose about the deck, thought Whittle. "I wonder when in the annals of history such a thing ever took place before. I venture to say never." But he thanked God for their success as they watched the conflagration in soft evening light. "To see the rigging on fire after it has burned in two and the burning ends swinging as the vessel rolls. Oh, it's a grand sight."

On 7 December 1864, Whittle wrote, "At an early hour this morning we made very high land ahead and made a most beautiful land fall from the SSW."

Precipitous emerald cliffs shrouded by fog and cloud lifted from the sea. The tiny volcanic island of Tristan da Cunha lay at 38° south—1,700 miles west of Cape Town, a few degrees below the latitude of the Cape of Good Hope and Buenos Aires, and about halfway between them. Tristan had been discovered and claimed in 1506 by the Portuguese admiral of that name, but not permanently occupied until 1816 when the British stationed a garrison there to bolster security for Napoleon Bonaparte, then imprisoned several hundred miles away on the island of St. Helena. The soldiers were withdrawn in 1817, but three chose to stay as founders of the community to be encountered by *Shenandoah.*

As *Shenandoah* rounded the point, the slopes of the northwest coast appeared to be dotted with cattle. A large English flag climbed a pole amid ten widely scattered stone houses where a small tableland shelves to the sea. *Shenandoah* ran up the Confederate flag, stopped engines, and hovered offshore from the single community of Falmouth. The prisoners piled into three captured whaleboats with their belongings and rowed ashore. "I must say I pitied the poor devils," wrote Whittle. It could be as much as a year between ship visits, and should he return ten years hence, the first lieutenant expected some of the whalemen would still be there. He was, however, glad to be rid of them. "I do not like to have strangers among our men. It is demoralizing." Lining felt sorry for Captain Worth: "There was a frankness and a freedom from all meanness which made us respect him. We gave him every thing we thought it right to do." Among other items, Whittle provided fishing line, a quadrant, and a book on navigation; the doctor contributed medicine and fishhooks. Captain Worth politely bid them good-bye with thanks for their kindness.

The thirty-five island inhabitants, mostly English, were divided into seven families, noted Whittle, and with some scarcity lived well enough on this productive island. Women seemed more numerous than men. They relied on passing ships to bring the mail from St. Helena. Visiting vessels, usually Yankee whalers, exchanged flour and clothing for beef and mutton. As many as seventy whalers had been near the islands simultaneously before the war, but now it was difficult to find a single one. "It is wonderful that even here, in this remote island, away entirely from our country, the people feel the effects of the war. . . . This proves to us our importance," concluded Whittle.

A boat arrived close aboard offering to sell cattle, chickens, milk, butter, eggs, sheep, and other provisions. The first lieutenant agreed to exchange flour worth eight dollars a barrel for beef worth eighteen cents a barrel. "This is paying dearly for our whistle, but that makes little matter." The boatman was from New London, Connecticut, the only American on the island; he had been there fifteen years. If there were any place in the world without Yankees, thought Whittle, this should be it. He would bet that the fellow not only had more money than the rest, but that he was a leading man among them. "He is a fine hearty looking man and has evidently had enough to eat." When asked who was governor, the Yank replied, no one; each man ruled his own family and if anyone did anything outrageous, they held a meeting and denounced him as a dog. Whittle considered them land sharks and thieves who charged exorbitantly for everything. "However, I can readily understand that to see new faces is such a treat that they hate to see the chance go."

Their arrival created great excitement, recorded Mason. Despite infrequent contact with the outside world, the people seemed informed about the war and recognized the flag. They were comfortably dressed in slop (sailors' issue) clothes obtained from whalers. Most wore shoes of raw bullock hide with the hair still on it. "All looked fat & sleek, had a great deal to say." Mason was quite anxious to go ashore, but the captain would not allow anybody over the side.

Dutchman Peter Green, a twenty-five-year resident, rowed out to complain that food and supplies on the island were inadequate to sustain the prisoners and asked that the captain either take them back or send provisions to serve them. Waddell agreed to land three months' rations: 400 pounds salt beef, 400 pounds salt pork, and 1,680 pounds of bread. Considering that Mr. Green was a sharp bargainer, Lining dispatched a note onshore to Captain Worth informing him that the provisions were for their use. He did not want it said that they abandoned captives on a nearly desolate island to the charity of people who had little to begin with.

Boats shoved off from shore with fresh provisions including over 700 pounds of beef along with sheep and ducks. The paymaster opened his store and drove a brisk trade with the islanders. At about 1 p.m., they got under way, steamed around the island eastward, then made sail to the royals and let steam go down. Lining saw for the first time great quantities of kelp in shallow waters. The weather cleared toward evening providing a clear view of the island as it receded into dusk.

A few nights later, with unfavorable winds and the engine turning, the captain's sleep was disturbed by a troublesome thumping in the propeller well. He and Chief Engineer O'Brien went on deck to investigate but nothing could be seen in the dark. At daylight, the propeller was hoisted clear for inspection. The brass band on the hub of the screw, which couples it with the shaft when lowered, was cracked and held in place by iron bolts in a repair obviously made before they acquired the ship. It was not clear if the crack extended clear through the coupling. A new coupling would have to be cast in a foundry; a temporary fix would be tenuous, and a loosely revolving shaft could seriously injure the shaft bearings and sternpost.

Cape Town was the only place short of Melbourne in which repairs could be made, but Waddell was leery of stopping. *Alabama*'s visit had created a sensation there in August 1863; *Shenandoah* could be entrapped by a Yankee warship, which is why Waddell had been instructed by Bulloch to bypass the Cape well to the south. He would cross the Indian Ocean under sail, "hoping to keep company with good luck."

Whittle stopped all other work to effect repairs that would allow use of the engine at least in emergencies. The roof of the propeller house was removed; the spanker boom was propped up by beams, and tackles were rigged from the mizzen mast head. Crewmen hauled the twelve-foot-diameter chunk of solid brass up on deck, a difficult task with a sea running. It was a great fuss, wrote Lining, "some thought that the propeller was ruined, & the house forever destroyed as far as looks were concerned."

Engineer O'Brien and assistants worked into the next morning through fog, damp, and cold that reminded Whittle of the Grand Banks of Newfoundland— a potential Yankee victim could be within six miles and be perfectly safe. "The truth is that I hate them so much that I find it hard to have my wants gratified. The more we catch the happier will I be." The engineers inserted new brass bolts in the coupler band, lowered the propeller in place, unrigged the pur-chases, and refitted the propeller house—all to the relief of the first lieutenant. He occupied the crew the rest of the day with scrubbing paintwork on the spar deck. The captain remained nervous about the propeller and was determined not to use it any more than he had to.

On Saturday, 10 December, Whittle fired the big guns for the first time but worried about their condition and the untrained crews. They would do their best in a fight, he thought, but he had little confidence and sincerely hoped that would not happen. James, the wardroom steward, complained to Dr. Lining that geese acquired on Tristan da Cunha were not eating and would die, so the doctor taught the delighted fellow how to manually stuff food down their throats. On Saturday evening as customary, the doctor drank to sweethearts and wives with his comrades and then another to his friends in England. Temperatures descended as they sailed south.

Whittle hoped Sunday would be a lucky day, only to be disappointed again as a nice breeze glided the ship along at eleven knots. They were alone in the great gray bowls of sea and sky. He held the usual inspection of men and ship at ten o'clock, both looking quite well, then spent the day with his Bible and letters from Pattie. "Oh how much would I give to hear from [her] if but to know that my darling is well. . . . God grant her health and happiness." Lining found it no longer pleasant to sit on deck in the mist and cold. "Nothing going on. No sail in sight. But as yet we are all good friends, have no quarrelling, but good jokes are going around all the time, & good spirits prevailing.

[Lieutenant] Smith Lee is the life of all and he is all the time getting off some joke or other."

―――――――――

The powerful sloop of war USS *Iroquois* (sister ship of *Kearsarge*, slayer of *Alabama*) made port at Montevideo, Uruguay, on her way to Batavia (Jakarta, Indonesia) and learned from Brazilian newspapers of *Shenandoah*'s captures off the coast five weeks earlier. Commander C. R. Rodgers dispatched a message to Navy Secretary Welles, hurriedly patched his failing boilers, and departed in the morning with intentions to touch at Tristan da Cunha, then sail on to the Cape of Good Hope "with all dispatch" in hopes of catching up with *Shenandoah*.[9]

―――――――――

On 12 December the wind hauled right aft; the sails no longer steadied the ship and she began to "roll like a tub," complained Lining. He spent most of the night in his bunk trying without success to hold a position so he wouldn't be tossed about and arose with sore neck and shoulders. The old shellbacks told him this was just a nice wind as they took heavy seas on both sides of each roll with the spar deck awash and gun muzzles plunging into swirling seas. "What an uncomfortable thing a rolling ship is." The wind mounted over the next days from a strong breeze through half a gale to a whole gale, blowing, wrote Whittle, "like blue lightning" with strong gusts. He had the ship under close-reefed fore and main topsails. She was behaving admirably, but the rudder made a great noise and he was anxious about it. "We shipped a good deal of water. She is decidedly a wet ship."

Lining noted small events in his journal, recording a "great sky lark" (fun, frolic) with Bulloch one morning, wrestling each other around the tossing wardroom. The doctor considered Lieutenant Chew an unlucky soul: first one of his trunks capsized in the cabin, broke open, and spilled everything about; another trunk that was airing on deck overturned and sent his letters into the sea. Chew was officer of the watch a few mornings later when, as the ship wallowed, he stumbled, slid into the lee scuppers, lost his cap, and nearly went overboard.

Chapter 6

"Running Her Easting Down"

Shenandoah turned eastward five hundred miles below the Cape of Good Hope in the "roaring forties" between 40° and 50° south latitude. Off the tip of Africa, mighty currents clash and powerful winds sweep around the globe unobstructed by land creating a cauldron of fierce storms. Although west winds prevail, they are not constant as in the trades—strong depressions punctuated by squalls and gales surge west to east with winds fluctuating capriciously in strength and in direction. Pushed by these depressions, blue-black waves pile up over hundreds of miles of open ocean and march eastward in towering ranks—as much as fifty to eighty feet from trough to crest and a quarter mile from crest to crest, heads curling and breaking in avalanches of spume and wind-borne spray. It is a wild and strangely regular waterscape of white-capped peaks in majestic and terrifying dreamlike motion accompanied by shrieking winds.

To anyone but a sailor, recalled Master's Mate Hunt, it would hardly have seemed possible that a vessel could live in such seas, but Shenandoah was an excellent sea-boat. Numerous birds soared in her wake, including albatross, cape pigeon, and stormy petrel, known among seamen as Mother Carey's Chickens. Over this mad ocean "our gallant vessel scud as easily as the birds skimmed the air astern." It was, however, anything but comfortable, and to dine "in Christian fashion" was becoming impossible. The steward struggled to place a meal on the table only to have a heavy lurch scatter dishes and contents in every direction. "Once, not satisfied with such a piece of impertinence, old Neptune sent a sea over our starboard quarter, which came pouring down upon us like a cataract, and the remnant of our dinner, previously disposed around the cabin floor by the first accident was, by the second, submerged under a couple feet of water."[1]

It was through the roaring forties that hard-driving clipper captains made fast passages across the bottom of the Indian Ocean to the Orient. In nautical terms, a sailing vessel's progress in one of the cardinal directions was known as "easting," "westing," "northing," or "southing," which could differ significantly from much longer distances actually traveled while tacking back and forth into a wind. The ever-shifting topography of the sea dictated that toward the wind was "up," reflecting the effort required to sail in that direction; and away from the wind was "down," normally an easier task. So, with the wind at her back—known as "running free"—and sailing generally east, *Shenandoah* was "running her easting down."

On similar occasions, *Cutty Sark* (the only surviving tea clipper) logged 984 miles in seventy-two hours for an average close to 14 knots, and the renowned *Thermopylae* made a best day's run of 358 nautical miles, an average 14.9 knots. British tea clippers were in effect the largest racing yachts ever built, and *Shenandoah* was one of them. Her designer was William Rennie, a noted naval architect responsible for several famous racers: *Black Prince*, *Fiery Cross*, *Norman Court*, and *Strathmore*. The roaring forties could bring out the best in these greyhounds, but they also could drive them under, never to be heard from again. The beautiful *Aerial* probably was lost thus in 1872.[2]

But Waddell was not sprinting to grab the first of the spring teas in Canton (Guangzhou) or Foochow (Fuzhou). Secretary Mallory instructed him to pass the Cape of Good Hope by 1 January 1865; he did so on 17 December "with a west wind following fast." The speed of the ship varied with the wind as the revolving gale (cyclone) hit; its path lay southeast, freshening with increasing violence. Sea after sea tumbled over the rails as the ship wallowed and struggled to free herself from water deep on deck. Heavy coal in her hold contributed to the rolls and, being down a bit by the head, she steered a little wild. All long, sharp, and narrow vessels have a tendency to roll deep, observed Waddell, while their great length gives stability to a wind. They were six thousand miles and two months south of their starting point on the Thames.

Men on watch huddled about the deck sheltering themselves behind bulwarks and deckhouse, spinning yarns and awaiting orders to reef or take in sail, or to replace one shredded by the gale, or to haul braces and trim sheets, adjusting the angle of the sails to the wind. The daily ration of grog provided minor relief. Officers wedged themselves into odd corners or secured themselves to stanchions, surveying every wave and giving helm and sail orders to keep her steady before the wind. Helmsmen were trained to hold their attention forward—not glance astern—as they instinctively and instantly adjusted the rudder to the violent motions of the huge machine. Only the most experienced sailors held the ship steady in these conditions; they could be required to lash themselves to the wheel. Captain and first lieutenant seldom left the deck. All focus was on the feel of ship: the oscillating cant of deck beneath the feet, the brutal shove of wind on back and cheeks, the varying resistance of a wheel spoke in the hand, the rumble of water rushing by, the shriek of the wind, the moan and vibration of straining lines, the almost bursting belly of sail, and the frantic shiver of the luff—the entire symphony of forces and stresses comprising the trim of the vessel as she rushed headlong.

———

At about this time in Annapolis, Ann Waddell (having returned to the United States after her husband's departure from Liverpool) was arrested by the Army provost marshal and held in her parents' home on Prince George Street with a soldier on guard around the clock. The charges and the length of her incarceration are not known. A neighbor wrote that Mrs. Waddell had been accused of passing intelligence of planned Union expeditions to her husband, but claimed she was innocent. "I think it is outrageous," the neighbor wrote, "that people cannot live in peace for the hateful Yankees. I hope they will be paid back in their own coin." Navy Secretary Welles must have learned by then who commanded *Shenandoah*, but what he hoped to gain by ordering the arrest of Mrs. Waddell is not clear.[3]

———

Mason was on watch in the evening of 16 December as the bell struck eight (8 p.m.). He had just gone to the poop rail to heave the log when, perhaps from bad steering, the ship swooped up into the wind and took a tremendous sea over the starboard rail amidships. A crest several feet high cascaded aft carrying everything before. Two 130-gallon water casks broke from their lashings at the mainmast and were flung bodily about the deck. Mason waded into the foaming water, directed crewmen in securing the casks and, at the end of his watch, went below to remove wet clothes. Just as the midshipman was about to jump into his hammock, there was another lurch to leeward. Several trunks and a medicine chest, some with rollers, charged across the deck fetching up on the other side and almost carrying Mason along with them, but he snatched hold of a hammock strap and swung clear of the wreck, much amused at the poor fellows who were awakened out of an agreeable sleep. The damaged medicine chest released a strong smell of ether and was set on deck to air out. Mason finally turned in and slept soundly in spite of the motion, concluding that a hammock is most comfortable in a heavy seaway, "for it swings about like the ship & one does not roll about as in a bunk."

Hunt described the storm as sublime beyond description. One mountainous wave surged down upon them, "and rearing its mighty crest, like a very demon of the ocean intent upon our destruction, discharged a cataract of water" whose weight he estimated at hundreds of tons. For Hunt, "it was a dreadful moment of fearful anxiety." The vessel shook and hesitated and settled as the storm screamed through the rigging and every sail, line, yard, and mast strained and moaned and rattled. The officer of the deck shouted for the men—half swimming in the waist-deep swirling, freezing seas on deck—to knock out gunport covers with axes. The mass of water, "which was pressing us down, like the hand of doom, into the treacherous bosom of the [ocean]," flowed out. She shrugged free and surged ahead, but the waves marched on, and this could happen again at any time. To add to their disquiet, the rudder continued thumping and jarring the stern; Dr. Lining was concerned that the whole thing would be wrenched off. The captain could not sleep and, wrote the doctor, "would give $5,000 had he never taken command of this ship, so much is he worried and bothered."[4]

During this cataclysm, Waddell chose to initiate what Lining called "a most disagreeable row." The captain already had provoked the first lieutenant by countermanding, without consultation, orders to the boatswain for rigging mizzen topgallant sheets. Whittle complained to his journal: Now a commanding officer can issue any order and revoke any order he wishes, but should do so through the chain of command. He regarded the captain as a "very unreasonable man in most things." Whittle was determined to ignore this incident for the good of the service and because, before departure, he had promised Ann Waddell to "keep out of all quarrels on the cruise," presumably with her husband. But the captain's lack of confidence in Lieutenant Chew and Lieutenant Scales lit the fuse. In the midst of the worst storm yet encountered, Waddell was determined to remain on deck all night during both men's four-hour watches, bluntly refusing the first lieutenant's offer to stand with one of them. He was a "regular self-made martyr," wrote Whittle. Then Waddell ordered that Master's Mate John F. Minor take Chew's watch, replacing a commissioned officer with a junior warrant officer. The captain informed Chew that he did not consider him competent and that he would respect neither his person nor his commission.

Lining advised Chew to do something to preserve his dignity and his position, so the young lieutenant asked to be relieved of duties, which Waddell granted. Whittle was apoplectic; although his routine journal entry was a page long or less, he filled six pages with pique over two days. This was an arbitrary and unwarranted act of authority; it would destroy esprit de corps; it implied that the first lieutenant was incompetent. He tried to have a friendly talk with the captain, to persuade him that such actions would force "a young man of fine spirit and sense" out of the ship. Waddell vacillated between bluster and conciliation; he claimed that he had not a friend in the ship and that the officers were all against him. Whittle demanded to know what was meant by this, but the response is not recorded, as he suddenly terminated the entry with "I can't write any more of this extraordinary conversation."

In the end, the captain restored Chew to duties. He instructed the first lieutenant to forget what had happened and to stand watch with Chew in heavy weather. Whittle hoped there would never be another such disturbance: "God knows I want peace for the good of the service." Chew, according to the doctor, was back to his old self with his face all lit up. Waddell's paranoia was childish and foolish, thought Lining. "If he would only act rightly we would all be with him." This was uncomfortably similar to the doctor's prewar experience in the USS *Cyane*. Chew recorded not a word in his journal, noting only that they encountered a gale: "It was not severe, nevertheless, we were under short sail."

By Sunday *Shenandoah* ran out of the storm and was going along more comfortably. Winds shifted from westerly to northerly, steady on the port beam and damping the rough cross seas. Whittle was surprised by the clement weather and did not think it would last, so he held the usual inspection at quarters. Tuesday was a delightful day, hazy early on, then clearing up with warm, cheering sun and light breezes. Lining spent most of the morning making a chessboard—they were weary of backgammon—and got beat in his first game. Then the winds veered east of north, making it difficult to maintain progress toward Australia. Waddell ordered a more northerly course seeking better conditions as Whittle directed improvements—the carpenter constructed a magazine for stowage of gunpowder, the gunner's people fired up the guns, the boatswain's mate and assistants prepared and fitted the topmast studding sail booms, and the sailmaker continued repairs to the damaged main topsail. With so few men, the first lieutenant found every job a long one but was thankful for what he had. However, he was getting heartily tired of not catching another Yankee: "This is too much sailing without a prize."

The CSS *Shenandoah*, that remotest and loneliest outpost of the beleaguered Confederacy, surged into the Indian Ocean about equidistant between Madagascar to the north and Antarctica. These Southerners were months out of touch, with only their orders, prayers, and thoughts of loved ones to comfort them. Five thousand miles of cold, storm-swept, and empty waters lay between them and Australia. On 18 December 1864, Waddell achieved his southernmost latitude—43° 29′ south—and was on the lookout for icebergs; air and water temperature were sampled every two hours. But so far the way was unobstructed. "I was anxious to see those immense bodies of ice," noted Chew, "but I did not bargain for a close proximity to them."

Mason continued studying for the lieutenant's exam among other activities: standing regular watches; working out the daily position, course, and distance for his training log; teaching French to Lieutenant Grimball and Assistant Surgeon McNulty. This would be only his second Christmas away from home. He thought the ship was "in a most discouraging condition," and despite the midsummer season in this part of the world, it was very cold in open ocean. Mason noted, however, "I am comparatively speaking perfectly happy. . . . I suppose we will find delightful weather in Australia." Sunrise in the morning watch of 23 December was one of the most magnificent sights he had ever seen, but the old proverb—"a red sun at night is a sailor's delight, a red sun in the morning is a sailor's warning"—held true. The sky quickly darkened over and by noon no glimpse of the sun was available for taking sights and figuring position.

That night Whittle stood a miserable watch with Chew. It was blowing hard and raining in torrents; the sleet was cold as hail. When Whittle faced into it, the wind stopped his breath and stung like nettles. Such a night, he wrote, "makes the poor mariner regret the day on which his destinies were linked with the sea. Oh how much would I not give now to be on shore, with our dear country at peace, and a certain little angel sitting by me as my wife. I would certainly be the happiest man in the world." He believed that Chew and Scales were gaining in experience and hoped it soon would be unnecessary to keep watch with them. Lining spent most of the day in bed to stay warm, noting, "I am also feeling quite badly. I don't know from what cause. Nothing of any interest going on."

Conditions worsened through Christmas Eve day as the wind backed to the west and another of those roaring forties gales blasted up behind. Whittle reported his first altercation with one of the warrant officers, Mr. Guy, the gunner. The ship was rolling heavily when the first lieutenant discovered that the chocking quoins (wooden wedges) were not properly inserted under the wheels of the guns. Asked about this dangerous condition, Guy had been argumentative and insubordinate, so Whittle reluctantly took him off duty. The gunner's insolence was explained: he and Assistant Carpenter Lynch were reported for being drunk on the berth deck; apparently they had been saving up their daily tots of grog for a grand blowout on the holiday. Guy's impudent refusal to go below led to a pushing and shoving match down the quarterdeck ladder, across the spar deck, and down to the berth deck. Whittle finally subdued him with the help of Midshipman Browne and Masters Mate Minor and, despite a strong temptation to thrash the gunner, decided to just stop his grog ration. Gunner Guy and alcohol would combine for trouble in the future.

Mason described the process of reducing sail starting in light airs of morning with all plain sail and progressing at stages through the day as wind increased. He would both supervise and assist, scrambling constantly up and down the tall, swaying masts and out on precarious footropes. Adjusting exposed sail area is the primary mechanism for maintaining equilibrium between speed and safety. *Shenandoah*'s largest and lowest sail, the main course, was over 2,000 square feet of canvas. The three topsails—fore, main, and mizzen—were from 1,200 to 2,000 square feet, and the smallest, the mizzen royal, was almost 300 square feet. The main yard was 72 feet long, 36 feet above the deck, and 50 feet over the sea. The highest yard, the main royal, was 32 feet long, 120 feet above the deck, and 134 feet over the sea. The others ranged in between. A man was a puny and vulnerable thing among these massive thrashing sails, huge swinging yards, and head-sized blocks—surrounded by a maze of lines, at the mercy of the winds, in constant motion, and all frequently in darkness and in rain. The danger and precision of these activities is difficult to imagine, and many were the opportunities for disaster, injury, or death if orders were given or obeyed slowly or incompetently.[5]

A racing skipper with a fully manned clipper would keep all sails on to the last minute and would set them immediately as wind subsided; a trained crew could be aloft almost continually to achieve best performance. But Waddell, shorthanded as he was, could not afford to endanger men or ship unnecessarily; and exhausted men make mistakes. The fore, main, and mizzen topsails were the main drivers, the first to be set and the last to be taken in. To prevent excessive heeling, other sails were taken in from the topmost, lightest sails—the royals—on down, and from the outermost headsail, the flying jib, inward, and would be set in reverse order. The courses were the hardest to handle and could be masked by high seas. By the end of the second dog watch (6 to 8 p.m.), they were left with topsails double reefed, the fore topmast staysail forward, and the main staysail ready for hoisting as a storm sail.[6]

Two large seas flooded over the rail in the afternoon but fortunately did not get to the magazine, although they inundated everything else. Mason had never seen such conditions and neither had the experienced men he asked. He thought the term "sea" much more appropriate than "wave." The latter "has too puny a sound for the ocean." "What we call a 'wave' on shore is but a molehill in comparison."

To the crew's delight, Whittle selected the largest pig in the pen—120 pounds—for their holiday dinner the next day. He was anxious to see them enjoy themselves despite the weather. This was a night, thought the first lieutenant, when cherished hearts in distant homes were wondering where they, the absent spirits, were, and his own dear Pattie must be thinking of him. "Most sincerely do I on the eve of the birth of Christ, invoke God's blessing and protection on my dear, dear country and all my dear ones. God bless them all." After ordering up preventer braces on the starboard side and splicing the main brace to warm the crew, Whittle retired early before standing the midwatch with Chew.

To Lining, it was worse than stormy Cape Horn: "Turned much colder at night & [temperature] went down to 42° which, books say, indicate an approach to ice burgs [sic]." He sat up until midnight wishing a Merry Christmas to all. They drank to sweethearts and wives and to a return of many Christmases. On deck, the midwatch seemed interminable to Chew, but finally ended. "Tired as I was, the motion of the ship was so great I could not sleep. It was only a doze."

Lining wrote, "Christmas at sea & Christmas on Sunday, a great beginning did we have." Scales recorded conditions in the ship's log: "From 4 to 8 a.m. fresh gales from the southwest; very heavy sea running; shipped several seas;

5:20 wind increasing, close reefed main topsail; 5:30 battened down hatches." Roiling walls of water swooped in from the starboard quarter, pushing the ship heavily to port, and then another from that side slammed them back again. The stern lifted and tilted skyward in a sickening corkscrew motion with the rudder high on the crest, even clearing it altogether, momentarily losing leverage. The thrusting deck buckled a man's knees, making him feel twice his weight while the forecastle buried itself in foam.

The waves surged forward, inundating the waist from one or both sides, men wallowing about clutching at lifelines. Then the stern plunged deep into the trough. Occupants and objects floated as gravity lost its force; the bowsprit soared to the clouds. In the valley between wet ramparts, horizons disappeared; the moan of the wind lessened and lower sails slackened, only to be awakened with a thunder of thrashing canvas as she surged upward again on the next wave. The sequence repeated wave after wave. At about 6 a.m. a big one again submerged the spar deck. Whittle hollered for all hands and knocked out the aft gunport on the lee side. The flood rolled aft and stove in the engine room skylight, showering the engines. It burst open the door to and inundated the wardroom, slopping into the staterooms and drenching everything.

Lining leaped from his bunk, placed his valise on a chair, and joined brother officers in the wardroom standing on furniture—shoeless, wet, and cold. Lee tried to block the water from his cabin with a mat, but gracefully resigned the task and returned to bed; Chew jumped between his trunk and his bed in helpless energy trying to "stare the water out of his room." Grimball's room was taken possession of by boots, basin, slop tub, and other objects floating around. He jumped up and commenced to shove the tide away from the door. "The water was terribly cold when I first put my feet into it," Grimbal recorded, "but they soon became used to it." The wardroom finally was cleared with the help of stewards. The doctor bailed out his stateroom with two pairs of stockings and then returned to his bunk in a useless attempt to get warm. He noted, however, "I never saw such good humour manifest. No cursing, all laughing and joking about our misfortunes." He hoped friends and relations at home were as happy as they on *Shenandoah*, albeit a bit more comfortable.

Coming off watch at midnight, Mason had gone below, awakened the idlers to wish them a Merry Christmas, and turned in, only to be disturbed at six o'clock by the noise of men hauling on the braces. When the big wave struck, the ship was forced up into the wind and commenced to roll "like je ne sais quoi." His hammock almost hit the overhead beams as water cascaded around the hatch cover setting everything adrift—chairs, books, tables, sofas, sextants "swimming about in the most admirable confusion." Mason tried to ride it out above the torrent snug in his hammock when, to his disgust, Whittle's cry for all hands echoed from above. "I must confess I thought things were getting rather bilious," concluded the midshipman.

But the danger seemed past as Mason dressed himself, lashed up the hammock to keep it dry, secured his books, and went on deck where men were at the pumps as wet as rats. The ship was put before the wind and scudded with the sea, rolling and pitching. Mason would go all day with feet in wet boots and no time to wash his face or clean his teeth, but he did manage to get a warm breakfast, which put him in better spirits. He spent the morning restoring order to his belongings, was able to shoot an altitude of the sun at noon despite the motion, and then stood the afternoon watch with Lieutenant Lee.

From aft on the quarterdeck, Mason watched the seas roar up and surge forward with crests higher than the foreyard. William West, captain of the maintop, was standing on the main hatch when one of these big waves from starboard snatched him up and flung him over the port rail well clear of the ship; an equally huge cross wave followed from port, catching him and disgorging him back on deck. No attempt at recovery could have been made. (Lieutenant Chew worried how he would feel as officer of the watch having to decide whether to witness a man perish or risk the lives of a boat crew.) "Now I grant that all this is a most magnificent thing to behold," confessed Mason, but "I should enjoy it a thousand times more were it not for the discomfort & dangers which are indispensable parts of a gale of wind; it is indeed wonderful how such a frail thing can stand such rough treatment."

Lining recorded that despite it having been sixty-seven days since they last dropped anchor, the wardroom cook and steward prepared a first-rate Christmas dinner including, among other delicacies, goose, fresh pork, corned beef, fresh potatoes, and mince pies. "We drank at dinner the health of the absent ones etc. & had a happy time." Cannon shot were heated in the crew's galley and carried to the wardroom to provide warmth, while Lining kept candles going in his cabin all day. (It was too dangerous to light their little stove in the rolling ship.) Scales ate and drank until red in the face, stood watch, and came down at 8 p.m. with a cramp in his stomach.

And so passed Christmas of 1864 at sea, noted the doctor. He wondered how friends in Europe were spending the day, longing to see them. "May God bless them!" He wished some of this plenty, which he saw wasting around him every day, could be shared with loved ones. "Ah! Me! What an awful thing this war is, & how terribly those at home have suffered. May it soon cease!" Whittle also thought the dinner a fine one but did not enjoy it much as they drank success to loved ones and the noble cause.

Chew was reminded of last Christmas, picturing himself again on the boulevards of his beloved Paris, looking at the sights, thinking of night scenes with a thousand gaslights and bright windows, but noted, "I would look up from this picture and everything was damp, dark, and gloomy, my ears were accosted by the row of the tempest without, the hissing of the angry waves against the ship's sides."

Hunt considered it the most miserable travesty of the festival he ever celebrated as thoughts reverted to home, to family gathering at Christmas dinner, to the old church with its decorations, and to the evening spent in fun and frolic. "In the place of pendant evergreens my eyes rested upon the smoky, swaying lamps, still dimly burning in the ward room, and instead of receiving the time-honored salutations from family friends, and bright-faced girls, whose lips give so sweet an intonation to the old phrase, I heard it from rough-bearded men, sunburned and swarthy, and in place of preparing for a gay holiday, I donned my sou'weaster and moodily made my way to the deck to stand a four hours' watch. . . . My solemn advice to the world at large is, never to go off the Cape of Good Hope in a cruiser to enjoy Christmas."[7]

Following the afternoon watch, Mason and Lee shared a late Christmas dinner—good mince pies and plum pudding with tolerable sherry. They had to keep plates in hand to prevent contents from being deposited in their laps. But the old ship got off pretty well with only a little water in the magazine. The crew had a good Christmas dinner and kept up their sprits remarkably well. "For there is nothing in the world like a good warm feed to put a man in a good humor. As I had the midwatch I went to my hammock (wet) at eight o'clock." Mason would console himself on watch, eating more mince pies from the steward's bountiful supply.

Toward evening, a sail was sighted off the port quarter steering east; there would be no chance of capture in such conditions. *Shenandoah* finally ran out of the gale into more genial climate north of 40° south. The wind moderated and was then nearly south, bringing occasional squalls of fine rain and more cross seas. Waves breaking against the sides had loosened the caulking and sent fine spray through open seams into the berth deck; the decks leaked dreadfully and all bedding was more or less wet. Concluded Waddell: "A wet watch is uncomfortable enough but to nod in a chair or be forced to turn into a wet bed is even more so."

––––––––

From Bahia, Brazil, 27 December, the commander of the USS *Onward* wrote to Secretary Wells that *Shenandoah* was thought to be still off the South American coast. Captain Libby of *Kate Prince* had provided a full report of his 12 November encounter and begged for an escort through coastal waters on the way home. Meanwhile, the U.S. minister in Brazil reported to Secretary of State Seward that *Shenandoah*, or any vessel Waddell commanded, was banned from Brazilian ports, although he was at a loss to explain this happy event. The minister had been demanding exclusion of rebel ships but made no specific case for *Shenandoah*.[8]

Apparently the government became convinced that *Kate Prince* had been taken in territorial waters and that Waddell had opened the ship's manifest breaking the seal of the Brazilian consulate. (Both assertions are unsupported by the record.) Despite his concern for American trade, Minister Webb feared that the small, lightly armed *Onward*, a converted merchant sailing ship, would be outmatched and hoped she did not encounter the Confederate vessel. *Onward* convoyed *Kate Prince* clear of the coast and immediately started in pursuit of *Shenandoah*. She cruised for eighteen days questioning all ships bound around Cape Horn. One rumor had *Shenandoah* sunk "at one of the Western Islands."[9]

On 28 December the USS *Iroquois* arrived at Tristan da Cunha from Montevideo just three weeks behind *Shenandoah*. Commander Rodgers immediately took on board the captured crews of schooner *Lizzie M. Stacey* and whaling bark *Edward* and sailed the same evening. "I shall push forward with all possible dispatch, and shall hope to get fresh information of the *Shenandoah* at Cape Town, where I shall coal as quickly as possible," he reported to Secretary Welles.[10]

Chapter 7

The Queen of the *Delphine*

On 29 December a cry of "sail ho!" interrupted the monotony of sea life, wrote Midshipman Mason—a sound not heard for three or four weeks. Enjoying fine weather and fresh breezes, *Shenandoah* was skipping along close-hauled on the starboard tack under double-reefed topsails, reefed foresail, and staysails. At first they paid little attention to the stranger closing rapidly from astern, but soon suspicions were excited. "Finally we hoisted the English ensign as a sort of a feeler, when to our infinite delight she replied by running up the Yankee colours." The problem was to stop her. She was upwind and under full sail while they had no steam up and no fire or even water in the boilers. Waddell jammed the ship up into the wind as the newcomer passed under the stern and surged on by the port beam.

The unsuspecting master held up a blackboard with longitude written on it, asking his fellow captain to verify their position (a common practice in mid-ocean). Down came the English flag; the Confederate banner ran aloft and the signal gun barked. The startled stranger kept on going, rapidly drawing ahead out of gun range. Waddell ordered the two long-range rifled guns cast loose and loaded. Gunners were scrambling to get off a shot when the target backed her mainsails and hove to, much to everyone's amazement and relief. Sailing Master Bulloch rowed across to take charge. She was the bark *Delphine* of Bangor, Maine, on her maiden voyage. Captain William Green Nichols was accompanied by his wife, Lillias, and six-year-old son, Phineas. When Bulloch boarded, Mrs. Nichols angrily confronted him: "I suppose you are going to steal my Canary birds, so you had better take them at once!" Her father was primary owner of the vessel, with her husband having a third share. They had departed New York with a cargo of wheat to London, but once there could get no return cargo because British merchants would not risk their goods under the U.S. flag.

Nichols finally received a charter from the same unlucky firm that hired *Shenandoah*'s first victim, *Alina*. *Delphine* sailed from London in early October on almost the same day *Sea King* departed that same port. She was seventy days out in ballast bound for Burma to load rice, which Waddell assumed would be supplied to federal armies. Once on board *Shenandoah*, wrote

Mason, Captain Nichols pleaded his wife's health, saying almost with tears in his eyes that it would be the death of her if she were moved in such a delicate state. "Captain Waddell, who is an exceedingly tender hearted man & believes everything one tells him, seemed almost disposed to bond the vessel." But Waddell sought Lining's opinion. The doctor thought it sounded like an excuse to get away and avoid *Delphine*'s destruction. "I told the Captain so & he rather reluctantly, I think, determined to burn her."

The boats returned about 6 p.m. with Mrs. Nichols and son along with the stewardess and her steward husband, two mates, eleven crewmembers, and personal baggage. As they rocked and bounced in the choppy seas, in danger of being crushed against the ship's hull, the crew rigged a sling from the main yard and hauled ladies and boy on board. "The Captain's wife, woman like, brought with her a canary bird in its cage," recalled Hunt, "and if a bandbox containing her best bonnet had been added to her baggage, it would have been complete." While hove to alongside the prize, Midshipman Mason and Midshipman Browne amused themselves by catching a couple of albatrosses circling the ship. Mason took one of the feet; after being carefully skinned and dried, it would make a nice tobacco pouch.[1]

The prize was raided for sheep and pigs and valued at $25,000. Waddell regretted not recovering additional stores, furniture, and other useful items that could not be transferred with the high winds blowing and heavy seas running. Night descended as *Delphine* was fired. Hunt described the scene: "Rapidly the flames gathered headway, casting a fierce, lurid glow over the heaving bosom of the ocean." "From doors, windows, and hatchways they burst forth like the vengeful spirit of destruction, wound up the spars, stretched out upon the yards, swiftly enveloping shrouds, sails, and halyards in one splendid, fiery ruin; and standing out, strongly revealed against the darkening sky, the burning vessel surged and tossed, a holocaust to the God of War." As *Shenandoah* sailed away, Hunt observed Captain Nichols pacing the deck with his wife, watching their vessel burn. "He probably had there invested the savings of half a lifetime of patient toil. To see the fruits of so many years swept away in an hour, might well try the philosophy of the best of men." The sky glow of the fire dropped below the horizon around three o'clock in the morning.[2]

Delphine's sailors were mostly Germans, for whom Waddell felt little sympathy. Six volunteered, increasing the *Shenandoah* crew to forty-seven. Whittle clapped the others in irons in the forecastle. The master and mates signed paroles, promising no disturbance, and were granted freedom of the ship. According to Dr. Lining, one of the mates, Captain Nichols' brother Irving, "was inclined to be uppish" but became cooperative when threatened with shackling irons. Another crewman asked to be placed on parole so he could formally swear not to take up arms against the Confederacy and thereby avoid Union conscription; however, he would not join *Shenandoah* because he was accompanied by his wife. A disgusted Whittle would do nothing for him. The man was a coward twice removed since he was a Missourian—therefore Confederate by definition—who would not fight and a traitor for being on a Yankee ship.

That evening Mason conferred with his journal: "On the whole we have a most promiscuous crew, men of every nation." Most of the foreigners could not speak a word of English, he complained, which was most troublesome at work and at quarters. Even stranger was the presence of three or four recruits from Maine, "as good Yankees as ever were seen." One stout, fine-looking fellow had been in the Union Army for two years. What induced them to join he could not imagine, but they were among the best sailors they had. Lieutenant Chew recorded that they had men from the Confederate States, United States, England, France, Holland, Denmark, Sweden, Norway, Russia, East Indies, Africa, Ireland, Scotland, and Wales. "What a medley!"

One captured goat, a young kid, provided a great deal of amusement on deck, but the pigs kept up a tremendous noise at night. Mason wandered forward to the forecastle one midwatch and noticed the newly acquired "Yankee" pigs had separated themselves from the "Confederate" pigs on opposite sides of the pen and were squealing at each other. The midshipman concluded that providence had smiled upon their endeavors: "This last fellow came right into the lion's mouth." Despite a four-week lull, this was *Shenandoah's* ninth prize in eight weeks but would be her last for several months.

The prisoners would be with them for twenty or thirty days until they reached port, there being little probability of encountering other vessels on this route; but reactions to their female guest were nearly unanimous: "A finer looking woman I have seldom seen, physically," wrote Lining; Mason noted, "The Captain's wife is quite a pretty woman but rather a strong minded one. . . . I rather think she wears the breeches"; Whittle agreed, adding that she was anything but an invalid, "At first she is a little frightened but we can soon drive fear away by proving by kindness that we are gentlemen."

Lillias Nichols was a down-easter from Searsport, Maine, where almost 10 percent of the 1,700 inhabitants were ship captains, including five of her uncles. "When she came off she looked mad as a bull, but it only amused us," wrote Grimball. The lady accosted Waddell in the wardroom, demanding in a stentorian voice to know where they would be landed. "On St. Paul, madam, if you like," he said, referring to an isolated island in the middle of the Indian Ocean. "Oh, no; never," she responded. "I would rather remain with you." Waddell was surprised to see standing before him a tall, finely proportioned woman of twenty-six in robust health. "It soon became palpable she would be the one for me to manage, and not the husband. A refractory lady can be controlled by a quiet courtesy, but no flattery." Chew's only comment: "We have the trouble of another woman onboard."

Shenandoah once again stretched her wings, all sail set on a bowline (close-hauled). Hunt recalled 30 December as one of the most beautiful days they had seen. The air was soft and balmy, he wrote, "like the month of May in our own sunny South." The heavy sea exhausted its mad passion and died away into long undulating swells.[3]

During the morning watch, Hunt conversed with Captain Nichols, who expressed chagrin for surrendering to such a weak foe. He had expected to find all guns working and men to fire them, able to blow him out of the water in five minutes. Had he shaken out his canvas, he would have given them the slip before they could have made sail or brought guns to bear. Nichols also confessed to Waddell his shame for having pleaded his wife's alleged illness as an excuse to save the ship, but did not feel that the lie was wrong under the circumstances.

Mrs. Nichols seemed to get over her feelings and appeared a ladylike person, noted Grimball: "She is treated with every consideration. I suppose she will abuse us in inverse proportion." The new goat with kid provided milk for tea every morning, during which the lady laughed and talked; her anger surfaced only when someone asserted her husband had been weak in his duty. The little boy ran about the decks playing with the goats. It was the last of the old year, wrote Lining, "and a pleasant year it has been to me, taken all in all. . . . But where will I be a year hence from today? Echo can only answer, where? Nothing of any interest going on." He had been suffering from a headache and would see the old year out with another drink to his little darling whom he longed to see. Whittle agreed that their lady passenger was becoming more sociable and "really seems to think that we are not all a parcel of piratical barbarians." He too would sit up to welcome in the new year.

Waddell resumed evening games of whist in his cabin. Mason enjoyed a round with Waddell, the first lieutenant, and Assistant Surgeon McNulty before retiring to the steerage, where someone brought out a brandy bottle and proposed a toast to sweethearts and wives followed by "success to the cause." The midshipman hurried to finish the day's journal entry before the master-at-arms could poke his nose in the door to say it was ten o'clock and lights out; but messmates made so much noise he couldn't concentrate. Thoughts wandered to Mrs. Nichols, her beauty and gentility. "But occasionally she brings out some ungrammatical expression which dispels the illusion; fortunately she seldom says much & the illusion lasts the longer."

Waddell reflected on the occasion and the war:

Thirty-first of December closed the year, the third since the war began. And how many of my boon companions are gone to that bourne from whence no traveler returns! They were full of hope, but not without fears, when we last parted. They had fallen in battle in defense of their homes invaded by a barbarous enemy. War, when waged by unprincipled and brutal civilized man, is always more savage and inhuman than when waged by the untutored savage of the woods. The Yankees in their invasion of the South, came with all the vices and passions of civilized men added to the natural ferocity of the savage. They had no magnanimity or chivalry; they fought on calculation of profit.

This fact never left my mind, and reconciled me to the destruction of property which was captured. I felt I was fighting them more effectually than if I were killing the miserable crowds of European recruits which they filled their armies with. For two years they waged war against the South without attempting to interfere with slavery; it was only when they found the Negro could be used for killing the white people of the South and serve as breastworks for Northern white troops that they declared him free; it was a new element introduced into the contest, and a very powerful one. They cared nothing for the unhappy Negro; they preferred his destruction to that of their white troops.[4]

Hunt was on watch at midnight when the new year, "wearing all the languid beauty of a Southern clime," opened. The weather was fine with a light, variable wind; the stars threw their silvery shimmer over the quiet water. Everyone but the officer of the deck, quartermaster, lookout, and the man at the wheel were wrapped in slumber. "Such were my surroundings when the ship's bell, striking the hour of twelve, announced the death of eighteen hundred sixty-four and the birth of eighteen hundred sixty-five."

At about 1 a.m. Dr. Lining was roused out of his bunk to examine a sailor who had fallen down the hatch. The crewman was stunned but not seriously injured.[5]

New Year's Day was bright, delightfully pleasant, clear and balmy; all sails were set with just enough breeze to fill them. "How propitious everything looked!" wrote Chew. "Can that day be taken as a specimen of the year in general?" It was the first day of the week and of the month, he noted, the first Sunday in the month, the first day of the new moon, the first time all sail had been carried with studding sails on both sides, and the first day their flag flew for an entire day at sea. "What an enumeration of firsts! May it not be the *last* time that they occur!" *Shenandoah* had been in commission two months, eleven days and had destroyed or ransomed more property than her original cost, recalled Waddell, "The case is without parallel." He called all hands to muster, read the Articles of War, inspected the ship, and wished them a happy new year. Providence seemed to smile upon them, thought Mason, and everything appeared auspicious. It was the first really fine weather they had experienced since entering the Indian Ocean. Mrs. Nichols' canary birds sang delightfully all day.

New Year's dinner in the wardroom included two splendid hams adorned with Confederate flags. It seemed a pity to cut them, wrote Chew, "however, looking at them was not sufficient for the voracious appetites of some of my messmates." Hopes for the future were tempered by thoughts of home. "What a waste of waters between me and the shores of my country!" They had a nice dinner, noted Whittle. "This is a day upon which all persons however separated think of their absent dear ones more than on any other. Oh! How my heart feels for my dear ones." He invoked God's blessing and wished for a better and happier new year: "My constant prayer is that a merciful God will guard, protect and cherish our dear country. That he will open the eyes of our enemies to the cruelty of the war they are waging against us and that he may teach them that they are wrong."

With the dawn, the nearly barren volcanic island of St. Paul rose above the horizon. Other than the quick stop at Tristan da Cunha in early December, this was the first land sighted since leaving Madeira. Mason noted that passing navigators had reported seeing fire flowing from crevices in the rock. Hunt claimed to have observed Mrs. Nichols in some distress over the prospect of being marooned there, and to have comforted her. (Hunt had a tendency to embellish his memoirs.) She told him of stories in the Northern press describing outrages committed upon defenseless men and women by rebel cruisers and produced a sample from an illustrated New York publication. The article compared the men of *Alabama* with dastardly pirates and renegades, but was, according to Hunt, full of blunders and absurdities that provided amusement in the wardroom for days.[6]

Waddell consented to tarry for the afternoon; they dropped anchor at the southern end of the island. Eight officers rowed themselves to the beach for a day of exploration and fishing. Whalers occasionally passed this way, so Waddell ordered them to destroy any property found belonging to citizens of the United States. To their surprise, they encountered three Frenchmen, part of a crew who remained for years, catching and salting fish and trading with Madagascar and African ports. The boat returned in the evening loaded with fish and with the excursionists in the best of spirits. But they paid dearly, recalled Hunt, with bright sunburns and hands blistered at the oars. They had hoped to capture a seal or two but failing this, found a penguin and "brought his aquatic fowlship off in triumph." The penguin had the bray of an ass, was covered by gray down, and walked with military erectness. Someone pinned a rag around its neck resembling a shawl, which amused them all, including Mrs. Nichols.

Chronometers were checked against the known longitude of the island and found to be only a few seconds in error. Sail was made and the propeller hauled up. Waddell shaped course for Cape Leeuwin at the southwestern tip of Australia, where American whalers were known to operate and homeward-bound merchants passed through on route to the Cape of Good Hope.[7]

The men (and woman) of *Shenandoah* settled into underway routine for the next three weeks with everyone anxious to get ashore. Variable conditions required constant sail handling and course adjusting, which kept the crew busy, but Waddell was frustrated by the calms and head winds. Friday, 6 January, was Lining's thirty-first birthday. He enjoyed conversing with Mrs. Nichols and viewing family photographs, but Captain Nichols got jealous and came poking around whenever the doctor was with her. "The fool and ass. . . . I shall now go on talking to her to plague him, if nothing else," Lining noted. Nichols frequently walked the quarterdeck with his wife, a privilege extended to no other prisoners. According to Hunt, "the old fellow made himself so continually and unmitigatedly disagreeable that our officers perforce avoided him." They were as anxious to be rid of him as he was to be elsewhere.[8]

Still concerned about Lieutenant Chew's seamanship, Waddell again relieved him of watchstanding duties, put Master's Mate Minor in his place, and assigned Chew make-work jobs beneath his rank. Chew accepted them because the captain wished him to, referring to the changes as a promotion in his journal. He would later record that the last three months seemed like six months to him: "I take no pleasure in destroying; my companions do not suit me. I sometimes wish to leave the ship, but when I think of the advantages of the cruise, it passes off." This was as close as Chew would come to an expression of dissatisfaction until late in the cruise.

Midshipman Browne and Midshipman Mason protested that one of them should have preference for Chew's watchstanding duties because they were senior to a master's mate, but Waddell's only response, according to Lining, was some sarcastic remarks as to what his officers would allow him to do. The doctor wrote, "[Chew] is certainly not the man I thought he was. Before I would allow such a thing to occur to me, they might take my commission." Sometime before midnight on 9 January, noted Lining, *Shenandoah* crossed the meridian just opposite on the globe from Charleston and so, every additional mile brought him closer to his home. It was a misty, foggy day with little wind.

———

Iroquois dropped hook in Cape Town where Captain Rodgers discovered to his dismay no trace of *Shenandoah*. A report had circulated that *Sea King* with Raphael Semmes in command had been lost near the Canary Islands, but Rodgers knew this to be false. A letter from Secretary Welles of 26 September awaited him with instructions to return to New York for repairs if he found no evidence that *Florida* or any other rebel privateer had gone to the East Indies. Rodgers replied that his boilers were in no condition for a long trip and that he had desertions among the crew. However, believing that *Shenandoah* had rounded the cape and was bound east, he was determined: "Thither, therefore, I shall follow with all dispatch, for in spite of the defective motive power of the *Iroquois*, I shall not abandon the hope that she may have the good fortune to arrest the progress of this new buccaneer." A detailed description of the rebel cruiser from the mates of *Stacey* and *Edward* was included.[9]

On 12 January Secretary Welles ordered the paddle-wheel gunboat *Suwanee* to search for *Shenandoah* on route via Cape Horn to join the Pacific Squadron near California, starting with *Shenandoah's* last known position off Brazil. "Every exertion must be made to overtake her, and, if successful, to destroy or capture her, provided an attack can be made without violating neutral waters or infringing upon neutral rights. . . . You are authorized and expected to follow her anywhere." The secretary placed higher priority on the blockade than on chasing Confederate raiders, and it can be doubted that he expected results, but Northern merchants were haranguing him constantly.[10]

About this time, a typical letter from H. H. Swift & Co. of New York complained vehemently of *Shenandoah's* capture and release of *Adelaide* off Brazil and requested protection both from Confederate cruisers and from Brazilian pirates. To mollify frenzied ship owners, Secretary Welles responded that two additional steamers were being dispatched to the Pacific and would search the Brazil coast on the way. However, it would be another month before *Suwanee* was ready to leave New York. In the meantime, Rear Admiral Dahlgren, commander of the North Atlantic Blockading Squadron, heard that *Shenandoah* was chasing American vessels off Charleston and sent another ship to look for her there.[11]

———

The doctor had taken a cold. He relieved boredom by tending his few patients, including the captain who also had a headache and was very blue. On Saturday, Lining attempted a tooth extraction, but every time he got hold of the tooth, the sailor grabbed his arm, so he gave up. Later, a block fell from aloft, striking one of the prisoners on the head and cutting it open, but not seriously: "If it had struck him fairly, it would certainly have killed him on the spot." But both he and Waddell were concerned about Sailing Master Bulloch's inflamed eyes, so the captain placed him on deck watch and assigned navigating duties to Chew. This was an important responsibility for a senior warrant, but not normally exercised by a commissioned officer. Chew thought it strange that Midshipman Brown or Midshipman Mason was not given the responsibility for training purposes. "But I suppose the Capt. has his reasons for giving it to me. I am not at all sorry for it. It is my first real navigating," having only practiced theory on the Savannah River. As navigator, Chew would write up the ship's official log, both draft and smooth copy. He had much to do, but was determined: "In the course of a week, I will have become accustomed to it."

Chew applied himself diligently and seemed to enjoy navigation. He had been keeping track of progress on a world chart, marking every day's run since leaving Liverpool as a souvenir of the cruise showing "the immense sheets of water traversed." Like Lining, Chew had noted the crossing of the meridian exactly opposite his home and was amazed to find himself in such a far-off place. He calculated that Melbourne and Lexington, Missouri, were distant from each other by the Cape of Good Hope 238° longitude, equal to 12,600 miles. They had enjoyed summer and fall in Europe and now in the southern hemisphere were having summer over again. "I suppose by the coming of the winter months, we will have [re-]crossed the line, thus having continual summer." His fundamental optimism asserted itself.

Whittle and Lining tried to persuade the captain to tarry in the western approaches of Australia in hopes of taking additional prizes, but, wrote the doctor, "He has his head set for port & is stubborn about it." Chew calculated that Cape Otway near Melbourne bore east by north, 1,100 miles. They celebrated Whittle's twenty-fifth birthday. Then the breeze died and the captain ordered steam up, which, groused Lining, was a useless and extravagant expenditure of coal—possibly unobtainable in the future—and the thumping of the engine kept him awake at night.

A vessel with American lines was sighted flying the English flag. They stopped her and Chew rowed across. The captain received him kindly, invited him into the cabin, and presented his papers. She was the former American ship *Nimrod*, sold to a London firm with a British register and captain and crew, but there was no bill of sale and the cargo bill of lading was not sworn to. This time Waddell concluded that the ship was a neutral and released her. The master was a grand-looking old fellow, recalled Hunt, with tremendous white whiskers like a polar bear. He brought a dozen bottles of fine old brandy as a present to Captain Waddell. *Nimrod*'s jovial master would rejoin them for further socializing in Melbourne.

The first lieutenant reported an uncomfortable encounter with Mrs. Nichols one morning in the wardroom:

"Well Mr. Whittle, I trust that we may soon have peace," she said, a sentiment to which he concurred.

"Do you think we can ever be friends?"

"No Madam, never," he responded.

"But Mr. Whittle, if after the peace was made you were to meet me, would you speak to me?"

"Certainly, Madam, I would speak at any time to a female."

"But would you not speak to my husband?"

"I might do so as he has never served against us."

The lady then expressed admiration for the Confederate navy uniform cap and asked if she could have one. Whittle felt compelled as a gentleman to acquiesce; he could say no to men but not to a woman. But they were Yankees, and their motives could only be mercenary. Whittle had no doubt she would hand the cap, if provided, over to her husband and he would sell it. He thought no woman with so little delicacy as to place a gentleman in such a fix should expect him to comply, "and on this principle I will let the cap alone." Mrs. Nichols apparently developed a grudging fondness for some of the officers but never took to the somewhat stuffy Virginian; she undoubtedly enjoyed teasing him.

Easterly winds continued to drive them northward with a current setting to the south and west, and in a day's run of 240 miles, they made only half that along their intended north-northeast course. Again under steam on Sunday morning, 22 January, they sighted a Swedish vessel, an English vessel, and a third appearing to be a large American-built ship that could be seen distinctly not two miles off; but the captain declared that it was again the English ship *Nimrod* and did not investigate. Mason subsequently would discover that the vessel was not *Nimrod* but *David Brown*, also owned by the Nichols family. After arrival in Melbourne, Mrs. Nichols informed him that they recognized the ship, and they "were shaking in their shoes for fear we would stop for her. . . . The sum total of all this is that we lost a fine prize."

Lining reminded the captain that the monthly British mail ship would depart Melbourne in a few days, hoping that Waddell would delay arrival until after it had gone, but to the doctor's disappointment, his advice had just the opposite affect: Waddell kept steaming at over eight knots. "This I think is culpable to a degree," wrote Lining. Besides wasting coal, steaming could further damage the propeller shaft, but more important, the mail steamer would spread word of their arrival all over the world. Whittle agreed: "I think that our cruise will be greatly inured." The mail packet service connected Melbourne with London and with Australian, New Zealand, and South Pacific ports frequented by Yankee traders and whalers. "As soon as they hear that we are in the neighborhood they will all run into port, and we will catch very few." On this point, the doctor and first lieutenant would be proven correct.

In his postwar report, Waddell justified the decision not to linger around Cape Leeuwin due to the weather and unfavorable easterly wind: "Working to windward was no easy task against a current, even for so fast a vessel as the *Shenandoah*." It was absolutely necessary that the vessel be dry-docked for permanent repairs to the propeller shaft, and he felt obliged to use steam even if it caused further damage to the bearings. Finally, he desired to reach Melbourne for the very purpose of communicating with the mail steamer.

The first lieutenant kept the crew busy sprucing up the ship: scrubbing, polishing, stowing, tightening, neatening, and painting. Both ship and men would don their best apparel—a shiny new coat of black hull paint for the former, clean uniforms for the latter. *Shenandoah* personified pride in their profession and the prestige, strength, and discipline of the new nation they represented in this faraway place. The first impression in a new port must be a good one. One evening Lining saw a comet to the southward—not very bright but with an immensely long tail—"May it be a harbinger of good news to us."

A new parole form was prepared for prisoners to sign before release in Melbourne, in which they promised not to serve against the Confederacy and not to provide information tending to the detriment of *Shenandoah*. Captain Nichols signed the form without protest, but not his wife. "She let loose with her tongue, pitching directly into her husband for telling her to sign it & say nothing," reported Lining. After signing the document, Mrs. Nichols turned to Lieutenant Lee and pointedly inquired, "Is there anything you want [my son] Phiny to sign?" Lee replied: "No, Madame, we are much more afraid of you than we are of him." Dr. Lining: "She went out in a towering rage. Not to get the vials of her wrath poured out on me, I kept quiet." The lady would not feel bound by parole given under duress and would pass on whatever information she pleased, which she subsequently did.

Chapter 8

End of the International Road

Under a shining sun and over a smooth sea, *Shenandoah* steamed toward Cape Otway. Lieutenant Chew had been careful in his morning, noon, and evening sights and was pleased to discover the resulting calculations were consistent throughout the day. His reputation as a navigator depended on making accurate landfall. He recommended an overnight course within ten miles of the cape and predicted that it would appear at approximately 5 a.m. Captain Waddell concurred but ordered a course that would give this dangerous southern tip of Australia—visible from twenty-five miles in clear air—wider berth. Chew retired anxious for first light. "I was certain of my work, but a current might exist, thus was my only cause of uneasiness."

Chew was on deck as dawn pushed back the night. Shorebirds flew about and the water had that peculiar color that indicates proximity of land. Many sails were visible inward and outward bound but were ignored inside British jurisdictional waters. At 5:30 the lookout on the topsail yard sung out "Land ho!" just ahead. "Imagine if I felt relieved!" wrote Chew. "The Capt. was on deck and complimented me for it." Towering cliffs sprouted from the sea crowned by the white column of the cape lighthouse. They steamed along the coast toward the headlands of Port Phillip Bay where a pilot came on board. "What a flocking around him to hear the news! . . . Joy & gladness mingled, yet the joy predominated." The pilot was just as curious about them.

Continuing through the narrow entrance, they paused while a health officer boarded to certify the ship free of cholera, typhus, yellow fever, and other diseases. *Shenandoah* proceeded up the bay with flags flying. Dr. Lining noted the splendid harbor, thirty miles long and quite wide, which could accommodate "all the fleets of the world." Word flashed to the city by telegraph, creating an immediate sensation. As they approached the anchorage about 6:30 p.m., numerous craft, large and small, saluted by dipping their ensigns; some gave enthusiastic cheers, which were cheerfully returned. Others threw newspapers on board or just circled. *Shenandoah* put her helm alee and rounded gracefully into the wind. The cable roared through the hawse as the anchor plunged into placid waters. Like a great bird coming to roost, she folded her wings and was at rest for the first time in almost four months.

The anticipation and relief of entry into Melbourne were palpable and rejuvenating—a striking transition between disparate worlds of contrasting sights, sounds, smells, and logic. The ship at sea was physically confining and mostly unstable in movement, but under reasonable conditions, the spirit could be liberated by unlimited horizons, the pleasure of lively motion in concert with impersonal forces of sea and sky, endless routine physical tasks, and a rigidly authoritarian, uncomplicated set of relationships among male shipmates. This state was, however, detached from normal human experiences, frequently tedious, and in adverse circumstances could be supremely dangerous and daunting. The land, on the other hand, had everything the ship lacked: females, (more) drink, better food, personal space, and freedom of action and opportunity. Yet while the land was physically liberating and stable, it was also emotionally confusing and stressful, with tight horizons, multiple choices and constraints, and all the complex and chaotic interactions of life.

The mariner tended to welcome this dichotomy, even to depend upon it. Coming or going, he might cross over with regret mixed with anticipation, joyful for the change and for shedding frustrations left behind. He might be content, perhaps even happy for a while until the opposite world beckons. After weeks or months on one side, he steps back through the mirror and begins the cycle again. For millennia such had been the life of seamen, wanderers on the world's oceans, often more at home there. A more esoteric calling could hardly be imagined, and there are few transitions in human experience more sudden or stark than arrival in port or departure from it. Worries of the sea temporarily behind them, the Southerners came together to confront an uncertain new world. They devoured news from home, even if months old, and launched loving communications on the long way back.

As word spread that evening of Wednesday, 25 January 1865, fleets of boats under steam, sail, and oar descended from every direction; flocks of sightseers streamed along the shoreline to view their first (and only) Confederate visitor. The captain would not allow guests on board until he was sure of a friendly reception from the authorities, but "if we can judge from outward signs," wrote Whittle, "we are likely to find a good deal of sympathy here among the people." Waddell dispatched Lieutenant Grimball to the vice-regal residence at Toorak conveying a letter to "His Excellency Sir Charles H. Darling, K.C.B., Captain General and Governor in Chief and Vice-Admiral, Melbourne." Approval from the governor, as the Crown representative to the British colony of Victoria, was required for a foreign warship to enter and be served in port. "Sir: I have the honor to announce to your excellency the arrival of the CSS *Shenandoah*, under my command, in Port Phillip this afternoon," wrote Waddell. He desired permission to make repairs, take on coal, land prisoners, and get to sea as quickly as possible. "I shall observe the neutrality. I have the honor to be, very respectfully, your obedient servant, Jas. I. Waddell, Lieutenant Commanding."[1]

Early the following morning, Waddell was awakened by voices in the adjoining cabin. Mrs. Nichols was preparing for departure and loudly demanding restitution of every book taken from *Delphine*. All were returned except *Uncle Tom's Cabin*, which Lieutenant Whittle threw overboard. The lady thanked them for their kindness, declaring she liked all the officers except Lining and Whittle. "I thought I was a kind of chicken of hers," concluded the embarrassed lieutenant, "anyhow I was very kind to her." Not sure whether to hold prisoners on board in a neutral port or to let them go before permission was received to do so, but also eager to be rid of them, Whittle made it known that shore boats were available for hire. The captives would not be restrained from taking them. The Nichols family loaded their luggage and shoved clear of *Shenandoah*. The men of *Delphine* rowed ashore while Mrs. Nichols with her maid and son crossed to *Jeanne Payne*, an American ship lying in harbor. Her parting shot: "I wish that steamer may be burned."

It was a fine day, the bay peaceful and quiet—at first. With permission from the captain, off-duty officers went ashore. Then the ship was besieged by visitors; the captain acquiesced and allowed them on board. The crowds went everywhere, complained Lining, and looked into everything; until nearly sundown the stream was constant. Even at dinner, duty officers could not keep them out of the wardroom. "Several very pleasant gentlemen came off, but a great deal also of riff-raff." Officers in town visited the legislative assembly during a discussion on tariff where, according to a local newspaper, they excited much attention from members of the house and public gallery. In the evening they attended a play called "A Match in the Dark" at the Haymarket Theater.

One of the first visitors to *Shenandoah* was Commander King, the British navy agent on board the royal mail steamer RMS *Bombay*, in the bay awaiting outgoing mail. After Waddell personally showed the commander around the ship "with the utmost courteousness," he reported to the admiralty: "The ship appeared to be in good order; Her officers a gentlemanly set of men, in a uniform of gray and gold; but from the paucity of her crew at present, she cannot be very efficient for fighting purposes." He noted that there were only 70 sailors on board for a proper compliment of 140. He suspected that she was the former *Sea King* but could not confirm it.[2]

At eleven o'clock that morning, Governor Darling convened a special session of his cabinet to consider Waddell's visit request. The clerk read dispatches covering Queen Victoria's proclamation of neutrality, official correspondence concerning *Alabama's* visit to Cape Town, and applicable orders to colonial governors based on laws of Great Britain and the maritime laws of nations. Her Majesty's ministers demanded that officials maintain both the fact and appearance of neutrality. The governor and advisers were acutely sensitive to the convoluted diplomatic and legal issues surrounding this unexpected and not altogether welcome visitor.

Belligerents had three superior rights in international law: the right to halt and inspect suspect ships of all nations on the high seas, the right to confiscate military supplies—contraband—intended for the enemy, and the right to blockade the enemy. In January 1862 the secretary of state for foreign affairs had issued a proclamation clarifying the rules during hostilities between the United States "and the states calling themselves the Confederate States of America." Visiting warships or privateers of either belligerent could take in only supplies necessary for immediate use and had to put to sea within twenty-four hours, or as soon as weather and safety-required repairs allowed. They were prohibited from engaging in warlike purposes and from obtaining warlike equipment.[3]

As specific as these rules were, events convinced both sides that the British flagrantly violated neutrality in favor of the other. There was no comfortable middle ground; old controversies resurfaced concerning the rights and responsibilities of neutral powers, while Confederates took every advantage of their status and insisted on their rights. Ships flying the rebel flag were to be accorded the same status as those of any other nation, including the United States, and were to be treated fairly with regard to assistance, supplies, and repairs in neutral ports. *Alabama*'s dramatic and destructive cruise in particular became a cause célèbre, an illustration of the pitfalls of neutrality, and a source of extreme acrimony between Washington and London.

The Melbourne *Argus* reported that the cabinet meeting was fully attended, and "so anxious were the Government to preserve the neutrality of the port" that more than two hours were spent in deliberations. Governor Darling decided to grant the stay request, its duration dependent on the nature of supplies and extent of repairs required. That evening, Commissioner of Trade and Customs James G. Francis, the official responsible for the port, communicated the permission through a letter that cited one additional order "with which it is requisite for you to comply." It directed that, in accordance with long-established practice, no armed vessel belonging to either belligerent shall quit her anchorage within twenty-four hours after any vessel belonging to the adverse belligerent, armed or unarmed, shall have left the same port. Australia depended on American trade and there were several U.S. merchantmen there at the time. Without such a rule, *Shenandoah* could lie comfortably in the neutral harbor until one of them departed, then follow her out for easy capture in international waters. Traders would avoid the port altogether for fear of entrapment with potentially severe economic consequences for the colony. That Commissioner Francis emphasized this particular provision illustrates the government's primary worry.[4]

Shenandoah's arrival occasioned a flurry of news gathering and speculation. The populace had eagerly absorbed stories of the war, which included the sailing of *Sea King* and her conversion to a Confederate cruiser. They read and believed that the vessel had been lost on a rock in the Atlantic or that Raphael Semmes commanded with a hundred of his old crew. The Southerners were asked constantly where Semmes was, noted Chew, and were reluctant to believe he was not on board. "Probably much of the excitement we created at Melbourne was due to this mistake." Waddell actively courted the newspapers to champion the cause, an unusual exercise in public relations not normally his function. The idea probably arose from the editorial wars in England and Europe as Southern representatives attempted to influence public opinion and decision makers.

On Thursday morning, the Melbourne *Age* reported, "Yesterday the community were startled by the announcement that a Confederate war steamer was in the Bay. . . . Our belligerent visitor is named the *Shenandoah*, after that valley in Western Virginia, where General Jackson won so many victories." The article summarized the cruise, listed prizes, and described the vessel in detail, undoubtedly from inside information. "As seen from the Railway Pier, she appears to be a very long ship, and lies low in the water. . . . She is well appointed, and is in perfect order." She also was, obviously, the former *Sea King*. The Melbourne *Argus* complimented *Shenandoah* as a remarkably fine ship: "Now comes an American representative to testify the reality of that fierce fratricidal contest which interests us all so much. . . . Though her demonstrations were of the quietest, the white ensign with the St. George's cross and stars bespoke her position in the Confederate cause. . . . The *Shenandoah* is regarded as the *Alabama redivivus*, or the Phoenix-like product of the wreck of that world famed vessel."[5]

In these accounts, we feel the isolation of an Australia where few warships sailed, far from centers of European affairs. Any such visitor was big news; this was bigger than most. Australians did not comprehend the complexities of the distant American argument, but in an age tinged with romantic notions of honor and valor, they related to *Alabama*. She had been a tangible manifestation of the Confederacy. Her exploits brought the contest to them in the language of ocean commerce and ocean conflict, which they understood very well because their welfare and perhaps their survival depended on the sea as part of the world's greatest trading empire.

Having no particular stake in the success of the Union or in understanding its concepts, many looked on the men of *Alabama* as valiant heroes fighting great odds. Captain Semmes was an international celebrity as much as Lincoln, Grant, and Lee. Despite vehement U.S. protests, *Alabama* and other rebel raiders had been welcomed warmly in British colonial ports such as Jamaica,

Trinidad, and Gibraltar—especially by colonial governors and army and navy commanders. *Alabama* caused a similar stir in Cape Town in August 1863 with parties and balls in her honor; and her mere rumored appearance off Port Philip Bay created a great deal of excitement in Melbourne. Much of this glamour transferred to *Shenandoah*, which is precisely what the Confederates intended.

With typical Victorian hyperbole, the *Age* issued a follow-up the next day: she was a clipper-built screw steamer, built on the Clyde, "which has become famous for turning out blockade runners, and does not appear likely to do discredit to the shipwrights of Glasgow." A wooden ship with iron frames, masts, and yards, she was no doubt built for and admirably adapted for the purpose. *Shenandoah* was a smart, trimly set boat—evidently a swift sailer— "but there is nothing rakish about the craft, nor anything that would rouse suspicion as to the pacific nature of her intentions were she to steam unheralded among the shipping of any port." The article noted that although large— 220 feet long and 33 feet in breadth—it was not obvious from a distance that the vessel had steam power. Her small armament was adequate for capturing merchantmen: "The guns, all new, are magnificently mounted, and are also in excellent order." The Whitworths could strike from three miles. On deck, the merchantman appearance vanished with "admirable order and discipline everywhere observable." Her officers reported that *Shenandoah* was a splendid boat and she behaved admirably at sea, "an assertion which is fully borne out by the appearance of the craft."[6]

The *Illustrated Australian News* declared, "They are dashing fellows and seem to take a great pride in their flag and their fine ship." One article described Captain Waddell as "a six-foot North Carolinian, with thick black hair and a weather-beaten face, the color of deep mahogany. He limped slightly from a dueling wound which he never discussed. He was proud, quick-tempered and aloof." According to the *Illustrated Melbourne Post*, the captain was in great favor with his officers and crew; he was "a gentleman of most prepossessing appearance and bears about him the frank expression of a sailor."[7]

Mr. William Blanchard, U.S. consul in Melbourne, read of the newcomer in his morning paper and was not impressed—comfortable routine was to be interrupted by the greatest crisis of his tenure. Blanchard was a Marylander, former editor of *The National Era*, an abolitionist newspaper printed in Washington, D.C. He never imagined the war would reach this far and was determined to conquer the enemy so impertinently plopping its anchor on his doorstep. Upon arrival at the consulate that morning, Blanchard discovered in his waiting room the captain, mates, and crew of the *Delphine*. He interviewed the former captives and prepared reports for the overseas mail scheduled to depart that evening on *Bombay*. Captain Nichols, true to his parole, and "not for want of loyalty towards the United States," refused to divulge information about *Shenandoah*'s armament and equipment. However, he stated his conviction that she was indeed *Sea King*. He had seen the name on knives, forks, and spoons, and Captain Waddell had told him so.[8]

The crewmen were not so punctilious about parole, providing a description of the rebel vessel and her guns, which went into the consul's report. Mail offices ashore were closed by afternoon, so Blanchard had his dispatches rowed directly to *Bombay* in harbor, one copy to U.S. minister Adams in London and the other to the U.S. consul in Hong Kong, "with a view to having a cruiser put on her track as soon as possible." The report concluded, "It is the general impression that she is not a formidable vessel. She is leaky, and requires two hours [per day] pumping out."[9]

Lining feared just such an eventuality when he advised Waddell not to enter port until after the mail steamer departed. That evening in his bunk, Midshipman Mason shared this concern: "As this journal is intended to be written without the slightest restraint, I intend to be perfectly candid therefore & say just what I think of things & what the feeling is amongst the officers in the wardroom." They assumed the captain would proceed first to whaling grounds around New Zealand, but apparently the skipper thought it important to get his report off to navy secretary Mallory, Congress, and the public. However, thought Mason, news of their captures off the South American coast would have reached home anyway, and they had only taken *Delphine* since. A better strategy would have been to conceal their whereabouts for a month longer. "So most everyone thought. A great many people of Melbourne said to me they wondered our Captain did not wait."

Waddell did not justify this decision in writing, but he might have wanted the world to know that *Shenandoah* was headed for the Pacific. *Alabama* had advanced as far as the South China Sea, and when she sailed into Singapore in December 1863, Semmes found twenty-two American ships lying idle in the harbor; he read of others bottled up at Bangkok, Canton, Shanghai, Japan, and the Philippines. With *Alabama* in the area, no shippers would assign cargo to a Yankee vessel. *Shenandoah* could have the same effect in the world's largest ocean while attacking the last concentration of enemy targets. The news from home was disturbing: Although Lee was reported to have won a great victory at Petersburg (which was false), Lincoln had been reelected. "This all looks like no end to the war," wrote Whittle. "God alone can tell when or how it will end." These lonely Southerners could serve the Confederacy as *Alabama* had done only if the people of both North and South knew what was about to happen.[10]

Whittle prepared a report to Commodore Barron in Paris along with personal letters, one to his father and another to his darling Pattie. He prayed that the letters would reach their destinations, would relieve anxiety produced by the report of their shipwreck, and would let them know they had done their duty under many trials. Waddell wrote to Secretary Mallory, "Sir: I have the honor to announce my arrival in this harbor, also to report the work done by, and on the condition of, this vessel, under my command." He summarized the cruise to date, noting that rough weather in the Indian Ocean had tested *Shenandoah*'s good sea quality. "She is strong for her kind, fast, very spacious and well ventilated." There were a few design drawbacks: Her boilers were eighteen inches and engine cylinders five feet above the waterline and thereby vulnerable to enemy fire. But he had succeeded in getting the guns to battery, built an excellent magazine, and quartered the crew on the berth deck.[11]

He would follow his instructions completely, continued Waddell. He would keep *Shenandoah* afloat as long as she was serviceable and then decide what should be done with her. "God has been very merciful and kind unto us, and in all of our danger and necessities stretched forth His right hand to help and defend us. I shall be detained here a few days, making some repairs and coaling, and will then proceed on my cruise. We are all well and cheerful, but anxious for an honorable settlement of our national difficulties." The correspondence was delivered to *Bombay* and accompanied Consul Blanchard's dispatches, Governor Darling's report to the Foreign Office, and Commander King's note to the admiralty out on the evening tide. It would take weeks for Waddell's missive to reach Richmond and it would be too late by then. Even getting out of Melbourne would not be nearly so simple as his words implied.[12]

Not content with catching the mail, Consul Blanchard fired off a letter to Governor Darling: "I avail myself of this opportunity to call upon your Excellency to cause the said *Shenandoah*, alias *Sea King*, to be seized for piratical acts." She did not come within the Queen's neutrality proclamation, he maintained, never having entered a port of the "so-styled Confederate States of America" for the purposes of naturalization and consequently was not entitled to belligerent rights. "I therefore protest against any aid or comfort being extended to said piratical vessel in any of the ports of this colony." This was the initial salvo of a fierce diplomatic war, a barrage of protests and affidavits on similar themes. The letter was delivered to the governor's office at 6:45 p.m., about the same time *Shenandoah* was receiving permission to stay.[13]

Captain Waddell, accompanied by Dr. Lining and Lieutenant Grimball and Lieutenant Scales in dress uniforms with swords, made the traditional courtesy visit to the governor at noon the next day. His Excellency not being in, the captain left a card and departed. They went to Scott's Hotel, laid aside their swords and walked through the town on a tour of inspection, returning to the hotel for drinks, socializing, and dinner. Dr. Lining thought the parliament buildings were quite handsome for such a new colony. First Lieutenant Whittle stayed on board to supervise ship's work and delivery of fresh provisions. "Oh!

How I did enjoy my first fresh meal. I am an epicure, but that is not necessary to make one, after four months at sea, enjoy something fresh." He commenced painting the ship and caulking the upper deck. Visitors were so thick that caulkers had to give their mallets a good sweep to keep them out of the way.

In the meantime, *Delphine* crewmembers informed Consul Blanchard that captured seamen had agreed to enlist on *Shenandoah* primarily to avoid imprisonment and punishment and that they would desert if protected from arrest. Blanchard directed that all such men encountered in town should be sent to him for shelter. Thus began an active campaign to lure sailors away from the Confederates, hitting where they were most vulnerable. Blanchard bribed deserters, put them up in boardinghouses, paid expenses, and provided substitute income. Quartermaster Hall told Waddell that he had been offered $100 to defect. Encouraging desertions from a legally recognized navy was itself a violation of international law. Whittle noted, "The general underhanded rascality which characterizes [Yankees] as a nation is showing itself here in the individuals who reside and who come from the U.S."

American officials applied similar tactics in ports visited by Confederate raiders. Raphael Semmes complained that deserters from *Sumter* at Cadiz in January 1862 "had [no] attachment to the flag, not being natives, or, indeed, citizens at all, and sailor-like they had got tired and wanted a change." It was considered routine for local officials to cooperate in apprehending deserters. However, despite Waddell's appeals to the police commissioner and much to his frustration, Melbourne police would not interfere, undoubtedly under the direction of a governor sensitive to delicate political considerations.[14]

Blanchard submitted another flowery, convoluted dispatch lecturing the governor on his responsibilities to uphold the interest of justice, the safety of universal commerce, and the honor and dignity of Her Majesty's government "too long contemptuously disregarded by those who, seeking asylum under it, only abuse an honorable hospitality to violate its laws and insult its sovereignty." It must be evident, he contended, that all presumptions of fact and law were against the legal character of the vessel, which had no legitimacy as a commissioned warship of a recognized nation. "The undersigned will not doubt, that . . . your Excellency will give so much weight, and no more, to a bit of bunting and a shred of gold lace, as they deserve." *Sea King*, continued the consul, was a registered British merchant ship; she came from nowhere, destroyed without adjudication and without necessity. "The undersigned feels assured that he will not be misunderstood nor his conduct be deemed too officious when the peculiar facts of this present case are duly considered." Great Britain's ports and coasts were being used to cover piratical enterprises against the lives and property of a friendly power. And were that to continue, "new claims and additional and serious complications unfortunately [might] arise between her Majesty's government and the government of the United States."[15]

Each day *Shenandoah*'s log recorded "crowded with visitors." The curious traveled as far as three hundred miles to swarm the ship, evoking a carnival atmosphere. Extra trains were laid on between Melbourne and the port of Sandridge near the anchorage, with seven thousand persons using them on Sunday alone. Every licensed boat and two or three steamers bore signs reading "one shilling to *Shenandoah* and back" while shuttling continuously between piers and ship. Many were refused permission to come alongside for lack of standing room.

According to Chew, an estimated ten thousand people visited in one day, comprising all ages, sexes, sizes, and conditions. As each steamer approached, he wrote, the young officers stood near the gangway watching for pretty faces and vied with each other to take them in charge. Attractive young ladies were invited into the cabin for the pleasure of a glass of wine. "I think some of our officers might have left their hearts in the 'Golden Empire.'" However, "let it not be inferred that old ladies & gentlemen were neglected, far from it; we flatter ourselves that all our respectable visitors received due attention." Some parties gave three rousing cheers upon departure in acknowledgment of their welcome. The stiff breeze caught one boat rounding the stern of the ship and capsized it, throwing a lady and two gentlemen briefly into the water to the amusement of all. Lining was one of the tour guides: "I walked until my feet hurt me & I felt perfectly exhausted." He received numerous invitations to visit and dine, some which he would be glad to accept, but saw few pretty girls. "Evening came & gave us rest again, & very glad we were to get it."

Whittle had never seen anything like the rush: "The[y] look at us with apparent surprise that we have not tails. If this is what we are to expect, the sooner we get to sea the less chance I will incur of going deranged. . . . The labor of showing them around is becoming very boring. If I have said it once that 'this is a 32 pdr of 57 cwt,' 'this is a sight,' 'this is a rifled gun,' I have said it 50 times." By Sunday evening, the first lieutenant was harassed, disgusted, and drained. With the captain out of the ship all weekend, everything fell on him and the duty officers. They came to refit, not to be exhibited as a curiosity. And there was the problem of security: "We have received warning that the Yanks are determined to destroy our ship by some means. There may be idle and boastful threats but they are of such a nature that we are on the alert." After the first few days' crush, visiting was severely curtailed much to his relief.

The Southerners were tourists as well as hosts. The commanding officer could come and go as he wished, and with permission of the captain or executive officer, officers were free to leave when not on their duty day. Crewmen were let ashore by sections or watches in the evenings and weekend days, supposing that work did not require them to remain. Whittle stayed on board most of the time, denying himself the opportunity to unwind. Normally an officer ashore strove to discard his navy persona, distance himself from responsibilities of uniform, and meld into the populace the better to relax. However, after being required to conceal their Confederate allegiance for over a year in Europe, it now was their duty to proclaim pride in naval and national identity. The officers were conspicuous in gray uniforms on the streets and in the public places and homes of Melbourne. Whittle noted, "As we have, as it were, the reputation of the Confederacy to make & maintain, it is very incumbent that every man an[d] officer should be circumspect."

Chew was surprised to see such a flourishing city. He knew of its size and its commerce and expected to see much. "Yet looking upon it, I could not but wonder and admire. In this remote quarter of the globe, one almost forgets where he is & thinks he is in England." Superb large houses with spacious streets conveying carriages of fine finish spoke for wealth. The Melbourne population was mostly English, he noted, but also included many Americans—Southerners as well as Yankees—and foreigners. A great deal of shipping occupied the harbor including eight or ten U.S. vessels, most of them for sale; two others arrived during their stay. The young lieutenant particularly delighted in socializing with local Frenchmen to show off his fluency in the "sweet language" and reminisce about his beloved Paris.

Chapter 9

The War Down Under

Melbourne sits four miles from the mouth of the Yarra River that runs into Hobson's Bay at the northern end of the larger Port Phillip Bay. On either side of Hobson's Bay, the towns of Williamstown and Sandridge connected with the city by rail. Barely thirty years before 1865, livestock ranchers, traders, and pioneers began flocking to the area, founding a city that represented—much more than Sydney or Hobart—the landed gentry, social groupings, and institutions, much like an English town. There was no aristocracy; nonconformist Scots and Ulstermen ran many shops and trades. The 1850s' gold rush flooded Melbourne with Europeans, Jews, and Chinese, and by 1861 the population was 126,000. Fine buildings and institutions were built on gold profits as trade flourished along with a vigorous democratic polity enabled by an expanding franchise. It was a frontier community, an opportunistic society increasingly based more on achievement and wealth than position, where working folk were well off by nineteenth-century standards. In terms of civic vigor and confidence, the people had much in common with citizens of Chicago, Denver, or San Francisco; Melbourne was the "Metropolis of the Southern Hemisphere." A visiting Englishman in 1870 declared that "the life and vivacity of the place were astonishing." He liked it immensely but thought Melbourne was "a little far from town," meaning London.[1]

Like the city itself, the three local daily newspapers, *Argus, Age,* and *Herald,* were exemplary reproductions of English models. Upon arrival of the monthly mail steamer, the editors copied, quoted, summarized, and rushed the news to print. The cry "Arrival of the English Mail!" echoed through the city. Boys bearing piles of newspapers ran through the streets hallooing at the top of their voices, "Hargus, Hage, 'Erald, 'stronary! Latest news from England!" Everyone with a sixpence exchanged it for a copy of the paper first to hand. The *Argus* tended to enthusiasm for the South while the *Age* cheered for the North and the *Herald* represented the neutral line of official British policy. But most war bulletins were short, inaccurate, and even false, reaching Britain weeks after the events by packet from New York or Halifax and, for the first two years of the war, almost uniformly describing Confederate victories. When the news passed through the muddy filters of the British press and arrived in Australia a month or so later, it presented an even less true picture.[2]

In elaborate Victorian prose, editors and citizens passionately expressed their views, informed and not—antipodal echoes of similar discussions in Europe. Many, especially among English ruling elites, became convinced early in the conflict and maintained their thinking until very late that the North could not prevail and the United States would split. Melbourne inherited the perspective of the homeland colored by great distance and by the peculiar perspective of the most isolated and thoroughly British outpost of the empire. Debate swelled on the streets, in public meetings, private clubs, law courts, and legislative chambers. All this excitement is partially explained by the close relationships between Australia and the United States. Americans by the thousands immigrated during the gold rush and eventually settled in skilled trades, business, or professions, giving the city the largest concentrations of Americans on the continent. Scott's Hotel, a favorite hangout for the Confederates, was owned by Americans as was the Batchelder and O'Neill photography studio where the men had their pictures taken.[3]

The sudden appearance of the rebel ship, wrote one newspaper, "has been like the explosion of a bomb-shell [in the expatriate community], and has fanned the slumbering feeling into a flame which will be productive of unpleasant results." Union men, including those of American vessels, were rumored to be plotting the ship's destruction. On board *Shenandoah*, armed watches were posted at all times, and "scarcely a night passed that there were not craft of more than doubtful character flitting around us," recalled Master's Mate Hunt. But regardless of their roots, many Americans found rationale for supporting the visitors. Those of Southern origin were joined by others with financial interest in the South or in the conflict in general. Currency speculation on the fluctuating wartime exchange rates between Great Britain and the United States generated great profit.[4]

James Maguire of Boston, for example, was a wealthy importer and manufacturer of shoes and boots. He was a Democrat who had been the first American consul in Melbourne until the new Republican administration appointed Blanchard in 1861. When massive quotas on footwear to outfit Union soldiers cut Australian imports to a trickle, the Maguire boot business boomed. He smuggled in Spencer repeating rifles despite the U.S. government's exclusive orders for the weapons. One newspaper wrote that Maguire "chaperoned" *Shenandoah*'s officers. Consul Blanchard stated that he "acted as counsel" to the Confederates. He was one of Waddell's primary contacts in the American community.[5]

One *Herald* correspondent rather condescendingly thought all the hullaballoo was a bit silly. Signing himself "An Englishman," he asked how many fools it takes to make a public, likening them to "rank noodles, full of the presumption, the bumptiousness, and the arrogance peculiar to the last stage of hopeless folly." Even worse, because of the warm sun, or because they drank too freely, or just because they were lazy, the locals were beginning to emulate their American cousins. The writer liked Americans; he admired "their earnestness, their originality, their quaint humour." But, he maintained, those in this dependency of Great Britain were under no obligation to imitate American ways of life or speech. "To give way to any public manifestation of feeling on this subject would be very improper, and very un-English."[6]

Most Melbournians, however, ardently supported one side over the other in the American Civil War. *Shenandoah* officers were feted as heroes by one faction and denounced as pirates by the other, while the governor and bureaucracy muddled and vacillated. A strong party of citizens and government officials adhered to the Union cause. The governor requested confidentially that Captain Charles B. Payne of the Victorian Volunteer Naval Brigade (and former Royal Navy lieutenant) visit and report on the ship's capabilities and armaments. Payne thought the state of the vessel on deck, aloft, and in the engine room both slovenly and dirty, not reflecting credit upon her officers. He observed forty to fifty slouchy, dirty, and undisciplined sailors; the number of officers appeared out of proportion to the crewmen. "Without disparaging the Confederate war-steamer *Shenandoah*," he concluded that she was simply an ordinary merchant vessel armed with a few guns.[7]

There appeared to be little public debate of the central issues—union, secession, states' rights, slavery. Pro-Union sentiment focused on repugnance for commerce raiding, dangers for the long and vulnerable umbilical cords of trade with Europe and America, and local issues such as land reform and tariffs. The Civil War generated economic uncertainty even in Australia—widely fluctuating prices and availability affected huge quantities of imports. The *Age* produced a rambling editorial condemning the rebel ship in language worthy of the most ardent Yankee: "We cannot regard the *Shenandoah* as other than a marauding craft, and her officers and crew than as a gang of respectable pirates. The vessel cannot claim to rank as a ship of war, nor ought the commissions of her officers entitle them to a place with gentlemen holding similar rank in the navies of recognized powers."[8]

The article further stated that she was *Sea King* under a false name and false colors, as defenseless as her victims against a well-directed shot from a true warship, and she owed her armament to a violation of international law. Her crew were not Americans but English, Irish, Scots, and Germans. "If the practice of enlisting the crews of captured ships be adopted, there is no check to piracy." She was in Melbourne to obtain from some resident Americans information to destroy the property of other Americans and to recruit crewmen in further violation of neutrality. She did not fight honorably in her country's defense but destroyed unarmed antagonists for plunder. "We shall presently hear of the corn-laden ships from California bound for this port having been burnt or sunk, to the loss, probably, of local capitalists, and, certainly, of the bread consuming public. . . . Who knows whether this vessel will confine her operations to ships sailing under the American flag? Our gold ships are very tempting."[9]

In the *Age*, a "Neutral Englishman" expressed shame and humiliation that *Shenandoah* was an English vessel, armed, equipped, and manned by British subjects. These Southerners could not advance the interests of the Confederacy, he maintained, even if they destroyed every federal vessel on the seas. Instead, their work would affect the poorer classes of the colony more than the Northern states, causing a rise in the already high price of flour and strengthening the monopoly of the corn trade. Why did she not protect the blockade runners, obtaining glory where it is to be found? Is it right that, by stretching a loophole in international law, such a system of buccaneering is countenanced? "If so, where is it to stop?"[10]

Nor did the *Age* accept the distinction between privateer and commissioned warship; whatever her pretensions, *Shenandoah* was a privateer: "The method may be strictly lawful, but it is exceedingly inglorious, and they who engage in it are entitled to no honor. . . . The day may come when the unoffending people of this colony may be made to suffer for the quarrels of nations in the other hemisphere." The well-being of their homes was at risk and Australians themselves must accept responsibility. "Except for British ports and British connivance, these piratical cruisers of the South would be unable to keep the sea."

These sentiments infuriated *Shenandoah*'s officers. Lieutenant Scales was tempted to engage the editor in a duel and even wrote up terms of combat, though ultimately not delivered; Dr. Lining retained the document as a souvenir.[11]

Despite these concerns voiced in the *Age*, it appears that the preponderance of sympathy was for the South. With tongue in cheek, "A. Z." ascribed the acrimony to the large number of resident Americans having Northern sentiments who, being suppliers of so many articles of daily consumption, feel free to dictate their opinions, "and if we do not think with them they will stop the supply of these articles, and put us to the inconvenience of making them ourselves." The North is merely trying to conquer the South, he continued, for the cotton Yankee merchants required while the South is engaged in a war of independence. The only stain upon the South is the curse of slavery, and this would be abolished before long. "And can anyone help admiring the gallant stand the South has made? Did we not admire the Italians? Did we not admire the poor Poles? We did not assist either; but may we not admire?" And finally with reference to *Shenandoah*'s mission, A. Z. noted, "the Americans reaped a great deal of glory from practicing the same treatment upon British merchant ships, but smart terribly now that they feel the lash themselves."[12]

An *Argus* editorial dismissed opposing arguments as "bunkum" reflecting Northern character and institutions, not the true sentiments of the community. The Washington government was characterized by mismanagement, divided counsels, boastful language, and political corruption. It was a vulgar tyranny, "which has kept no faith with her enemies and . . . has broken every promise to its friends." Under the pretext of a crusade against slavery, the United States "has committed crimes against civilization more detestable than any slavery." Eighty years ago in America, rightful rulers had been despised and rebels honored; now rebels were traitors. As insistently argued by Southerners, why shouldn't the Confederacy do to the United States what the colonies had done to Great Britain? These were natural rights of revolution, freedom, and consent of the governed.

The *Herald* noted that the old Stars and Stripes were hoisted over many places of business in the city, apparently in compliment to the Confederate cruiser, "which now flaunts her flag bravely in our waters." Despite virtuous indignation from Yankee sources, "had the Confederates a merchant navy, it would, in vulgar parlance, be served with the same sauce." And the Union could not claim innocence; blockade runners routinely were seized by Union warships.[13]

The *Herald* cited the controversial demise of the CSS *Florida*, news that had just reached Melbourne. *Florida* (also English built and sent forth by James Bulloch) accumulated a record second only to *Alabama*, until, that is, the early morning of 7 October 1864—the day before *Sea King* and *Laurel* sailed from England. As *Florida* lay in the quiet harbor of Bahia, Brazil, the USS *Wachusett* suddenly rammed and attacked the sleeping vessel and after a short but hopeless resistance towed her out of port while a Brazilian warship and coastal forts opened fire. Hailed as a great victory in the North, the act was condemned by Confederates as yet another example of Yankee perfidy. But Secretary of State Seward was obliged to disavow it as a flagrant violation of Brazilian neutrality. So angry were locals that a mob sacked the consular offices in Bahia and dragged the U.S. flag through the street. "The '*trick*' was eminently Yankee," wrote Raphael Semmes, "and I presume could not possibly have been practiced in any other civilized nation of the earth." There is evidence that Lieutenant Robert Carter suggested to navy secretary Mallory that *Florida* join the proposed Pacific expedition, and so she might have done.[14]

"Peace is what the southerners ask for; peace meaning recognition and a new empire," concluded the *Herald*. "The Federals declare there shall be no peace without submission and their dictatorship." Australia need not trouble itself either way, but the editors wished to be clear: Europe had acknowledged the Confederate States as belligerents and ought to have declared them an empire. "Australia, the child-giant of the English press, and a continent that may ere long sway many destinies, can at any rate do no less than welcome the gallant outcasts of a distracted country." While deploring the misery caused by such destruction, the *Herald* stated, "we cannot but recognize and fraternize with the brave men who uphold their country's flag at the risk of being hanged at the yard-arm, or shot after a short shrift."[15]

Meanwhile on *Shenandoah*, Chew wrote, "How can I do justice to the many kindnesses, the warm sympathies for our cause manifested by almost everybody?" The officers could not go ashore without being approached by would-be friends extending the greatest civilities; societies and clubs vied in courting them. Lining encountered a Mr. Hart with whom he had traveled on another ship in 1860. An elderly man, Mr. Weymouth, approached Whittle during a ship tour and enquired about an acquaintance who turned out to be Whittle's uncle, Arthur Sinclair, a Confederate navy commander. Weymouth had known Sinclair as a U.S. Navy midshipman on the Pacific station thirty-four years earlier and, overjoyed to discover his old friend's nephew, extended warm invitations. "He is one of the most perfect old gentlemen I ever met," wrote Whittle. "He tells me to make his house my home." That evening, he and Lining dined with the family in South Yarra. The doctor was impressed by their host's colorful past: he had been a trader and silver smuggler in Mexico and South America and was pressed into the Peruvian army.

The Confederates knew that public opinion was fickle; they had much experience with it in Europe, and some of their welcome seemed more superficial than real. The pro was flattering and the con frustrating. However, public debate was not crucial to their mission while official support was. And there were real problems: After three days in port, Mason worried about the behavior of some warrant and petty officers. He considered them good-for-nothing fellows who went ashore in uniform, got drunk, raised a row, and disgraced the ship. He was almost ashamed to show his face on shore. While such actions were not unusual sailor behavior, Mason expected better from the more senior men even if they were not Southerners.

Sailmaker Henry Alcott overstayed his shore leave and was suspended from duty temporarily. On another occasion, two midshipmen, Browne and Mason, were dispatched to haul an inebriated Assistant Surgeon McNulty back by force. Warrant Officer Guy was refused permission to go on shore but stole over the bows anyway and returned the next morning. He had been marked as a deserter and was not to be allowed on board, but once there refused to leave. Bulloch shoved him down the ladder, tore his shoulder straps off, and kicked him into the boat. Waddell, after hearing of derogatory statements Guy had made on shore, later invited him back on board and arrested him.

On Monday, 30 January, Governor Darling's private secretary responded to Consul Blanchard's letters: As advised by Crown law officers, there was no evidence of piratical acts, and whatever the previous history of *Shenandoah*, the government was bound to treat her as a ship of war belonging to a belligerent power. The consul immediately fired back another protest. Not to put too fine a point on it, Blanchard concluded, "The said vessel is nothing more than a pirate, which the nation whose vessels she robs and destroys has a right to pursue, capture, or destroy in any port or harbor in the world."[16]

The British never accepted the pirate thesis. Commissioning of warships fell under national rather than international laws; there was no requirement to have originated in or even visited a home port. This representative of a recognized belligerent had arrived in peace, made reasonable requests within the rules, and enjoyed extensive local support. Nothing could be gained and only trouble would ensue by taking the extreme position advocated by the consul. The governor ignored Blanchard's implied threat to take *Shenandoah* by force. Remembering the outraged British response to the *Trent* incident, the consul undoubtedly understood that a repetition of *Florida*'s capture, however tempting it was, had he a warship to do it, would have grave repercussions.

In his correspondence with colonial officials, Waddell was sensitive of his position. Pride and honor were close to the surface to the point of occasional testiness, but he was careful not to alienate the authorities and risk denying himself the help so desperately required. The Southerners blamed Commissioner of Trade and Customs Francis for much of their troubles, claiming that he was part owner of a store selling American goods and was a close business and political friend of Consul Blanchard. Underneath the formality of official communication ("Sir: I have the honor to acknowledge receipt of your letter of . . . I have further in command to inform you . . . I desire to communicate to you . . . I have the honor to be, sir, your obedient servant.") the strain is apparent even on routine matters of supplies and repairs.

Waddell engaged the marine engineering services of Messrs. Langland Brothers & Co. while other work progressed rapidly. A diver examined the propeller shaft, reporting that bearings, castings, and coupling band supporting the shaft and propeller were in serious condition. It would be necessary to discharge coal and stores and haul the ship clear of the water to ascertain the full extent of damage and caulk the hull inside and out. Repairs would take at least ten days. Mason wondered that the whole stern post had not been torn out and continued to blame Waddell for employing the engines in a rush to catch the mail, which undoubtedly exacerbated the problem. To the captain's further frustration, Commissioner Francis appointed his own board of engineers.

Waddell requested and was granted supplies—fresh meat, vegetables, and bread daily in port, and sea supplies of brandy, rum, champagne, port, sherry, beer, porter, molasses, lime juice, and light material for summer clothing. Forcing a false civility, the captain said he would extend every facility to the commissioner's engineers. In his responses to Francis, Waddell avoided specifics regarding the eleven prisoners; he was uncertain of their official status and concerned about further entanglements. The commissioner prodded him for a list of the captives, implying that they had been landed in violation of regulations. Waddell retorted that the prisoners "left this vessel of their own free will, without consulting the 'regulations enforced in this colony,' unmolested, unassisted, and not in any boat belonging to this vessel." After a third request, he produced the list, but complained about delay caused by the unnecessary engineering survey. He hoped the governor would consider these entreaties in "the spirit of a law-abiding man and impatient to be about his country's business."[17]

On Wednesday, 1 February, Commissioner Francis received his commission's report confirming the repairs required. However, Francis pointedly explained, the slip (a marine railroad with a large cradle and steam engine to pull it) was leased by the government to private individuals. No government assistance, direct or indirect, would be applied, and no government facilities or appliances would be used. This was an attempt—ultimately unsuccessful—to isolate the regime from culpability in Shenandoah's subsequent activities. The commissioner also required the Williamstown harbormaster and the Melbourne collector of customs to observe carefully and provide daily reports of progress "without unseemly obtrusion or interference"—a standard that, in Waddell's opinion, they utterly failed to meet. The officials were to note apparent abuses of permissions, especially those prohibiting extension of or improvements to the vessel's armaments. Waddell also asked to sell surplus stores for needed cash, certifying that these were purchased and not captured items, but the council denied the request as not within the strict observance of neutrality.[18]

Invitations and gifts poured in for the officers from enthusiastic local elites, making the Southerners comfortable in their proper milieu. The railway company provided free open tickets for use throughout the visit. A deputation arrived from Ballarat, one of the principal mining districts in the hills above Melbourne, inviting them to visit at the hosts' expense. They were voted members of the cricket club and of the prestigious Melbourne Club and were invited to a dinner in their honor. The dinner was attended by Captain Waddell, two lieutenants, Lee and Scales, Midshipman Mason, Paymaster Smith, and Dr. Lining. According to the doctor, sixty gentlemen attended and it was a very fine dinner. "There was no putting of fellows 'under the table,' & our crowd especially behaved very well."

Two toasts were offered: "the Queen," which all drank standing, and "the Captain and officers of the Shenandoah, our guests of the evening," followed by three cheers, for which the citizens stood while the guests remained seated.

Although the toasts notably omitted any reference to the Confederacy, the cheers were unprecedented as club rules forbade such demonstrations. To the relief of all concerned, the club president had informed Waddell in advance that no words of his own would be expected or necessary; it would have been politically embarrassing had the Confederates toasted or spoken formally in defense of their cause, which they would have been honor bound to do if called upon.

The Melbourne Club included all the first people of the town, noted Mason, including members of parliament and judges. The dining room was magnificent and the dinner was excellent with all sorts of fine wines and food. "Enjoyed myself very much but in a reasonable manner." Dr. Barker, a jolly old fellow seated on Mason's right, invited Mason to visit his lunatic asylum in the suburbs and then waxed eloquent on the advantages of placing a hangman's knot behind the neck rather than beside the ear for a quick and humane death. The young midshipman listened attentively for politeness' sake and decided if he ever was to be hung, he would beg the executioner to act accordingly. (The proposition would seem less remote and theoretical later in the cruise.) After dinner they retired to smoking and billiard rooms for conversation, then departed about midnight. The captain granted permission for the officers to stay overnight in town, a rare treat. Mason went around with the rest of the crowd on a "bit of a lark" and then turned in at the Albion Hotel.

The gathering inflamed the controversy. The *Age* editor, particularly incensed at this egregious violation of neutrality by prominent citizens, considered them "soft headed flunkeys" collaborating in a fraud on the British government. Captain Waddell was there to injure Australian commerce with the aid of British subjects "who, by cajolery, or, if report speaks truly, in some instances by force, have been induced to become buccaneers." Was *Shenandoah* just a joint stock speculation whose only object was plunder? Merchants who provided coal and provisions paid for by goods seized on the high seas were conniving in the presence of the Confederate cruiser. What would happen when their coasts swarmed with American privateers, depriving the colony of intercourse with foreign countries? Instead of feting these people, they should be helping the government get rid of them. The *Age* editor threatened, should difficulty arise about compliance with government orders, the harbor defense raft mounting one or two guns with a dozen volunteers would put *Shenandoah* under water in less than twenty minutes. Waddell took the sentiments seriously, although the scenario was doubtful under normal circumstances.[19]

Also on 1 February, debate in the colonial legislature about the true identity of *Shenandoah* made evident the prevailing sympathy. A Mr. Berry believed ample information existed showing the ship to be *Sea King* and therefore, under the proclamation of neutrality, "had the Shenandoah returned to any

English port after having destroyed other vessels, she would have been instantly seized and condemned." Burned and sunk vessels had been loaded with English cargo and owned by Englishmen, he claimed. (Some cargos arguably were English owned, but none of the captured ships were.) Berry continued that the neutrality proclamation made it illegal not only to arm and fit out such vessels but also to send them to sea with a view of handing them over, by sale or otherwise, to either belligerent. Even if loosely interpreted early in the war, the proclamation was being more tightly enforced, as evidenced by confiscation of the Laird rams and other government actions. In addition, all ships destroyed by *Shenandoah* would be subject to claim by the American government (as indeed they were). He therefore wished to enquire why confiscation of the vessel was not carried out, a sentiment to which Commissioner Frances responded with "Hear, hear."[20]

Mr. McCulloch arose to counter these points: Mr. Berry had produced no real proof concerning *Sea King*. The colonial government already had discussed the issue at length, and there was no justification for treating *Shenandoah* as a pirate. Strict neutrality should be enforced, but beyond allowing the ship to take on stores and effect repairs, the government could not act. These remarks were punctuated by frequent cheers and calls of "Hear, hear!" Mr. Berry's attempt to read the deposition of a former lady prisoner (undoubtedly Lillias Nichols) was greeted with shouts of "Order!" and "No, no!" and overruled by the chair. Mr. O'Shanassy pointed out that the French government had allowed *Florida* and *Alabama* to refit in their ports and therefore "the honorable member [Berry] might as well have let this matter alone," which brought cheers from all parts of the house. A Mr. Lalor stated his belief that only the governor had full powers to treat with a vessel belonging to a foreign power. There the matter was dropped.[21]

Disappointed by this debate and the governor's unhelpful responses, Consul Blanchard consulted with several American merchants and decided on a new tactic: an indictment in admiralty court. He employed a firm of solicitors, Messrs. Duffett, Grant & Woolcott, submitting to them affidavits and witnesses respecting *Sea King*. "My solicitors considered there was abundant evidence," he reported to Secretary of State Seward, "and that it should be laid before the Crown law officers, which I authorized them to do."[22]

In the meantime, socializing continued. Lining, Scales, and Paymaster Smith dined at the home of architect Francis Maloney White. Mason described a fascinating four-hour tour of the asylum hosted by Dr. Barker for him and Lieutenant Lee. And by special invitation, several officers attended a performance at the Theatre Royal of *Othello* starring the famous Barry Sullivan. Mason thought the theater crowded and the performance miserable. During the intermission, the band struck up "Dixie." Many in the audience cheered while some contributed hisses and groans, "all of which was excessively annoying to ourselves." He departed at the earliest opportunity, went down to Sandridge in the eleven o'clock train, and returned to the ship.

On Saturday, 4 February, with work continuing feverishly in preparation for going on the slip, a steam tug towed *Shenandoah* across the harbor to Williamstown where she was moored to a buoy between the breakwater and adjacent railroad pier. The ship lay there snugly for a couple of days in calm conditions with caulkers and joiners at work and a gang of stevedores removing cargo and coal into lighters alongside. No visitors were allowed even on Sunday, which Mason thought was uncivil to the hospitable inhabitants of Victoria.

Through his solicitors, Consul Blanchard was granted an audience for Monday with Minister of Justice Archibald Michie and Attorney General George Higinbotham to present his case for action by admiralty court. He was accompanied by his attorney; was supported by Mr. J. B. Swasey, an American merchant; and carried ten affidavits from men, and one lady, of *Delphine*, *Helena*, *Susan*, *Lizzy M. Stacey*, and *D. Godfrey*. In dry legal language with lots of "saids"—"the said steamer," "the said officer," the "said voyage"—the depositions reflected careful transcription. They had seen the name *Sea King* on the ship's wheel, buckets, bell, and other locations; several of them had worked to file off the words. As Mrs. Nichols had warned her captors, she held nothing back, but she also swore that she had been welcomed on *Shenandoah*, was treated with kindness and consideration by Captain Waddell, and was frequently in conversation with him. "He left his wife in England; and . . . on leaving England he told her that he was going on a cruise, and that she would most likely hear a great many things to his detriment, but not to believe them."[23]

George Silvester, an original crewman from *Laurel*, summarized the damning details of the entire cruise. Blanchard asked Mr. Duffett to read this particular affidavit aloud to the minister of justice and attorney general, but to no avail. After much discussion, both gentlemen seemed to admit that *Sea King* (*Shenandoah*) would be liable to seizure and condemnation if found in British waters but not in Melbourne unless she violated neutrality, and if she did, they would take immediate action. In a subsequent letter to the governor, Blanchard pointedly inquired why a violation of law in one part of Her Majesty's dominions did not constitute violation in another part. Thoroughly disgusted, he gave up on admiralty court.

Chapter 10

Charley the Cook

D r. Lining and Lieutenant Whittle again dined ashore with the Weymouths and, much to Lining's surprise, Whittle "got exceedingly tight, neither knowing what he was doing, or where he was going." The doctor walked Whittle around for a while until they boarded the train. By the time they arrived at the ship, Whittle was able to take care of himself and apparently no one other than the officer of the deck noticed the inebriated first lieutenant. This is the only recorded occasion when he let off steam. He seldom left the ship.

Shenandoah was heaved clear of the water the next day on the slip, resting on keel blocks with the hull shored up. Stages and platforms were erected along the sides to complete caulking the hull as mechanics immediately began work on the shaft, all "busy as bees" according to Mason. Everything was in such confusion with quarters torn to pieces, carpenters and joiners at work everywhere, and caulkers banging over his head all day long, that the midshipman could neither read nor write. The wearisome work progressed rapidly for nearly a week.

Captain Henry Walke of the USS *Sacramento* reported from Lisbon that *Shenandoah* was thought to be in Vigo, Spain, but he did not find her there. He might have been confusing her with the ironclad ram *Stonewall*.[1]

During the first two weeks in February, Melbourne papers reported war news eight to eleven weeks old, dating from 18 November to 19 December 1864. The ship *Osprey* crossed the Pacific with copies of *The San Francisco Herald* containing telegraphic bulletins and articles based on eastern editions; *Albert Edward* brought papers from Puget Sound. Other vessels carried information around Cape Horn or the Cape of Good Hope from New York and England, sometimes via Sydney. Rumors and speculation jumbled with facts, then were repeated, excerpted, and summarized from the *New York Times*, the *New-York Tribune*, the *New York Herald*, the *New-York Evening Post*, the *New Orleans Times*, the *Daily Richmond Examiner*, and the *Richmond Whig* among others. Some items were not attributed at all, making it difficult to distinguish truth in these reports from wishful thinking, misconceptions, and bias. "As usual, the operations of the armies have been attended with varying success and no decided results," reported the Melbourne *Age*. "The Federals, as usual, are reported to have sustained some reverses, but for the details we must await the arrival of the mail in the Bay."[2]

Articles speculated where General Sherman was going after taking Atlanta and about Philip Sheridan in the Shenandoah Valley; they discussed efforts of Confederate generals Hood, Beauregard, and Early to stop both Sherman and Sheridan. A dispatch from the Associated Press, dated New York, 18 November, reported that Richmond was full of rumors concerning Sherman's movements, that he was meeting with great success, and that there was panic in gold. The *New-York Evening Post*'s correspondent reported that the *Richmond Whig* stated Sherman had sent a large part of his army toward Selma indicating a move on Mobile. The *Whig* also demanded that Confederate authorities call out a special force of 75,000 men to annihilate Sherman and Sheridan, believing that could be done and assailing the Confederate congress for incompetency.

The *New-York Tribune*'s Army of the James correspondent wrote that rebel papers expressed great anxiety at reported movements of Sherman's army and the gravest apprehensions concerning powder mills, shops, and arsenals at Augusta, Macon, and Columbus, Georgia. It was rumored that Robert E. Lee dispatched both generals Longstreet and Early with 35,000 men to intercept Sherman, which was not true. Jubal Early's army was said to have been in wretched condition and ready to abandon the lower Shenandoah Valley, which was true. It also was correctly reported that Grant was receiving reinforcements. He was reconnoitering the Confederates and massing on Lee's right near Petersburg. "He is confident, and fully prepared."[3]

The papers variously followed Sherman from Atlanta to the sea. "Confederate accounts . . . represent his march through Georgia to be marked by desolation." Later unattributed reports had him surrounding Savannah but claimed that Union troops were short of provisions, and that, under command of Beauregard, the hero of Fort Sumter, Confederates were massing to oppose them. Southerners concluded that the interior of Georgia had seen the last of invasion while their forces reoccupied Atlanta, and that the federals, by quitting Georgia, so weakened their grasp of East Tennessee they could lose the whole state. Contrary to these accounts, Sherman had occupied Savannah on 22 December; he was moving 60,000 men north through the Carolinas on the final leg of his destructive campaign.[4]

Other tidbits falsely reported Beauregard advancing on New Orleans instead of opposing Sherman in North Carolina; Sherman was expected to meet Georgia governor Brown at Augusta to arrange for that state's readmission to the Union; rebel general John Bell Hood advanced into middle

Tennessee, cutting off all communication for Union-occupied Nashville; the city was short of supplies and federals under General Thomas had been thoroughly defeated, losing five thousand prisoners and thirty guns. Reality differed, however: Hood had dashed his army to pieces against Thomas' veterans at Franklin and Nashville (30 November to 16 December). The once proud Army of Tennessee fled into northern Mississippi and by February no longer existed as an effective fighting force.

There were rumors of a commission including George McClellan for the North and Vice President Alexander Stephens for the South to negotiate a peace, which later was said to have failed. Secretary of State Seward sent an apology to the authorities of Brazil for violating their neutrality during seizure of *Florida* and then insisted upon reparation or apology for firing on the U.S. flag. "If our cruisers were contravening her laws, she knew where to find us and how to adjudicate her claims, but the act of opening fire upon our vessels will be rebuked."[5]

According to reports, Confederate cruiser *Tallahassee* had been driven ashore near Wilmington and was a total wreck, while *Chickamauga* was repairing at Bermuda after destroying "an immense quantity of shipping." Actually, in a three-week cruise out of Wilmington, *Chickamauga* captured only four ships, returned through the blockade, and was burned by the Confederates as the city was overrun.

The men of *Shenandoah*, expatriate Americans, and people of Melbourne on both sides of the issue read their prejudices into every report. They could not know about the dramatic turnaround in the North after the fall of Atlanta—from deepest despair to confident determination—or about the pending collapse of the Confederacy. No one in the Antipodes could conclude that the war was almost over or who the victor would be.[6]

Three days after *Shenandoah* finally departed Melbourne, the *Argus* reprinted an undated article from an unnamed San Francisco paper that noted *Shenandoah* had been the common theme of conversation in that city, that the threat to commerce "caused not a little uneasiness" among businessmen. However, continued the article, there were three federal vessels on the coast; *Shenandoah* probably would aim for Mexican or Central American waters to capture American treasure steamers and sailing vessels and then run into a South American port for coal and supplies.[7]

Waddell and his officers feared for their homeland, but the situation would have seemed no worse than the sickening reversals of spring 1862, and not much different from the previous winter. The government controlled roughly the same expanse of territory: most of Tennessee, much of Louisiana, the banks of the Mississippi River from Memphis to Baton Rouge, and the Trans-Mississippi states. The U.S. Navy had taken Mobile Bay, but the city was safe.

Georgia had witnessed the passage of Union soldiers but was otherwise unoc-cupied. Aside from a few Union enclaves along the coast, North and South Carolina remained in Confederate hands.

As far as they knew, the federals had not been able to take Savannah and Charleston, and blockade runners still ran into Wilmington with supplies from Europe. Other than Grant's fifty-mile line holding Lee in front of Peters-burg and Sheridan's occupation of the lower Shenandoah Valley, Union forces controlled little of Virginia. An isolated and lonely group of Southerners in a faraway place clung to hope and duty. They were not inclined to a gloomy out-look that would render their dedication and sacrifice meaningless; they took what information they had as an incentive to greater effort in their country's cause.

That weekend, Dr. Lining, Lieutenant Grimball, Sailing Master Bulloch, and Paymaster Smith accepted invitations by two American-born miners to visit Ballarat, "the greatest mining region yet discovered in Australia." They joined prominent citizens for dinner at Craig's Royal Hotel, toured the Black Hill quartz mine and a gold mine, and viewed the huge, noisy steam machin-ery for crushing ore and dewatering mine shafts. The United Extended Band of Hope Alluvial Company Shaft No. 2 was reportedly the deepest gold mine in the world, producing 130 ounces of gold a day. They donned oilskin suits and went down 420 feet in a rickety elevator. "It was a horrid sensation," noted the doctor, "that of going down, certain death if any accident had happened, for if the fall had not killed us, the chain falling on us certainly would." It was dark, wet, hot, smelly, and stale in the underground bed of an ancient river. The doctor dug for a few sparkling pieces of sand, which they told him was gold. They later enjoyed a boat regatta at Lake Wendouree.

The Southerners attended a grand Buccaneer's Ball as guests of honor at Craig's Royal Hotel. Grimball thought it an exceptionally handsome entertain-ment; as usual, Lining evaluated the ladies with a practiced eye, particularly the daughter of a Major Wallace; Bulloch found his flame in a young lady from Geelong; and Smith got his hand squeezed in a most tender way by some fair admirer. They had a fine supper and danced until four in the morning, contin-ued the doctor, "by which time I had nearly danced my feet off & was quite content that it should stop. . . . Strange to say although liquor flowed in profu-sion, I did not see a single case of worrisome drunkenness during the evening." The next day was spent lounging and conversing. Lining was taken for a pleas-ant carriage drive through the Zoological Gardens while Bulloch went visiting and received a kiss from the young lady he met at the ball. After dinner they took the four-hour train ride back to Melbourne and the ship, much pleased with the visit but also very tired. Chew—who in their absence was required to stand additional duty—was happy to see them.

On Friday, 10 February, U.S. consul Blanchard discovered another seaman waiting at the consulate: John Williams, who testified that he had been taken from the bark *D. Godfrey* on 7 November 1864. He had served as cook under compulsion and punishment, and on Monday last, he swam ashore to obtain protection of the consul. Williams swore that he observed fifteen or twenty persons concealed in different parts of the ship—men who boarded after arrival in Melbourne and who expressed an intent to join as crewmembers. They worked in the galley and engine room, and some wore the ship's uniform. "I can point out all the men who have joined said *Shenandoah* in this port."[8]

This information provided Blanchard a new weapon from the Foreign Enlistment Act: that provision forbidding subjects of the Queen from enlisting under an alien flag in a conflict to which Great Britain was not a party. If Blanchard could prove complicity in evading the act, *Shenandoah* might be liable to seizure. He forwarded Williams' deposition with a note to the governor and for the first time received a rapid and substantive reply: John Williams was to attend on Monday morning next at the office of the Crown solicitor, "and if he can give evidence sufficient to support a charge of misdemeanor" against any persons concealed on board *Shenandoah* or against any of the officers, "proceedings will be taken immediately." The attorney general instructed Police Superintendent Lyttleton to initiate a formal investigation.[9]

Two days later, First Class Detective D. S. Kennedy delivered a report concluding that Captain Waddell intended to take forty hands on board during the night and to have them sign articles once outside the Heads. It was understood that the captain wished to ship only foreign seamen or Englishmen who had assumed a foreign name. Three boardinghouse keepers—McGrath, Finlay, and O'Brien—were said to be recruiting crewmen and receiving £6 a month in wages and £8 as head bounty. A shipwright had been offered £17 per month to ship as a carpenter; a waterman named McLaren had enlisted. Although Kennedy found no evidence of efforts to load ammunition, a resident clerk reported overhearing a plot that an old vessel, *Eli Whitney*, was to take on board sixty men and a quantity of ammunition, clear Melbourne before *Shenandoah*, and meet her outside the harbor to transfer the same. When Mr. George Kennedy responded to an *Argus* advertisement for "two or three respectable young men," he was asked about his capabilities and experience with big guns, plied with drink, and given every inducement to join *Shenandoah*.[10]

On Sunday, Midshipman Mason and Lieutenant Scales visited a little chapel called St. Peters just behind the Parliament House. It was the first time Mason had heard the service of the Church of England, and it reminded him of a Sunday afternoon at the Church of the Holy Cross in Troy, New York. The building was plain and nice, he thought, while they were being shown into a pew with two young females who were "not at all pretty" but very civil and offered them a prayer book. "The 'honest' Melbournites stared at us with gaping mouths and starting eyes, as if they were astonished most *amazingly* to see two of the '*Piratical gentlemen*' in the house of God." Mason found the sermon ordinary; Scales declared that it was "excessively stupid" and could scarcely keep awake.

Monday, 13 February, Blanchard would put his new case before the Crown solicitor, but not in person. He induced another "loyal American merchant," Samuel Lord, to accompany and support John Williams and four other deserters with similar stories. Lord was a wealthy trader from New York who had been elected to the chamber of commerce in 1853 and had served as acting U.S. consul. Mason cited him as one of those most influential in opposing *Shenandoah*. John Williams testified that he had been forced to join and had been punished seven times for upholding his country, including being triced up by the thumbs. He claimed to have told Whittle that he was a veteran, and had his former ship, the USS *Minnesota*, been present, *Shenandoah* would have been blown from the water. (The *Shenandoah* log contains an entry noting that Williams had been double-ironed and gagged for drunkenness and disorderly conduct, and a few days later he deserted by swimming ashore.)[11]

Walter Madden, from Boston, as was Williams, served as captain of the hold (a petty officer position). He swore that he joined for six months under threat of being put in irons and confined in the coal bunker and that he was sick at the time. Also like Williams, Madden certified that *Shenandoah* was *Sea King*, that he had seen men hidden in the forecastle and working in the galley who had come on board since arrival, and that "the officers pretend they do not know that said men are so hid." Thomas Jackson, a native of Yorkshire, England, who claimed U.S. citizenship, swore that he was taken on board *Laurel* in Liverpool under the influence of drink, and then shipped on *Shenandoah* having been again well supplied with rum.[12]

Hermann Wicker and Charles Behucke, from Lübeck and Hanover, Germany, respectively, shipped together on *Alina* and were captured on 29 October. Wicker claimed to have been intimidated and, not understanding English, replied yes to everything and signed in fear for his life. After being placed in irons in the forecastle along with sheep and hens for over thirty hours, Behucke also consented, "against which impressment I now protest." Wicker and Behucke swore that they worked with and could identify new men in the crew. Most important, Wicker identified a particular man known by the name of Charley who said he would join as cook after the ship departed.[13]

Mason attributed similar testimony in the newspapers to the intrigues of their numerous and influential enemies. No doubt the men were well bribed, he opined, for they were induced to swear all sorts of atrocious things. "Of course there are always plenty of shallow brained flunkeys ready to swallow all such improbably & preposterous things, never supposing for a moment that a man who deserts his flag is capable of any falsehood however gross it may be."

The solicitor reported to the governor, who reacted that same day with uncharacteristic decisiveness, instructing Attorney General Higinbotham to enforce the requirements of neutrality. A note to Blanchard assured him that the matter had engaged the earnest attention of the government. Now that he had a name, the attorney general issued a warrant for Charley's arrest. Police Superintendent Lyttleton boarded *Shenandoah* to execute the warrant. Blanchard provided Walter Madden as witness, stipulating that Madden was to be escorted and returned to the consulate so that he could not be seized as a deserter. The officer of the deck, Lieutenant Grimball, informed the policemen that the captain was ashore and refused their request to search the ship. Grimball showed them the shipping articles, which contained no signatures since their arrival, as evidence that no illegal recruitment had taken place. The policemen decided to return the next day and pursue the question with the captain.

On Tuesday morning Commissioner Francis again requested a date that *Shenandoah* would be ready to depart. The captain responded that he would be ready for launching from the slip the next morning at 4 a.m. and, barring an unforeseen accident, would sail on Sunday, 19 February. He had yet to take in stores and coal. Superintendent Lyttleton returned that morning with the arrest warrant and was, according to Waddell, kindly received. Lyttleton inquired if witnesses brought onto the ship would be arrested for desertion. Waddell replied that the deck of *Shenandoah* represented Confederate territory and every violation of law or usage of the sea service committed on her deck would be punished by the laws that governed her. He refused to allow a search and the policemen departed without satisfaction. Lyttleton reported to the police commissioner that the captain had allowed him on board only by courtesy, that Waddell considered the affair a great insult—believing his word should be preferable to deserters'—and that the police were there only to annoy him at the instigation of the American consul. Furthermore, if the police took one man, they might come back for fifteen or twenty. Waddell would, quoted Lyttleton, "fight his ship rather than allow it"; and if overcome he would surrender *Shenandoah* to the Melbourne government and report the matter to his government.[14]

At 3:30 p.m., after deliberation with his executive council, the governor issued a proclamation directing that all work on *Shenandoah* cease immediately. The police chief informed the lessee of the slip and dispatched his forces with instructions to prevent the launch of the vessel "at all risks"; however, the police were strictly enjoined to avoid confrontation with officers and men of *Shenandoah* and to not obstruct their movements in any manner. Governor Darling felt duty bound to make every effort to prevent violation of the law, but he was afraid, "looking to the very strange language which Lieutenant Waddell had employed . . . and to the sympathy with the Southern cause . . . which was known to prevail in this community," that local workmen would assist in launching *Shenandoah* in defiance of the government.[15]

At 6 p.m. a special messenger delivered to Waddell a letter from Commissioner Francis, accusing the captain of refusing the execution of a lawful warrant. The government had a right to expect that those receiving aid and assistance as a belligerent under the Queen's proclamation should not in any way oppose proceedings intended to enforce the maintenance of neutrality. As instructed by the council, Francis appealed to Waddell to reconsider his position. A special train left Spencer Street station bound for Williamstown with a detachment of royal artillery and a force of policemen armed with loaded carbines under the command of Superintendent Lyttleton. The artillerymen manned the Williamstown battery and reversed the guns toward the slip. Thirty to fifty police took possession of the slip engine-house; they assumed positions on adjoining ships and lighters and on the platforms running down each side of the ship within ten feet of the hull. The gun raft *Elder* with two 68-pounders moored nearby ready for action.[16]

The Confederates were outraged, their personal and national honor affronted in the most egregious manner. With armed policemen surrounding *Shenandoah*, her guns dismounted and half the crew ashore, officers and crewmen were helpless. They could come and go as they pleased, but local workers were instructed to leave the yard. Lining never felt more humiliated: "Everybody seemed to share this feeling, even the men, & a general wish was expressed to resist if possible." Chew considered it a contemptible affair from beginning to end; Mason was anxious to know the wherefores of this most unwarranted proceeding; the action was a display of "intellectual military weakness" that Waddell was not prepared to witness. However, so long as the government did not attempt to search the ship, he concluded, nothing should occur to occasion loss of blood.

But some workmen remained and, from the incessant clanking of hammers, appeared hard at work repairing the screw and preparing the vessel for launching as boats busily delivered provisions. Despite the governor's edict, one of the city's wealthiest and most influential men provided resources and labor to complete the job. "The excitement caused by this event was most intense during the evening," reported the *Age*, "and there were constant rumors of a collision having taken place." Unnamed *Shenandoah* officers expressed to a reporter their desire to cut the lines holding the ship in her present awkward position. However, with the slip gates closed and with insufficient water to float, she would stick on her side in the mud. It turned out that guns of the Williamstown battery could not bear on *Shenandoah* due to intervening high ground, so the artillerymen returned to barracks. Waddell noted that there were cannon at the pier itself, which to his surprise were not manned.[17]

The rapidity of these actions suggests determination but not necessarily a united front. According to Mason, Commissioner Francis had taken responsibility for the affair while other members of the colonial government disclaimed connection with it. Francis was partial to the Yanks, concluded the midshipman; he had strenuously opposed the policy of allowing repairs and was only too glad to have a pretext for detaining the ship. Public conversation ran on few other topics, declared the *Argus*: "Strong sympathy was expressed for the officers of the ship, and also strong hopes that the Government had made a mistake; for Northern sympathizers were so few as not to be heard in the expression of a prevailing warm feeling towards our visitors."[18]

The *Herald* reported a fever of excitement. Streets of the city were crowded with persons anxious to hear the news. Considerable amusement was aroused by the appearance of *Victoria*, Australia's first warship, which moored close by with her solitary gun pointing at the Confederate vessel. Consul Blanchard found the town full of rumors that evening, and at about 5 p.m. he jumped on the Williamstown ferry to find out for himself, encountering on the way the captain of the British ship *Nimrod* (who had been so hospitable when boarded by *Shenandoah* in January). The Englishman told Blanchard that he had been drinking with the officers in their wardroom when Waddell entered with a printed paper in hand and informed them that the ship had been seized.[19]

Waddell again consulted his officers in a crisis, laying Francis' letter before the three lieutenants Whittle, Grimball, and Lee, and Dr. Lining, and requesting opinions. As on previous occasions, the officers took a hard line while the doctor credits himself with providing important counsel. They agreed that a police search would not be permitted under any circumstances and also that a letter should be written to the government denying that the man was on board. Before this was done, however, Lining suggested a thorough search just to make sure. Grimball and the master-at-arms combed the ship and found no strangers. Lining then sat down and wrote the letter, reading it out in parts and taking suggestions from the others.

At about nine o'clock, Mason departed with the captain's reply: "I have to inform his Excellency the governor that the execution of the warrant was not refused, as no such person as the one therein specified was on board; but permission to search this ship was refused." According to the laws of nations, he continued, the deck of a vessel of war represents the majesty of the country whose flag she flies. She is free from all executions of local law except for crimes committed on shore, in which case the police may present a warrant to be executed by the ship's master-at-arms. He had allowed authorities to review the crew list. Two officers made a thorough search and sent all unauthorized personnel out of the ship. Therefore, as commander and representative of his country, Waddell certified that there were no persons on board except those whose names were recorded in the shipping articles, that no one had enlisted since arrival, and that he had not in any way violated the neutrality of the port. "And I, in the name of the Government of the Confederate States of America, hereby enter my solemn protest against any obstruction which may cause the detention of this ship in this port. I have the honor to be, sir, your obedient servant, James I. Waddell, Lieutenant, Commanding, C. S. Navy."[20]

Soon afterward Bulloch reported to Lining that he knew of stowaways on board. Whittle initiated another search; four noncrewmembers were discovered and immediately ordered out. Around ten o'clock that evening, a constable of the water police observed a boat leave *Shenandoah*, followed it to the pier, arrested the men, and carried them to Superintendent Lyttleton, who said to one of them, "I believe you are the very Charley I want." The prisoner laughed and said it was a great joke on board about Charley, but "I am not the man." The prisoners stated that they had been on board a few days unknown to the captain and when discovered, they were ordered ashore.[21]

Waddell disposed his small force to secure against boarding, then decided to push the issue and ordered the ship launched as scheduled on the 4 a.m. tide. The steam tug *Black Eagle* appeared but Lyttleton ordered it away. The slip manager informed the captain that he was prevented from launching by order of the government. When Lining arose the next morning, he looked out to see bobbies still surrounding the ship, "keeping watch & ward over us." The morning paper reported that the men sent out of the ship had been arrested and were to be tried for violating the Foreign Enlistment Act. At the request of Lyttleton, Blanchard sent witnesses to the jail where they identified Charley and his companions; the miscreants were to appear in Williamstown Police Court the next day.

Consul Blanchard delivered another legal broadside of over fifteen hundred words, a "summary of facts derived from . . . testimony, with my view of the law applicable thereto," defining *Shenandoah* as "an illegal and criminal rover-of-the-sea." Referencing those provisions of the Foreign Enlistment Act that forbade Her Majesty's subjects from fitting out, equipping, or arming ships for combat in wars about which Britain was neutral, Blanchard cited as precedent the hotly contested case of the screw steamer *Alexandra*. In spring 1863 Thomas Dudley, the American consul at Liverpool, learned from his spies that *Alexandra* was being built as a Confederate cruiser and convinced British officials to seize the ship. The Crown lost the case following lengthy court proceedings, and the ship was returned to her owners. The government could not prove they planned to present the ship as a gift to the Confederate government (which they did), rather than to employ her as a passenger boat, mail boat, or yacht (as they maintained).[22]

The result was a tactical victory for the South, but it marked a turning point in attitude toward Confederate ship procurement. The British walked a fine line between proper discharge of international obligations and protection of lawful private enterprise. British firms were making great profits selling ordinance to both sides—dozens of blockade runners had been converted or built, shipyards were inundated with profitable contracts, and ships were legitimate products of industry and trade. However, anti-British sentiment in the United States over the raiders became intense. After Confederate defeats at Gettysburg and Vicksburg in July 1863, it began to look to the British as if the Union might actually prevail. They started watching rebel shipbuilding activities much more closely, thus the Laird Rams and other vessels were confiscated and *Shenandoah* narrowly escaped.

Blanchard maintained the *Alexandra* case was lost only because the government could not prove owner's intent. But *Alexandra* and *Sea King* were fitted out under similar circumstances for the same purposes, and proof of intent was that it was carried out—post hoc, ergo propter hoc. The hostile cruise, and therefore the offense, was still in progress, interrupted in Melbourne only to make it more effective thereafter. The vessel now lay in reach of British law and should be seized. On the inconvenient technicality that fitting out, arming, and equipping had not been accomplished in British territory as stated in the law, Blanchard claimed that *Shenandoah* was prepared in England as a transport or stores ship for a cruiser and then became a cruiser.[23]

Like her sisters, *Shenandoah* represented a new breed: not ships of battle in the traditional sense and not licensed privateers. International law had not caught up with the concept. The Foreign Enlistment Act of 1819 was simply inadequate to the circumstances; it provided no comprehensive guidance and there were no court precedents prior to *Alexandra*. Blanchard wanted it both ways: if *Shenandoah* was a cruiser in international law, then she violated the Foreign Enlistment Act; if she was not a cruiser, then she was a pirate. The consul would receive a less eloquent reply soon after *Shenandoah* escaped his clutches: the letter provided no grounds for altering the governor's views on the subject.

Chapter 11

"On the Bright Blue Sea"

Waddell fired his own diplomatic salvo requesting that the governor justify the stop work order. He dispatched Grimball with another letter to Commissioner Francis, ordering the lieutenant not to return without a reply: "I therefore respectfully beg to be informed if this seizure is known to his Excellency the governor, and if it meets his approval." Privately Waddell did not think the government actions amounted to seizure, but in a bid for public support the captain spoke bitterly to his friends ashore. Unless the embargo were removed, he would haul down his flag, abandon the ship, and send crew and officers home. The controversy circulated widely. The *Argus* editorialized, "He had thought that the bleeding condition of his country was an appeal to the generosity of the English. He had begun fairly, by doing nothing except by permission of the Government, even in his crippled state, and he ought not to have been entrapped to the slip where he was utterly unprotected."[1]

Attorney General Higinbotham concluded that Waddell's claim of exemption from local jurisdiction was not a natural right of international law, but was conditional on the behavior of the visitor within municipal law; enforcement of statutes such as the Foreign Enlistment Act would be impossible otherwise. Charley's offense hardly could be committed without connivance of the vessel's commander and officers, who may be liable as principal offenders. The attorney general advised, therefore, that the claim might be disallowed "even if it be assumed that the *Shenandoah* belongs to a recognized foreign state within the meaning of the rule referred to."[2]

Convening his executive council, the governor invited opinions as to whether the object of the work suspension had been achieved. The contradictions between Waddell's word that no noncrewmembers were on board and the apprehension of local men leaving the ship were noted. However, recorded the minutes, this was an unpleasant subject "upon which his excellency and the council have no desire to dwell." The lessee of the slip, Mr. Chambers, informed Francis that *Shenandoah* was ready for launching. If a gale of wind should arise, he would be compelled to launch her or run the risk of serious damage, and, most alarming, he gave notice that the government must now assume all resulting expenses. A government lawyer opined that a foreign warship is indeed exempt from jurisdiction of local courts. The government's action was not seizure; it was, however, an unauthorized detention. When pressed, the law officers expressed doubt that an arrest warrant could be executed "at all hazards." So the governor, citing safety reasons, instructed Francis to lift the work suspension. One might read between the lines that the imminent departure of *Shenandoah* was an outcome devoutly to be desired, even at risk of conceding a valid point of law.[3]

The bluff had succeeded, gloated Mason. If Waddell should abandon the ship, "[the authorities] would be in the same predicament as the man who drew the elephant in the lottery." The pro-Union *Herald* expressed frustration that the government, ever in a muddle, had exposed itself "to the ridicule and contempt which ever attach to ignorance, rashness, and rudeness in high places." The Melbourne correspondent for the *Illustrated London News* reported that the colony had not raised her character in British estimation. The government did either too much or too little; it ought to have been sure of its information before acting and then should have retained possession. "By their conduct they have equally offended North and South."[4]

Commissioner Francis wrote to Waddell justifying the procedures and chiding him for swearing that the fugitive was not on board: "It thus appears plain, as a matter of fact, that the foreign-enlistment act was in the course of being evaded." Nevertheless, Charley had been secured; he was the only person for whose arrest a warrant had been issued, and Waddell pledged he had enlisted no British subjects in Melbourne. (Here the commissioner quoted back word for word the promise from Waddell's first letter.) Therefore, "his Excellency the governor has been pleased to revoke the directions issued yesterday." Francis expected that the captain would "exercise every dispatch" to ensure departure as previously stated, that is, the coming Sunday.[5]

An embarrassed Waddell conveyed in return his appreciation for the governor's observance of the rights of belligerents. However, he stated, the men in question were on board without his knowledge, were stowaways, and were caught only through the vigilance of the ship's officers. "But in no way can I be accused, in truth, of being cognizant of an evasion of the foreign-enlistment act. In conclusion, sir, allow me to inform you that I consider the tone of your letter remarkably disrespectful and insulting to the Government I have the honor to represent, and that I shall take an early opportunity of forwarding it to the Richmond Government." He needed no prodding on the central issue, assuring them every effort was being made to get *Shenandoah* to sea at the earliest moment.[6]

In naval tradition, a sea lawyer is one who persistently asserts the letter of the law for the purpose of obscuring his intentions to violate the spirit of the law. The men in question were stowaways because they had not signed the shipping articles. Whether or not the officers were "cognizant" of them depends on how hard they looked. Waddell reasoned that he and his people were not custodians of British law and that if the authorities failed to enforce those laws, it was their problem. If the governor had no proof of wrongdoing, he could not expect the Confederates to help him find it. "The law of nations, as laid down by every authority, justifies foreigners in refusing their aid to carry out laws which are repugnant to their own interest. . . . I was therefore justified in refusing to submit to the humiliation of a search."[7]

Captain Semmes faced a similar recruitment problem with *Alabama* in Cape Town in September 1863. "There was my good friend, her Majesty, the Queen—I must not be ungallant to her, and violate her neutrality laws. What monstrous sophists we are, when interest prompts us?" His sailors had gone on shore and refused to return; when he applied to the police, they told him, "so sacred is the soil of England, no man must be coerced to do what he doesn't want to do." Therefore, Semmes reasoned, because a warship is part of the territory to which she belongs, if subjects of the Queen should think it proper to come into his territory and refuse to go back, "I may surely apply the same principle, and refuse to compel them."[8]

Upon arrival in Melbourne, Waddell had written to Flag Officer Barron in Europe, "I shall get all the men I want." By the late 1850s, gold fever had settled into steady production, so unemployment was common and willing volunteers abounded; sailors and landlubbers alike were looking for adventure and escape from the obligations of shore life. One recruit thought it would be better than gold digging: "The pay is nothing to boast of, but there is a chance of making a good deal in the shape of prize money." Others claimed to be Southerners asking to fight or for their sons to fight for the homeland. The repair and supply of the ship occasioned a great deal of coming and going, some legitimate and some not, some open and some furtive.[9]

On the other hand, Waddell had to be cautious. "Every effort was made to entangle me in legal difficulties." He received forty-seven letters, many of which were bogus applications for service as paymasters, doctors, clerks, or marine officers. A few informed him that the ship would be destroyed at her anchorage if a constant watch was not kept. The captain made no reply to these communications, but asked protection of the police. One elderly lady descended on him several times in the city with her twelve-year-old grandson in tow, claiming that she was born in Mobile and that she was too infirm to support the child, asking that he be enlisted. Waddell referred her to the attorney general and she was not heard from again. He implied that Consul Blanchard and other U.S. citizens were behind these machinations, as they might well have been.

With all this official activity, the court of public opinion also was in session. On the afternoon of Wednesday, 15 February, placards posted in the town advertised a public meeting at the Criterion Hotel, the most luxurious American rendezvous in the city. With a long bar and marble counters, imposing decanters, spittoons, red plush furniture, gilt-emblazoned wall mirrors, décolleté ladies, and bartenders in snow-white shirts, the facilities were available to anyone, not just the upper classes—an American example Australians were quick to follow.[10]

As reported in the *Herald*, a large, impromptu, jocular meeting convened with self-appointed leaders who followed semiformal rules of order, leading a lively exchange. Issues were hashed over and resolutions debated. The primary question was, had the government acted in accordance with the principles of international law? One participant—to loud cheers of agreement—maintained that colonial authorities would never have threatened the ship if she had flown the U.S. flag or that of even the most trivial European power; a dissenter responded that they could seize a pirate; another countered that *Shenandoah* was not a pirate, that the Southerners were of Anglo-Saxon stock, and if they unanimously demanded self-government, they should be allowed—it was an act of cowardice for any government to seize a ship belonging to such a struggling confederation. Another speaker noted that emissaries of the United States offered *Shenandoah* seamen sums varying from £50 to £100 to desert and inform against their captain.[11]

Mr. Francis Quinlin, barrister-at-law, presented himself as a friend of all downtrodden nationalities, of those who strove to be free. He maintained that the casus belli was not slavery but an issue of free trade versus protection. The valor and unanimity of Southerners pursuing independence entitled them to be considered an independent state de facto and perhaps even de jure. Like American colonies, the Confederacy would prevail; recognition was not necessary to its existence as an independent state. Mr. Quinlin offered a resolution that the government action interfered with their happy relations with what was likely to become a great nation. Doctor Rowe seconded the motion, adding that the government had been guilty of a breach of hospitality. Australia was a colony itself and should take notice of this struggle as similar to one it itself could face one day; it was simply a demand for self-government. Another citizen countered that the Southerners had no more right to send out such privateers than those who carried on the Irish rebellion.

The confusion here reached its climax, continued the *Herald*. Mr. Herberson remarked that those preceding him had erred in addressing the audience as gentlemen—eliciting hisses from the crowd. He strongly protested that the government had dragged the public through the dirt to be made subjects of ridicule for the English press and had no right to act as it had presumed to do.

A motion censuring the government was made and carried amid loud cheers. A vote of thanks to the chairman and three cheers for *Shenandoah* brought to a close "one of the most disorderly meetings which has ever been held in Melbourne."[12]

The *Age*, however, thought the conveners should be heartily ashamed of themselves. The whole issue was "one of those cock and bull opinions in which the question suggests the answer, and the answer takes for granted the whole matter in dispute." It was based on the premise that the government could not search a foreign ship of war; but the Confederate States were not a "power," just a belligerent with no accredited representatives and with no means of holding its people accountable to international law. Had a similar difficulty arisen with a federal ship, the American consul would have aided local authorities and preserved the reputation of his flag. If Captain Waddell harbored a fugitive from British justice, continued the *Age*, he forfeited his rights under international law. Even presuming comity had been established with the Confederates, an infringement of international law would destroy it. Failure to act on evidence presented by the American consul was itself a breach of neutrality for allowing enlistment by one side. "Captain Waddell is aware of the very dubious position in which his honor and good faith as an officer and a gentleman now stand."[13]

And so it went, politics both as serious business and as entertainment and everybody with an opinion. Ironically, sympathy for the Confederacy in Great Britain was concentrated in ruling elites of title and wealth who identified with aristocratic Southerners and feared Yankee democracy—the "tyranny of the mob"—while so many British colonials of Melbourne, more in tune with radical politics and the expanding franchise, favored the South as a champion opposing tyrannical central government. These Melbournians were on the wrong side of the war and the right side of history.

In the afternoon of 15 February with work completed, tide up, and everything ready, police surrounding the ship disappeared. The *Age* reported a considerable number of people crossed over from Sandridge, expecting some sensational scene, but the launch passed off quietly. *Shenandoah* once more attained her natural element, cheered by a crowd of spectators on adjacent wharves. The *Victoria* and other vessels lowered their flags in salute. The cheers were returned with a will while the Confederate banner dipped in response, the last such recognition it would ever receive. "How proud we felt as soon as clear of the slip!" wrote Chew. "We were masters of the situation; they were at the mercy of our guns." Midshipman Mason noted, "Once afloat we all felt very independent, as we could then bid defiance to officials & get to sea as soon as we liked." They hauled alongside the collier *John Fraser* and commenced loading fuel all night and the next day. (*Fraser* was owned by Fraser, Trenholm and

Co. of Liverpool and may have been sent out by James Bulloch specifically to supply *Shenandoah*, but no confirmation has been found.)

Meanwhile, Charley and his companions appeared in police court. His real name was James Davidson of Scotland; he was twenty-two years old. Arthur Walmsley and William Mackenzie, both Englishmen, were twenty-two and seventeen. Franklin Glover declared himself an American, aged twenty-four. Consul Blanchard's witnesses—Williams, Madden, Behucke, and Wicker—provided detailed and consistent testimony under oath that Lieutenant Whittle and Sailing Master Bulloch coached Davidson (Charley) to hide in the forecastle while visitors were on board, emerging only in the evening. Davidson had expressed the desire to enlist, wore uniform pants and cap, slept on board (unlike other local workers), cooked for the officers, and was supervised directly by the boatswain and master-at-arms. They saw Walmsley and Mackenzie similarly employed. About twelve noncrewmen were housed and fed in the forecastle under lock and key during the day, their meals served through the port that the anchor chain passed through. Davidson and Walmsley declined to make statements; Mackenzie said he was not aware that he was breaking any law and just wanted work. The judge committed all for trial at the Supreme Court except Glover, who was released as a U.S. citizen not subject to British law.[14]

The *Argus* published letters from *Shenandoah* officers arguing that the evidence of deserters was, in Whittle's words, "utterly and entirely false." Bulloch admitted that there may have been a Charley in the galley who gave him a light for his cigar at meal times, but the area was crowded with workmen and other strangers. He had refused all requests to enlist even from supposed Southern citizens, and he utterly denied advising anyone to stow away or hide. Master-at-Arms Reid declared that he locked the forecastle only once to confine Williams in double irons for being drunk and insulting visitors, but he never served out rations to persons hidden on board. Despite these public denials, revelations of illegal activities tended to turn public and editorial sympathy against *Shenandoah*. The three men were convicted a month later after a trial that garnered a great deal of public attention. Davidson and Walmsley were sentenced to ten days' imprisonment but released due to time served; Mackenzie was released in deference to his youth.[15]

Consul Blanchard saw *Shenandoah* coaling when he was on the ferry crossing the bay to attend the trial. A fellow passenger, customs official McFarlane—also no friend of the Confederacy—informed Blanchard that they were loading two hundred additional tons. Blanchard complained to the governor that the Confederates were taking on more coal than was permitted by the rules. His Excellency curtly replied that Her Majesty's instructions allowed a belligerent vessel to take on coal sufficient to carry her to her own country or to some nearer destination. The governor disregarded Blanchard's wry observation

Captain James I. Waddell
Naval History and Heritage Command

From left: Midshipman John
T. Mason, Midshipman
O. A. Browne, Lieutenant
William C. Whittle,
Lieutenant Sidney Smith Lee
*Museum of the Confederacy,
Richmond*

Lieutenant John Grimball
Museum of the Confederacy,
Richmond

Lieutenant Francis T. Chew
Museum of the Confederacy,
Richmond

Lieutenant Dabney M. Scales
*Museum of the Confederacy,
Richmond*

Shenandoah in Hobson's Bay, 18 February 1865
State Library of Victoria, Melbourne

Shenandoah in Hobson's Bay, 23 February 1865
State Library of Victoria, Melbourne

Visitors on board *Shenandoah* in Melbourne
State Library of Victoria, Melbourne

Bourke Street, Melbourne, ca. 1870
State Library of Victoria, Melbourne

Bourke Street East, Melbourne, 1865
State Library of Victoria, Melbourne

Ball at Ballarat

State Library of Victoria, Melbourne

Shenandoah at Williamstown Dockyard, February 1865
Naval History and Heritage Command

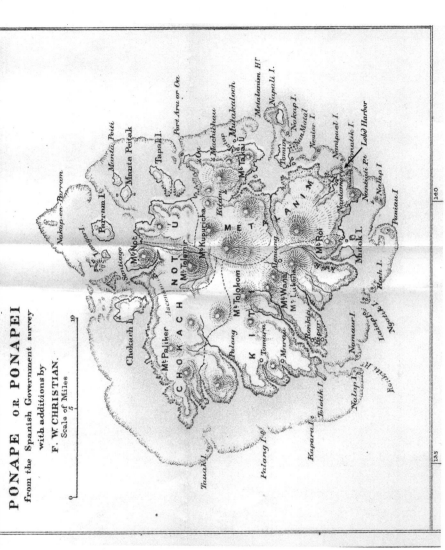

Pohnpei Island, ca. 1895

F. W. Christian, The Caroline Islands: Travel in the Sea of the Little Lands

(London: Methuen & Co., 1899)

Pohnpei Shore, ca. 1895

F. W. Christian, The Caroline Islands: Travel in the Sea of the Little Lands
(London: Methuen & Co., 1899)

Chief's nephew, ca. 1895
F. W. Christian, The Caroline
Islands: Travel in the Sea of the
Little Lands *(London: Methuen &
Co., 1899)*

Ruins of Nan Madol, ca. 1895
F. W. Christian, The Caroline Islands: Travel in the Sea of the Little Lands
(London: Methuen & Co., 1899)

Shenandoah at work in the Arctic
State Library of Victoria

that *Shenandoah* could go anywhere she desired under sail and did not need fuel at all. Again, the government would take no action.

But Waddell's troubles were not over. He gave the crew twenty-four-hour liberty to amuse themselves ashore where "a Negro, sixteen Germans, and an Irish-American" were induced to desert. His application to the chief of police for their arrest again was denied, a discourtesy he assumed would never have been applied to a federal vessel. A carpenter installing a new bureau in Waddell's cabin said he heard Americans in a restaurant discussing the feasibility of smuggling themselves on board and, after the steamer was at sea, capturing her. If they tried, responded the captain, he would "hang every mother's son of them."

By eight o'clock that evening, stores were loaded from lighters alongside and coal from *John Fraser*. Dr. Lining had a final dinner with friends ashore. He found none of the ladies especially noted for beauty or talent, but the dancing and singing followed by a "pretty good" supper made for a pleasant visit. The next morning the SS *Great Britain* pulled in with mail after a two-month voyage from England; the Confederates looked forward to letters and news from home. The *Argus* reported a rumor, which it then contradicted as ridiculous, that Raphael Semmes was on board under a false name. (The story that Semmes took command of *Shenandoah* in Melbourne persisted for years.)

The afternoon of Saturday, 17 February, found *Shenandoah* at single anchor, steam up, propeller lowered, and, except for carpenters still banging away in the officers' cabins, ready for sea. The harbor police appeared to be keeping strict watch and all seemed peaceful, but Waddell was not taking chances. All hands were ordered to remain on ship. Four officers with sidearms and half the crew with loaded revolvers and muskets close at hand were kept on watch; the guns were ready loaded and cast loose. Boats approached the ship with men requesting to enlist, but all were rebuffed.

————

On that same day, Secretary Welles ordered the USS *Wachusett* (captor of *Florida*) to proceed from Boston around the Cape of Good Hope to the East India Station with headquarters in Macao, to relieve the USS *Jamestown* as protector of American commerce in those waters. She was not to deviate from the most direct route "except for the purpose of pursuing piratical vessels," should she hear of any. The sailing sloop of war *Jamestown* was the only American warship in Asia and had been on the lookout for *Alabama* in late 1863 and early 1864. In February 1865, she was protecting American citizens and showing the flag in Japan. There are no indications that her captain was aware of *Shenandoah* until long after she disappeared into the Pacific.[16]

————

That evening, an informant told Blanchard that he had conversed with a group waiting on the Williamstown pier to board the bark *Maria Ross*, which would transfer them to *Shenandoah* at sea. The consul's frantic efforts to apprehend these men were blocked at every turn: A crown solicitor's official curtly declined to address the matter, the police commissioner was not in, the attorney general was in parliament and requested a written affidavit, Chief Detective Nicholson took a statement but required a warrant, and Police Magistrate Sturt listened politely but desired corroborative evidence, suggesting Blanchard go to the water police across the bay and confront the men directly. At that point, the witness refused to proceed further, fearing retribution from those on the pier. *Maria Ross* was searched by customs before she departed, and no unauthorized personnel were found.[17]

A police investigation after *Shenandoah* departed revealed that approximately six boatloads of men and luggage departed the wharf at Sandridge during the night for *Shenandoah* and boarded through the propeller hoist hole. *Shenandoah* officers in civilian clothes were on the railway pier directing the men into boats; when the police came by, the officers hid in the scrub. While this was going on, water police were not seen on the bay. Captain Sears of the American bark *Mustang* later told Blanchard that he had stood on the pier and watched all this. Police Commissioner Standish claimed that his officers were unable to interdict these activities, but it is more likely that they were instructed to look the other way.

The governor stated he would refuse any future claims of belligerent privileges from Lieutenant Waddell or any *Shenandoah* officer, and he forwarded investigation results to governors of the other colonies. Blanchard completed a detailed report to Secretary of State Seward with enclosures of all correspondence, affidavits, and newspaper articles to back him up. He began, "Sir: It is my painful duty to report . . ." and ended with "There are eyes that do not see and ears that do not hear, and I fear that this port is endowed with such a portion of them as may be required to suit the occasion." As U.S. consul, he was baffled and obstructed by local authorities. This lengthy document would be key evidence for the international tribunal in the *Alabama* Claims case.[18]

With impressive Victorian invective and a long list of grievances, Waddell expressed similar frustration, referring to "all the understrappers" of government who "imbibed that driveling spirit for petty annoyances" and engaged in "overzealous and scrupulous" conduct. He concluded that the majority of the governor's council were inimical to the South, and many engaged in trade with the North. Repairs and supplies cost about $15,000, almost emptying the strongbox—less than $5,000 remained and he had no additional letters of credit. Waddell's postwar writings show he felt honor-bound to specify how little of Confederate funds were in his hands at the end and, because his accounts were not subject to official inspection, that he wished to acknowledge his responsibility to the people of the South.

On one of those last evenings, a representative of the *Argus* visited the captain and requested copies of correspondence with the intention to publish, which was done. Waddell found this gratifying, for he wanted the opposition party in Melbourne to be aware of the facts and actions of the government. "I was treated rudely by Sir Charles Darling and his council, but the good people of Melbourne were kind and did not forget we were strangers and distinguished from all other visitors on account of our peculiar position politically." One gentleman had donated a hundred tons of coal without cost; another leading citizen and wealthy miner, Mr. Throckmorton of Virginia, placed at their disposal without payment several tugboats and harbor lighters he owned, saving several thousand dollars.

———

Commander Rodgers in *Iroquois* made port at Point de Galle, Ceylon, on 18 February after struggling with his boilers all the way across the Indian Ocean. The RMS *Bombay* passed through the port, so Rodgers learned from Australian papers that *Shenandoah* was in Melbourne. An informant from the mail steamer told him of rebel activities, including plans to take on additional guns and enlist a hundred more men. "I should sail for Melbourne immediately if I could hope to reach that place in time to overtake the *Shenandoah*," Rodgers reported to Secretary Welles, but it was nearly five thousand miles with no coaling stations en route and directly in the teeth of the southeast trades. "I could not expect to arrive until she had sought some new field of pillage and destruction. I shall therefore hasten through the Strait of Malacca to Batavia and the Strait of Sunda, and shall thence strike in the direction where I can best . . . intercept the *Shenandoah*, being influenced by the latest information I shall receive."[19]

Of those American warships actively chasing *Shenandoah*, *Iroquois* came closest—*Wachusett* was too far behind, *Suwanee* was proceeding via Cape Horn to the wrong side of the Pacific, and *Jamestown* could not overtake them in any case. In late March, Welles would dispatch Commander Bankhead with the USS *Wyoming* from Boston. His "chief and first object" was to pursue, capture, and destroy *Shenandoah*. He was to headquarter at Batavia, concentrate on the "straits and passes to China," and cooperate with *Wachusett* based in Macao. But *Shenandoah* was going nowhere near these well-traveled routes as *Alabama* had done.[20]

Welles apparently did not recall an intelligence report of April 1864 that plans for *Sea King* included a visit to Australia and attacks on Yankee whalers in those waters. Semmes remarked in his memoirs, "It was indeed remarkable that no protection should have been given to [whalers], by their Government," which unlike merchant vessels congregated within confined, well-defined hunting grounds and remained there for weeks at a time. It was "the most obvious thing in the world" that they should be attacked, but the whalers, "like the commerce of the United States generally, were abandoned to their fate."[21]

If Rodgers had been directed to, or had thought to, take *Iroquois* from Cape Town to Melbourne or Sidney rather than Batavia, and if his boilers had been in reasonable working order, it is interesting to consider the outcome—a rematch of the *Alabama–Kearsarge* contest? Probably not, even though the contestants were roughly similar in size and armament. Raphael Semmes sought combat in June 1864 because his worn-out ship and crew had no other chance of avoiding the enemies surrounding him, and he wished to go out fighting after a long and successful cruise. Waddell, on the other hand, had every reason to avoid battle along with advantages in speed under sail and steam. His command was in the best shape ever, and he was just beginning the vital part of the mission. The crew was not well drilled at the guns, having never fired them in anger. Only a disabling accident or unusual circumstances would have prevented *Shenandoah* from outmaneuvering and outrunning her pursuers, as Semmes had done on several occasions in both *Sumter* and *Alabama*.

———

While Rodgers sat pondering in Ceylon that morning, *Shenandoah's* officer of the deck, Lieutenant Chew, received orders to call all hands and get under way. "Soon the cheering notes of the boatswain's pipes, & the clanking of the windlass were heard. . . . Come gale, come calm (infinitely prefer calm), in fact anything, rather than be subjected to such indignities as we received in Melbourne." All guns were loaded and bets were offered that they would not pass through the Heads in safety, but nothing occurred. *Shenandoah* sailed quietly out after twenty-five days in port. Dr. Lining had had some very pleasant hours along with very disagreeable ones, but at any rate they all were glad to be rid of the vexation experienced there. "There were few if any who sailed in the *Shenandoah*, who will not carry to their graves many pleasant memories of the days they spent on the shores of Australia," wrote Hunt.[22]

"Once more on the bright blue sea," recalled Waddell, "standing away from the land, feeling as free as the ship let loose to the breeze in chase to the westward." The pilot left them with good wishes but not with feelings of home, mused the captain. "No letters or words of affectionate recollections were to be conveyed through him to those we had left behind; a feeling of impatience hurried him over the side, and no regret was entertained for the separation."

———

On this same day in South Carolina, Confederate troops evacuated the cradle of the Confederacy to the encircling host of General Sherman. Charleston had endured 567 days of continuous attack by land and sea. Five forts—Moultrie, Sumter, Johnson, Beauregard, and Castle Pickney—were abandoned during the night as remaining Confederates marched northward toward Lee's belea-guered forces around Petersburg. Southern ironclads *Palmetto State*, *Chicora*, and *Charleston* were fired on and blown up. The largest of the ironclads, *Columbia*, went aground abandoned near Fort Moultrie to be salvaged by the Union Navy.

––––––

After *Shenandoah's* departure, the people of Melbourne returned to routine, continuing a march to independence of their own and a close friendship with the United States of America that endures to this day. Reported the *Argus*: "We may now speak of the confederate war-steamer *Shenandoah* as something that has come and gone. With all the sympathy we may have had with her as the representative of those who are fighting against long odds, she, in the fulfill-ment of a warlike errand, was most unwelcome in our still peaceful port, and we are unfeignedly glad of her departure. . . . Our latest news of her represents her as having cleared the Heads at noon, steering south-west for about twenty miles, when she altered her course to south, and was lost sight of in thick mist, at half-past two p.m. . . . It is not impossible yet that we shall have further news of the *Shenandoah*."[23]

Waddell's recollection called forth a bit of poetry from Edgar Allen Poe's *The Bells*. "Soon after night closed in, the steamer's head was turned toward Round Island, in Bass Strait. The moon shone beautifully bright, the atmo-sphere was clear, cool, and the sky looked more distant than I had ever before observed it,

> *While the stars that oversprinkle*
> *All the heavens seemed to twinkle*
> *With a crystalline delight.*

Chapter 12

"The Abomination of Isolation"

A surprise waited outside the harbor, recalled Master's Mate Hunt. The ship's company had received a mysterious addition of forty-five men. Materializing from hiding places in the hollow iron bowsprit, dry water tanks, and lower hold, they were mustered forward and the captain was called. Hunt had been on watch part of the preceding night with strict orders to prevent anyone but crewmembers from coming on board. He claimed in his memoirs to have been annoyed over the affair: "How such a number of men could have gained our decks unseen was a mystery to me then and is still." But all were sorely needed and quickly enlisted. "Good men and true they proved, and very useful before our cruise was ended." Lieutenant Chew also was caught unaware: "They were hid away by the men who of course cared for nothing but seeing their numbers increased, thus lightening the work. . . . We were well pleased with what they had done, although we could not have countenanced it in Melbourne."[1]

Midshipman Mason and Surgeon Lining, however, did not seem particularly surprised. Mason blandly reported that "the stowaways" (his quotes) appeared on deck that morning, while the doctor thought they were a funny sight in every conceivable dress from gentleman to sailor. Lining and Lieutenant Lee each acquired a steward; others were assigned to serve the officers in the wardroom. "This gave us a quite respectable crew although not yet our full complement," concluded Mason. No account by Lieutenant Whittle of the stowaways exists because the relevant pages were cut from his journal, perhaps to avoid postwar incrimination. Waddell would state officially that he "never enlisted any seamen at any British port, or within the jurisdiction of Her Majesty's government. He never asked any seaman what his nationality was, and had no knowledge whatever on the subject."[2]

One of the new men, Irishman John C. Blacker, held a British master's license and was reported to be a first-class pilot for the Australian, Indian, and China Seas. He had commanded the merchant vessel *Saxonia*, which he abandoned in Melbourne. Blacker was assigned as a second captain's clerk to get him on the books and pay him, but performed no such duties. He would become unofficial adviser to the captain—a strange arrangement perhaps symptomatic of Waddell's insecurity and estrangement from his officers.

The new men were, Waddell recalled, "equal to any emergency, all quite homeless and accustomed to a hard life, more in search of adventure and fun than anything else." New Englanders were among them. "Where is it one does not meet with that class of humanity? To find a genuine Yankee on the deck of a Confederate war ship, manifesting delight in the destroying of his country-men's property, was droll indeed." A sergeant, corporal, and three privates formed a nucleus for a marine guard, and uniforms were made up for them. The new sergeant, George P. Canning, claimed that he had been an aide-de-camp to General Leonidas Polk and received a ball through the right lung at Shiloh in 1862, a festering wound that would eventually kill him.

Shenandoah was in her best state—caulked, painted, provisioned, repaired, and coaled. The sail-handling departments (forecastle, foretop, maintop, and mizzentop) were up to almost half strength, divided into port and starboard watches with a sufficient number of petty officers, so the ship was at least man-ageable. Newcomers filled out the engineering department as firemen and coal heavers, and for the first time there was a marine detachment to manage pris-oners, assist with discipline, provide armed boarding or shore parties, and help man the guns. Morale had been boosted by a run ashore and by the renewed state of the vessel; once again the world contracted to an isolated, mobile com-munity confined between wooden bulwarks, sea, and sky and so very far from home.

On 19 February 1865 *Shenandoah* ran through Bass Strait separating Melbourne from the island of Van Diemen's Land (Tasmania). Dr. Lining noted, "Set all sails, let steam go down & hoisted up the propeller, much to our delight." On Monday it was back to work. Lieutenant Whittle had the deckhouse on the spar deck dismantled. (Lining had considered it unsightly, useless, and "very unlike a man-of-war.") They now had clear deck from poop to forecastle for hauling halyards and braces and for handling the big guns. The ship's galley, formerly in the deckhouse, had been reconstructed on the berth deck below. But the doctor worried about heat in tropical regions.

Rugged Cape Howe appeared about midday. The cape marks the southeast corner of Australia from which the coast trends north-northeast up to Sidney. Whittle fretted about rounding the headland with the wind against them: "I trust that the dull monotony of beating to windward will be occasionally relieved by catching a Yank. Oh! How anxious I am to pick up some more. Our crew, greater than at any former period, seems to be a good set of men, but they have been stowed away so long that it is hard to give them enough to eat. After we get them well filled up, we will be all right." The wind shifted next day as they headed north and east in light breezes for the coast of New Zealand.

Whittle's entry for 22 February reflected on George Washington's birthday: "And sad is the thought that the very spot where 130 years ago this 'father of his country' was born is now flooded with blood of his countrymen fighting against the hordes from the North." Should the vandals be successful, he ruefully predicted, they undoubtedly would celebrate old Abe's birthday just as they do Washington's. The miserable Yankees were fighting against the very rights they thought so sacred in the revolution, but induced only by desire for wealth while sacrificing everything else—principle, life, and honor. "I regard them collectively & individually a pack of scoundrels consummated in every variety of rascality."

The date of 22 February was also the fourth anniversary of Jefferson Davis' inauguration as president of the Confederate States. Whittle could celebrate only by drinking a glass of sherry, doing his duty, and praying for the cause— hardly able to realize his sister Jennie was having her twenty-first birthday. "Only a short time since and I thought & looked upon her as a little child. God grant me many happy returns of this the anniversary of our first father's birth, and of the inauguration of our first President, or second father." He was compelled that evening to punish a wardroom cook who got too much grog in him and neglected his duty. "I punish myself when I punish one of the men who I know would stand by me at any time, but I must rule or he—both cannot." Lining drank to the health of President Davis and reported, again, nothing of interest going on.

Whittle exercised the crew in lowering all three royal yards to the deck and sending them back up at the same time—one of the more difficult seamanship evolutions that he proudly reported was accomplished without difficulty. The holds had been haphazardly stowed in Melbourne, so it took him several days to rearrange them. The gunners fired the two rifled cannon for the first time; they behaved splendidly. He appointed three new petty officers—captain of the maintop, captain of the hold, and ship's cook. It was discovered that the greater portion of the rum had leaked out, which Whittle attributed to bad handling of the barrels. "There is nothing which conduces more to contentment of the crew than the ration of grog. I am very tired."

First Lieutenant Whittle's relationship with his captain deteriorated dramatically: "I do not at all like the way in which things are being conducted. Of all men I ever saw, Waddell has the most provoking way of meddling." The captain continued to cut him out of the chain of command, passing orders to subordinates without consultation—Whittle did not know what was being done. Waddell was, complained Whittle, impulsive, weak, and vacillating, going always by extremes. "I feel the importance of our being in perfectly good terms, but if he throws up the gauntlet, what can I do?" The theme repeated day after grinding day; the captain acted like a man who had lost all his friends; he was "as dignified as weak men become when dignity ceases to be a good quality." Saddened at the apparent loss of friendship and mutual respect, Whittle felt a deep sense of wrong. He pitied Waddell but was more concerned that the captain's impulsiveness had alienated the other lieutenants. "I trust he will relent, for this state of things does the ship's discipline great harm."

On 25 February Captain Boggs of the USS *Connecticut* reported to Secretary Welles from Bermuda: "There is also a rumor that the [Confederate] ironclad with two turrets, called the *Stonewall* (last heard from at Madeira), is expected soon at the port, where she will be met by the *Shenandoah* with the intention of making a raid on the coast."[3]

The wind continued fickle as *Shenandoah* worked her way across the Tasman Sea toward New Zealand, bypassing Lord Howe Island and Norfolk Island, the latter a former British penal colony. Chew complained that the captain considered the area unworthy of notice after a petty officer with seven years in whaling—part of it on these grounds—told him they could have made five or six captures at least. Dr. Lining also believed they were going to look here for prizes but instead were pressing right on: "How I do wish some people could stick to one thing at a time & not be as vacillating as the wind." Waddell later wrote that he would have lingered had the wind been favorable, but it was important to nurture the supply of coal. And he assumed that the whalers dispersed and took shelter in port or fled to the Arctic after having been forewarned during *Shenandoah*'s delay in Melbourne. Valuable time spent looking for them would be wasted.

According to Whittle, at this point the captain ceased altogether conversing with his officers except in strict performance of duties and did not speak with his first lieutenant at all, officially or privately. Waddell interacted only with "clerk" Blacker and began putting all orders in writing. Whittle feared for the efficiency of the ship: "Why what is the matter with him? Alas! I fear it is irrational. I did not know him before." It was "childish foolishness that a boy of ten would be ashamed of." Waddell left no indications of his feelings during this period.

They continued jogging along without sighting a single sail. Whittle hoped the next prize would be something like a fast bark of about 400 tons; he would ask to be given command of her as another raider. Such a vessel would do quite as much damage as *Shenandoah*, he thought, and the probability of capture would be remote; they could pass right through a Yankee fleet without suspicion. "Oh how I would glory in such a chance." He would call her the *Dixie* or, after his hometown, *Norfolk*. Both lieutenants Lee and Scales and Sailing Master Bulloch would go with him, wrote Whittle. "In fact I could take any of [the officers] as all would like to go"—one indication that other officers were disaffected.

In late February and early March, American whalers loaded supplies in ports along New Zealand's east coast before cruising the vast hunting grounds to the north. *Shenandoah* attempted to round the northern tip of the islands, but wind hauled to the southeast, right in their teeth. They beat to windward for several days with light and baffling airs, making scarcely any headway. Waddell opted for a northerly course toward the passage between New Caledonia and the Fiji Islands, almost a thousand miles away, hoping to overtake slower whalers en route.

Assistant Engineer McGuffney and Fireman Rawlinson became intoxicated, but the source of the alcohol was unknown until Chief Engineer O'Brien searched the bowels of the ship and emerged with a bucket of rum. The sailors had forced open the bulkhead of the propeller shaft alley, exposing the head of a rum cask in the hold on the other side. They bored a hole in the cask and had been helping themselves. This was the rum Waddell thought had leaked from the barrels. Whittle triced up Gunner's Mate Crawford for insolence. "Then he gave in and was as polite as you please."

By 5 March they were making good time east of the islands of New Caledonia when the storm hit. Waddell immediately wore to the port tack under storm sails and struggled off to the southeast. He could not lie to on the starboard tack or run before the wind because either alternative would push them westward toward islands "whose exact locality was too indefinitely ascertained." Whittle noted that this was President Lincoln's inauguration day and thought it fitting that they should expect a gale. Father Neptune had been good to them so far, but this would be a bad one.

On that same date in Washington—5 March—the new president approached the podium on the east front of the Capitol just as the rain stopped and the sun burst through in shafts of brilliant light. Abraham Lincoln took this as a good omen and began his second inaugural address, speaking of the approaching end of conflict: "With firmness in the right as God gives us to see the right, let us strive on to finish the work we are in." On the other side of the world, the men of *Shenandoah* would strive longer than others.

The gale worked westward as they struggled out of its direct path. Waddell had never seen such a succession of violent squalls. "She was enveloped in salt mist and tossed about by an angry sea like a plaything. . . . Her easy motion, stability, and dryness increased my admiration for the little ship." For nearly two days they lay to. The fore storm staysail carried away; it was repaired and replaced only to go again, and in its place crewmen suspended a tarp in the weather rigging to prevent the ship from flying up into the wind. On the second day, a heavy sea came rolling in forward, striking the ship a terrible blow, making her tremble in every part and carrying away part of the bulwarks. The spar deck was inundated again. The deluge cascaded aft, upset one of the guns, broke its lashings, and fetched it up against the lee bulwark. The first lieutenant rushed out with his men in waist-deep surging water, passed a line around the gun, and secured it behind two iron bits—a good example of a "loose cannon." Dr. Lining: "Everybody uncomfortable, ship rolling, wind howling, everything & everybody wringing wet."

The storm broke on 8 March, and the bowsprit pointed northward once more to make up several lost days and several hundred lost miles. All plain sail was set under beautiful skies as everyone enjoyed a drying-out. "Oh what a joyous thing is a pleasant day after a heavy gale," noted Whittle. "Truly it is one of those pleasures which cannot be estimated except by experience. Little does the landsman know the hardships of the sea. Oh how much I would give to hear from my darlings. God protect them, I pray."

Still doubting Chew's seamanship, Waddell assigned him to keep all forenoon watches (8 a.m. to noon)—the best time to keep an eye on him—while other officers, to their frustration, stood more dangerous and tiring evening and night watches. In his time off, Chew was to take care of captured navigational instruments and keep chronometers wound—busywork below a commissioned officer's responsibility. Waddell explained to Chew "in a very confidential manner" that these were important duties for the good of ship and mission. Dr. Lining: "I pity [Chew], and yet can't feel sorry for him, as he has not any self-respect and independence." Chew either was unaware of the negative connotations in this unusual arrangement or chose not to be candid about it to his journal.

Day after day masthead lookouts sighted neither land nor vessel as *Shenandoah* crawled along over an infinite dark-blue disk under a pale blue bowl, occasionally blemished by wispy white clouds. She could have been standing still with wind and water flowing by. What winds there were came from the direction they needed to go. Constant orders to the helm were "full and by," holding the ship as close to the wind as possible, and still they could not make their course. Waddell decided to get up steam, lower the propeller, and stand to the north and west. Chew again disagreed as there would be no coal where they were going: "We are now steaming up 'among the islands' as the Capt. says. He is continually talking upon this subject & we hope someday to see these islands. . . . There in the region where a fresh S.E. trade should be blowing, to have light & variable winds from the north'ard! And then no sail in sight! A sail! A sail! My kingdom for a sail!"

Trade winds finally emerged on Sunday, a day of rest, passing rain and tolerable breeze. A squall interrupted the captain's reading of the Articles of War. In the privacy of his cabin that afternoon—Sunday was the only time he had for relaxation, if then—Whittle read religious services and thought about darling Pattie and family. Chew described various wardroom diversions, including chess games in which one player showed no pieces on the board, blinding the opponent to his moves; and he worked on his French studies and read a great deal. They celebrated birthdays and continued the Saturday evening tradition of toasting sweethearts, wives, and country.

As *Shenandoah* approached the equator, temperatures soared and it rained a lot. Pitch bubbled from the deck seams, making it sticky to walk; clothes grew moldy and required continual airing out. Whittle oversaw repair of bulwarks, rigging, and sails damaged in the gale. All hands appeared to be in good spirits, but maintaining the ship was an interminable task and even Whittle's best endeavors left him feeling blue. "I have worked as hard and as continuously as ever any man worked in the world." It was one thing to be first lieutenant of a regularly equipped and manned warship, but it was altogether different on an impromptu vessel with a third of a crew. He made up his mind never again to go to sea in a man-of-war. "While this war lasts, my whole effort, my life and all I have shall be my country's, and when it closes, my whole effort shall be to make myself worthy of her whom I love far more than life. Oh! How happy I should feel to be able tomorrow to make her my own. . . . We have had a nice breeze the whole day and our gallant old ship has been skipping along beautifully."

The New Hebrides were a couple hundred miles to the west and the Fiji Islands a little farther to the east. Chew occupied an afternoon reaming out fuse holes and filling 8-inch shells with powder, stowing them in a temporary shell room just below his cabin. "Quite pleasant companions to have near you. However, should they explode, I will be as safe as anyone else." Oppressive heat continued, punctuated by hard squalls—the "floodgates of heaven"—as temperatures climbed to 118° Fahrenheit in the shade but cooled as the sun descended. On one soft evening, a party of officers sang in the lee gangway as the crew vocalized forward. "What a crowd of remembrances came pouring in upon me," wrote Chew, "while looking upon the long, undulating waves silvered by a full moon, & listening to some old, familiar song! And what pleasure I experienced when they sang a sweet, melancholy song my own dear sister used to sing in years gone by! It is the dead of night in my far Eastern home. Mother, sister, nieces, all are quietly, sweetly sleeping perhaps dreaming of the wanderer who is full of thoughts of them."

The captain spent forenoons on deck, frequently conversing with Chew during the watch. Waddell spoke to Chew of missing the whalers around New Zealand; he was following them north to hunting grounds among the Solomon, Fiji, Gilbert, Ellis, and Caroline groups. Next he would head for the polar seas to seek the North Pacific whaling fleet. "Now there is the program," noted Chew with a hint of sarcasm. "Let us see how it will be carried out." He was anxious to sight the Fijis and hoped the captain would not pass them unseen too. Waddell resumed talking with the officers generally, and on 15 March Whittle had a long chat with him. The captain had a bad case of the blues, wrote Whittle, complaining that having to be on deck so much of the time was breaking him. "He takes an exaggerated view of his troubles which are far fewer than others. He has not sufficient confidence in the ability of his officers, in which he is wrong. For I never saw a better set, and one who learned so rapidly."

The first lieutenant had a few disciplinary problems. He triced up Able Seaman Fegan for refusing to obey the master-at-arms. "I think he is trying the sailor's well known experiment, 'to see how far he can go.'" Two men got drunk and into a fight while restowing the after hold; he disrated one of them, the captain of the hold, and stopped the grog of both. In Melbourne Whittle had not employed the usual practice of searching men and boats to prevent smuggling of liquor on board, something virtually all sailors would do at every opportunity. "If you treat sailors as men, instead of rascals all will go on well, taking good care to punish all violations of discipline."

He had other worries: the terms of the original six-month enlistees, many of whom were experienced petty officers, were to expire soon. Asking for discharge, as was their right, would be foolish way out here, thought Whittle, when they could reenlist for good pay and treatment, but sailors were singular beings. Thanks to the "stowaways," however, he probably would be able to continue. The sailors' meager clothing allowance was always wet, and the heat was beginning to tell on their health with the sick list longer than ever. The officers seemed to be passing around another eye infection—both Lining and Grimball were suffering severe inflammation; Assistant Surgeon McNulty was reported ill, probably drunk; and Whittle was badly fatigued.

The captain chose this time to worry about Lieutenant Scales as he did about Chew—Waddell said he had to be on deck at all hours when Scales had the watch, so Whittle volunteered to stand with Scales also. The first lieutenant was on deck from early morning to late evening in addition to standing in for Grimball who was still on the sick list. If Whittle stood watch also with Scales, much of it at night, he would have very little sleep. "But if one is to break down it had better be me than him, and I shall stand it as long as I can walk." The situation brought forth a bit of grim humor in his journal. After being up all day and night surrounded by rocks, islands, and doubtful shoals requiring intricate navigation, what if *Shenandoah* should be wrecked on the Fijis or New Hebrides? They probably would be eaten by cannibals. "I am decided that in such a case I would cover myself all over with coal tar, curl my hair and I might pass as an uneatable Negro. With this dark bright idea, I will say 'bon soir' & bad luck to the yanks."

The previously loquacious Lining recorded little, only commenting briefly on the weather, the state of his dispensary, and "nothing of interest going on." Over succeeding days, Whittle's anxiety escalated. They were "almost out of the world" near the Fiji Islands, twisting and turning among neighboring groups. "Oh! If we could take a prize, it would revive us all." They had not seen a single sail since Australia after two thousand miles in the track of the whalers. "This is disgustingly remarkable." Later: "Even the sight of a Dutchman would cheer us up. . . . The day has been terribly hot, with frequent rain squalls. The thermometer was 92 in my room." Finally: "Monotony, Oh! Monotony. No yanks in sight. No sails in sight!! No anything in sight!!!"

They were between the Solomon Islands to the west and the Gilberts to the east—virtually empty ocean a thousand miles in any direction. They had not gotten closer than three or four hundred miles to any of numerous islands dotting that part of the Pacific, complained Mason. "Indeed I believe we have found a portion of the world that no mortal ever explored." Chew would take a telescope into the main top and sweep the horizon, but to no purpose. "In fact," wrote Lining, "the region seems to be the abomination of isolation." The very birds had deserted them, nor had even a fish been in sight. "Of course we can't expect to catch a prize in such a place as this." Inflamed eyes prevented Lining from reading or doing anything.

On 24 March, one degree below the equator and five degrees from the 180th meridian, land was sighted right ahead—Drummond Island (the native name is Tabiteuea), the largest of the Bishop group of the Gilbert Archipelago (now the independent nation of Kiribati), about thirty miles long and four wide. It was low and thick with coconut trees; there was no harbor and it did not seem safe to approach within less than six or eight miles. Several canoes came off under sail, and one holding three natives approached the ship. The men were "the most miserable looking set," thought Whittle, perfectly naked and heads bare. "They had straight, coarse black hair, were of a dark copper color, and looked very like the American Indian, except that in the face they had few signs of intelligence." They had in their boat nothing but a few fish, some of which were purchased in exchange for tobacco. A sailmaker's mate named Glover could speak enough of the language to communicate, trying his best to get them to come on board, but they were afraid.

Lining thought the natives were a horrid looking set of devils, "more like monkeys than men." Viewing through a telescope numerous huts with no vegetation other than coconut palms, he wanted very much to go on shore and see these people in a state of nature. Hunt thought it was too fair a spot to be inhabited by cannibals, "still among the most ferocious and degraded of the Polynesians." Chew, the romantic soul, hoped to take a stroll beneath the palm trees, see the people, and collect shells for his sister. But the islanders had not seen a ship for a long time and Waddell wasn't wasting time here. As *Shenandoah* got under way, claims Hunt, the natives paddled curiously in the wake beneath which the propeller was revolving, trying to discover what made the ship move. At a hint from the officer of the deck, the engineer performed a stirring solo upon his steam whistle, when, "with every appearance of consternation, they took to their paddles and only paused when they had placed a safe distance between themselves and the screaming monster." "Imagine our disappointment," concluded Whittle, "at not seeing or hearing of a single Yankee. Oh the terrible, terrible monotony!!!" Discouragement was pictured on every countenance, noted Chew; some doubted the very existence of a whaling fleet in these deserted regions. Dr. Lining again ascribed the situation to bad management.[4]

Two days later, *Shenandoah* reached the equator, the doctor's fourth crossing. There was no ceremony. Apathy had taken the place of enthusiasm and pride in the ship. "All I care for now is to have the cruise over, & a chance of once more getting out of her. Weather very rainy & variable again." Chew wrote, "Can a place seem more out of the world where we are? I frequently look forth and imagine I see the whole expanse of this ocean, with its many islands, all calm and peaceful, nature uninterrupted by the wickedness of man."

Early in the morning the shouting of Lieutenant Lee reefing topsails awakened Whittle. He dressed quickly, donned great boots and storm hat, and rushed on deck where it was raining heavily and blowing freshly from the east with every appearance of a terrific gale. They prepared for the worst as the wind suddenly chopped around to the northeast, taking the ship flat aback. Bringing her around on the other tack, however, all were delighted to discover not a gale but the forerunner of the northeast trades providing a steady wind putting them on course at about nine knots. Whittle noted, "We were all much excited and elated this evening by the report of 'sail ho!' but found it only to be a cloud. . . . No sails in sight. Oh! The monotony!!" Lining considered that furtive cloud to be the Flying Dutchman omen of bad luck.

Just as it lightened up at 4:45 a.m., Friday, 29 March, the joyous sound of "sail ho!" roused them all to find a little schooner on the port beam. Chew recorded, "What an event! A sail! A sail! Everybody rushed to the deck to see how a sail appears. . . . Officers and men seemed to have a new life infused into them." They stood in chase and at six o'clock caught up and hove her to. She ran up the Hawaiian flag and upon boarding proved to be the trading schooner *Pfiel*, five months out exchanging whiskey for furs and ivory. *Pfiel*'s master reported no ships at nearby Strong (Kosrae) Island, but several American whalers had been anchored at Ascension Island as late as three weeks previously. (One of them was *Charles W. Morgan*—now moored in Mystic Seaport, the only surviving American wooden whaling ship—but she departed the island with two others before *Shenandoah* arrived.)[5]

Chapter 13

"Upon a Stone Altar"

"Oh what splendid trades!" wrote Lieutenant Whittle. "We are fairly ripping along on our way to Ascension. . . . I trust we will make some prizes here!" By 9 p.m., about twelve miles from the island, he wore ship to the east and reduced to close-reefed topsails awaiting daylight. In the misty glow of dawn, 1 April 1865, *Shenandoah* approached under steam and sighted four vessels lying quietly at anchor, three flying American flags and one flying the Hawaiian. Midshipman Mason: "The poor Yankees evidently displayed their bunting with the greatest confidence, little dreaming that we were a Confederate Man of War." They were one thousand miles north of Australia, one thousand miles southeast of Guam, and three thousand miles southwest of Honolulu.

The natives called their home Pohnpei, "Upon a Stone Altar." Rising out of the ocean at 7° north, 158° east—nearly opposite London on the globe—the island presents a striking contrast to the many coral atolls dotting the western Pacific. It is the tip of an extinct volcano, 14 miles across, a roughly circular 277 square miles of black basalt rock dissected by 11 mountains over 2,000 feet high. Steep ridges and deep valleys cascade outward and downward to a shoreline with little coastal plain. Soaring peaks rake moisture from heavy clouds engorging more than 40 rivers tumbling over ethereal waterfalls into quiet pools shaded by lush tropical forest. Mangrove swamps encircle the shoreline, sprouting from brackish water where rivers meet the sea. The climate is hot and humid and rainy, tempered from October to May by trade winds blowing fresh and clear from the northeast. Pohnpei is verdant, abundant with food and fresh water, and a welcome sight to mariners after long months at sea.[1]

The people kept history alive through sacred stories, songs, and prayers. A favorite creation song opens with "A canoe set sail from a foreign shore." Seven men and nine women—perhaps escaping oppressive circumstances—assisted by divine wind and directed by an octopus named Litakika arrived at a submerged reef. With supernatural skills and heavenly assistance they built upon it a stone altar, created a surrounding reef, encircled it with mangrove trees, covered it with soil, and watched it grow into their new homeland. The legend has echoes in the American creation story with small ships fleeing injustice and John Winthrop intending to carve a city upon a hill out of the Massachusetts wilderness. Like that community, Pohnpei was from the beginning considered to be divinely sanctioned. "*Pohnpei sapw sarawi ehu*, 'Pohnpei is a holy land,' is the first statement Pohnpeians today make about their island."[2]

Successive immigrations established new clans while the island developed into an independent, self-sufficient world. As in North America, the land defined the character of human activity, determined the range of possibilities, and shaped values and beliefs. Population pressures, limited resources, and internecine feuding led to tribal warfare, a dark period identified by Pohnpeians as "the other side of yesterday." But survival required cooperation, accommodation, and conciliation. The island took in weary voyagers from distant places, nourished them, and over time made them into *Mehn Pohnpei* or the "People of Pohnpei." New ideas, animals, plants, and technologies merged into a way of being called *tiahk en sapw*, "the custom of the land," that provided a cultural unity while allowing traditional distinctions in beliefs and practices. *Pohnpei sohte ehu*, "Pohnpei is not one," is the way Pohnpeians explain it today. A cultural order finally evolved that was flexible and resilient enough to accept alien forces, neutralizing their more threatening aspects and incorporating their best features.[3]

How familiar this evolution should seem to Americans. Had the men of *Shenandoah* known the history, they could have understood instinctively; they would have recognized the difficulties when integrating customs of the land appeared to be failing under the centrifugal forces of seemingly irreconcilable differences. One could say the history of the United States is a passage from the other side of yesterday to a *tiahk en sapw* identified by the people as "e pluribus unum." The year 1865 was a particularly catastrophic phase in this process.

For centuries Pohnpei had been a mirage to Europeans; a few explorers reported sightings but did not stop. By the nineteenth century, adventurers and scientists sailed the western Pacific; and in the 1830s and 1840s scores of vessels arrived, primarily American but also British whalers and traders. The USS *Vincennes*, flagship of the North Pacific Exploring Expedition, anchored briefly in 1854. On board was John Brooke, principal author of *Shenandoah*'s cruise plan. As the north Pacific fishery developed, Pohnpei became an ideal place to rest and restock, and by midcentury around fifty ships anchored each year, with over a hundred in 1855 and 1856. Freshwater was the most critical need while dense forests provided lumber for repairs. Desertions and white beachcombers were common, the occasional ship losing a significant part of its crew during the night.

Pohnpeians adjusted, developing accommodations that took at least as much advantage of the newcomers as the other way around. Conflict occurred over such basic concepts as property, honor, and etiquette; there were the usual villains on both sides. Captains occasionally found themselves with armed sailors employed as pawns in clan wars or political maneuvering among chiefs. However, violence was not an inherent feature of the relationship because both sides more easily obtained what they wanted without fighting.[4]

The barrier reef surrounding the island formed a protected lagoon with islets and atolls, many uninhabited. Lieutenant Chew recorded his observations, noting the importance of the reef in breaking the seas and enabling natives to paddle and sail around the rugged island terrain to any point on the periphery. *Shenandoah* made for Lohd Pah Harbor on the southeast coast. The Dauen Lohd River descends a mountain gorge and dumps into the top of the harbor—a long, narrow channel flowing between coral reefs and mangrove forest with a single narrow shelf of dry land below the brow of a hill named Kamweng. The anchorage was small with plenty of water and good holding ground; northeast trades were fair for entering or departing, so this site was frequented by whalers. Luxuriant tropical foliage extended to the water's edge, and, marveled Chew, from the ship this mingling of green and bright aquamarine gave "a cool refreshing appearance to the harbor." The six-hundred-foot-wide channel gradually widened, but a large coral head in the middle provided little clearance to swing a two-hundred-foot ship around a single anchor with forty fathoms of cable out and four vessels already anchored.[5]

As *Shenandoah* neared the opening, a boat pulled out to meet them; Waddell hoisted the English flag, stopped engines, and took the boat alongside. A disreputable-looking white man clambered on board claiming to be a pilot and saying that he could take them in. This was agreed for a price of $30, but with the understanding that if he ran the ship ashore or let any accident happen to her, he would be instantly shot. Waddell and Blacker strapped on pistols and walked the pilot up to the forecastle to direct the operation. "I would not engage to do anything under such a threat as that," wrote Lining. Chew noted, "The poor pilot was frightened out of his wits." He was a Yorkshire Englishman named Thomas Harrocke, thirteen years on the island after escaping from Sidney as a convict. "[I] could scarcely conceive a more degraded looking object," recalled Hunt. Harrocke had adopted island habits and taken a native wife who bore him two children; his body was tattooed with fantastic designs, and he spoke his mother tongue with difficulty. The savages apparently treated him with kindness, "but the torrid climate, with unnatural and . . . oftentimes disgusting food, had made sad inroads upon a naturally robust constitution, and it was plain to see that he was descending by slow but sure stages to the grave."[6]

Harrocke and others like him were castaways of the ships' world, living alone or in small groups with native families on the fringes of the island and of the social order. The beachcombers encouraged prostitution and introduced liquor production; they could be rowdy, corrupt, violent, and ruthless. But

Pohnpeians managed these vagabonds more effectively than they could those viewing the island contemptuously from their ships. Beachcombers served as pilots, interpreters, and trading liaisons, earning considerable return for the Pohnpeians in payments received for food, water, wood, and sex. The high chiefs occasionally adopted and treated them as their children. Harrocke would serve as intermediary and translator throughout this visit.[7]

Shenandoah proceeded through the narrow channel under steam for maximum maneuverability. Waddell stayed with the pilot until the ship was secure—anchors down off both bows in fifteen fathoms. He ordered hawsers run out from the stern and secured to trees on the banks, holding them safely in place and blocking the passage out. The first mate of a nearby whaler thought the visitor was a Russian corvette until his second mate, a Union Army veteran, pointed out the officer in Confederate uniform on the forecastle. Whittle launched four armed boats, a lieutenant in charge of each, with orders to take control of the prizes. "Oh! What an April fool to the poor Yanks," he wrote. "We fired a gun & ran up our flag. What a time!"

From his overflowing bases on the James River at City Point, General Grant outflanked Robert E. Lee's thin lines southwest of Petersburg in the Battle of Five Forks, then ordered an all-out assault along the entire front. Also on April Fool's Day 1865, *Iroquois* dropped hook in the Dutch harbor of Batavia (Jakarta, Indonesia) on the island of Java. Commander Rodgers had passed from the Indian Ocean through the Strait of Malacca into the Java Sea. He investigated the coast of Sumatra and the Strait of Sunda and visited for two days in Singapore. This had been *Alabama*'s cruising ground sixteen months earlier, but there was no word anywhere of *Shenandoah*. Rodgers concluded that foreign merchants and captains spread rumors of rebel vessels just to discourage shippers from trusting cargoes with American competitors. He would repair his troublesome boilers and set out again, hoping to receive additional intelligence from mail steamers out of Australia, British India, and China to guide his movements. Rodgers would continue this intense search for another three months, finally reporting to Welles on 24 June that "*Shenandoah* was no longer to be looked for on this station."[8]

Chew was drenched by rain when he arrived alongside the Yankee vessel and climbed the side. "What a sight met my gaze; a small, dirty whaler, rugged, ruffian looking set of men, the crew, and a great number of natives. I took a hasty glance around me in wonder, but recovering myself, I proceeded to business." He demanded to see the captain. The first mate, somewhat worse for drink, reported that the captain was not on board and refused entry to his locked cabin where the papers were kept. Chew promptly descended to the cabin with every intention of breaking in, so the mate produced the keys. Mate and papers were sent off to *Shenandoah* while the lieutenant surveyed his surroundings. She was the bark *Pearl* of New London, three months from the Sandwich Islands, having nothing on board but wood, water, and provisions.

The ship was surrounded by canoes, her deck covered with men, women, and children on board for trading. "These simple creatures looked on me in great wonder, my gold lace, sword & pistol seemed to attract their regard." They appeared to be the same race as those at Drummond Island, but with some pretensions to dress. "The fashions of the good people of Ascension are quite plain, simple and not at all costly." A wreath of flowers adorned each head. The men wore skirts of bark strips sewed to a girdle, which made quite a rattling sound when they walked. Many had on shirts, some hats. Women wore two simple pieces of cloth secured about the shoulders and around the waist. All were tattooed on the back of the legs and arms only, the women more so than the men, with a black nut juice that appeared dark on tawny skin. Men, women, and children were smokers and, having no pockets, pierced holes in their earlobes and stretched them to carry their pipes. Chew considered them ugly; but with beautiful jet-black hair, symmetrical limbs, and delicate feet and hands, they were fine models for painter or sculptor.

The boat returned from *Shenandoah* with orders to send off what provisions Chew could find along with whale line, books, charts, and navigation instruments. Chew completed these chores by sundown, carrying also a collection of shells, a curious spear from the Fiji Islands, a large whale tooth, native beads, and a multivolume *History of the French Revolution*. Alongside *Shenandoah*, a dozen boats were loaded down to the water's edge with every conceivable sort of plunder. Midshipman Mason accompanied Lieutenant Lee on board another whaler: "We pulled up alongside & on boarding the vessel were received by a strapping big Negro, who proved to be the chief mate." But all four captains were absent, having gone off early that morning by boat to visit the American missionary in another part of the island. The captured mates were put in irons in the forecastle under guard of a marine with loaded musket.

Waddell condemned three of the vessels. *Pearl* (evaluated at $10,000) had been out since November 1862 and sent home via Honolulu 1,483 barrels of whale oil and 5,600 pounds of whale bone, but was now empty. The ship *Edward Carey* (evaluated at $15,000) was originally from Nantucket but had sailed last from San Francisco. The ship *Hector* (evaluated at $58,000) left New Bedford in May 1861. Both *Carey* and *Hector* were full or nearly full, with 280 and 300 barrels of oil, respectively. The bark *Harvest*, however (evaluated at $35,000), was a problem. She had sailed from New Bedford in May 1859 and operated since from Honolulu with her last departure on Christmas Eve 1864.

She carried 350 barrels from twenty-one whales. But according to her captain, *Harvest* had been sold to local interests in 1862, and if legally registered in the independent kingdom of Hawaii, she was neutral and must be released.[9]

Waddell was particularly gratified with nautical charts found on the prizes showing their tracks and where they had been most successful, which would help him locate the fleet "without a tiresome search." He also collected eight chronometers, two sextants, and five quadrants along with muskets, ammunition, and two dozen U.S. infantry uniforms intended as trade goods but which would be used to clothe his marines.

Late in the day a whaleboat rowed into the harbor, its unsuspecting occupants—after a hearty round of drinking and socializing ashore—pulling along leisurely, laughing and talking and looking over the new arrival. Whittle again ran up the Confederate banner and dispatched Grimball to intercept. The lieutenant hailed the boat, ordering her alongside *Shenandoah*. The men objected, but seeing muskets pointed at them, complied. Over the gangway climbed captains Edwin P. Thomson of *Pearl,* Amos A. Chase of *Hector,* George O. Baker of *Edward Carey,* and John P. Eldridge of *Harvest.* "When they learned what we were they were astounded," wrote Whittle.

The first lieutenant withdrew his remaining men from the whalers. When *Shenandoah* came in, the pilot had recognized the flag, claimed to be delighted in their arrival, and ensured Waddell that they would be welcomed by the natives; but they were surrounded by canoes and would take no chances until assured of that friendly reception. With the island under local authority, with "no civilization," and with everything under their guns, Whittle had no worries about neutrality laws or American consuls. One cargo of 300 barrels of oil alone was worth $40,000. They had taken a total of 13 Yankee vessels, of which 11 had been or would be destroyed and 2 bonded. "This fully repays us for our monotony," he wrote, "and is not a bad haul. . . . The Yanks were certainly caught napping this time. I only wish there were 50 instead of 4."

The whaler captains sat on the poop with saddened expressions, looking at their stores coming over the side and conversing occasionally about the misfortune. One was "disposed to be impertinent" and was clapped in irons. Another claimed a Virginia mother, although he was considered a New England man, and gave Waddell a good deal of information about probable locations of the whaling fleet. Crewmen of the 4 prizes numbered about 130, mostly Hawaiians, whom the captain considered "a timid, mongrel race, easily imposed upon and cheated, but suiting the purpose of such men as command whalers." These sailors were not considered a threat and were allowed to look out for themselves. Mason observed them among the islanders and in the huts, sitting quietly with women and mending their clothes, apparently well treated and content.

Waddell pondered the fate of *Harvest*. She was a typical specimen: 360 tons, 104 by 28 feet, built of live oak, and, according to her former first mate, in first-class condition with five boats, outfitted for a year's whaling. *Harvest* was built in Middleton, Connecticut, in 1825 with a carved American eagle on the stern. Although Captain Eldridge claimed a lawful transfer to the Hawaiian flag, he could produce no Hawaiian registry and no bill of sale. He and his mates were American citizens who had been in charge since long before the alleged sale, and the vessel's name had not changed. The purported transfer appeared to be a ruse to escape capture and therefore, concluded Waddell, she was a lawful prize. (This decision further enraged Yankees and Hawaiians and would come back to haunt him in his postwar career.) Lining and Mason disagreed: even absent a bill of sale, they believed they had no right to condemn lawful property of citizens of Hawaii.[10]

The mates of *Harvest* were ordered to retrieve their gear from the doomed ship. First Mate Hamill would claim in a postwar affidavit that his writing desk, papers, letters and other possessions—including $270 in Mexican dollars, gold, and greenbacks, a gold watch, chain, and gold ring—had disappeared. His chest and trunk were broken open with contents scattered about and navigational instruments confiscated, leaving him only bedclothes and mattress. He also stated that Waddell attempted to recruit him, saying it was a shame for the young man to be on a whaler. Hamill retorted that he would rather serve on a whaler than go to sea with a crew of Englishmen under the Confederate flag. The captain responded that the United States was ravaging the Shenandoah Valley and he was doing what he could "to pay them up."[11]

The island and its natives were unique experiences for these Southerners, arousing keen interest. Chew expounded in enthusiastic detail: The population of the island was about 8,000, divided into five tribes each with its king or chief. The people fished and gathered coconuts and other tree fruit along the coast, while interior valleys and plateaus offered trees suitable for canoes and houses. Waddell recorded what the pilot told him: their currency was the coconut, metal money had no value; they were fond of finery, tobacco, liquor, powder, and shot; and "no principle of honor controlled them in their intercourse, but fear of injury made them respect whatever they solemnly entered upon." They were semibarbarous and either had no knowledge of a Creator or disregarded Him. Although their king (chief) was adored, Waddell could not see that they showed him particular respect in common intercourse (presumably as compared with European royal etiquette). The pilot claimed to have read of the war in newspapers from visiting ships and to have informed the chiefs about it. They were, according to him, great admirers of Jefferson Davis. Waddell: "The clash of southern arms . . . electrified the minds of men in the remotest parts of earth, its heroism and dash were 'borne upon the wings of the morning' and wafted by the breezes into the very habitations of the isolated barbarians."

Waddell was determined to observe diplomatic protocols even if of doubtful utility, and so the next day he dispatched Harrocke with an invitation for the local chief to visit *Shenandoah*. After a long wait, the cutter shoved off from the beach with several "darkies" (Mason's quotes) accompanied by a swarming cloud of fifty or so outrigger canoes. The boat arrived alongside. The chief, apparently reluctant to come on board, cautiously climbed the companion ladder to the top of the rail, squatted at the head of the gangway, arranged his apron, and looked around. The natives did not appear to be afraid, thought Mason, but they had been sternly warned off the day before and probably were a bit uncertain. The chief's son clung to the hull outboard on the ladder, unable to climb on board; Harrocke and the remainder of the party were in the boat. The captain waited, unable to communicate with his guest, until with repeated head and hand signals, the chief was induced to step down off the rail to the deck where he stood perfectly erect as if expecting a submissive bow from all present. His retinue followed, arranging themselves in proper order around their sovereign. The pilot presented his majesty to the captain with a backward motion of the head and, "That's the king, sir." The visitors smelled intensely of coconut oil, noted Waddell, "a protection against mosquitoes and almost anything else."

The chief and a few others wore garlands on their heads made of yellow flowers similar to lilacs, wrote Mason. As a child, he had often made lilac wreathes, stringing them on brown straw. The native flowers (presumably orchids) were six times as large with a much stronger perfume. "This odor is very sweet but so very powerful that it is sickening." Lining wished he could make a photograph, describing the chief as a man around forty years of age, not tall—about five feet eight inches—but well made. He had a dark complexion with "not at all an intelligent countenance" and black hair of moderate length; he wore a circlet of beads around his head and a collar about his neck. The lobes of both ears were bored and stretched so as to easily admit a finger, and in one of them a clay pipe was held in place by a half turn. A broad, worked belt girdled his waist, which with the clout finished his costume. Subchiefs were dressed similarly, and all were "slushed down well with oil, until they shone & smelt! Whew! Whenever they leaned up against any place they left a mark."

Waddell invited chief and suite to his cabin with his officers as witnesses, "for such things are interesting; the absurdity makes it so." Conversation was postponed while pipe and Schiedam schnapps were passed. A few glasses drew forth friendly sentiments from his majesty, and he became quite at ease, apparently impressed by captured objects in the cabin. "The whole affair was very ludicrous," noted Whittle. Waddell informed his guests (through Harrocke) that they had come to capture Yankee ships. The chief was delighted, asking that the prizes be destroyed in harbor so his people could remove copper from the hulls. Waddell promised the chief whatever they could take from the whalers, on condition that the hawsers securing *Shenandoah* to trees ashore not be disturbed and that no thievery occur before the vessels were made ready to burn.

The captain presented the chief with a few dilapidated muskets and an old sword, which was buckled around his naked waist with the blade dangling about his legs, "much to the injury of his shins." The visitors were escorted on a tour of the ship. Although astonished by the big guns, thought Whittle, the chief showed a good deal of sense while examining them. As they began a descent through the hatch into the engine room, his legs became entangled with the sword, so his son removed and took charge of it. The engineering machinery excited surprise and amusement, communicated by a cluck of his tongue, which was echoed by the retinue. The chief rested against a part of the engine and became smeared with white coating used to prevent rust. Observing the process of condensing freshwater from salt water, the visitors were at first incredulous, but after tasting the warm, fresh product, wrote Mason, "their wonder & admiration knew no bounds." After viewing everything that excited their curiosity, the party ascended to the main deck to smoke another pipe, sitting down on the grating near the wardroom door and smearing the bulkhead with "this horrible cocoanut [*sic*] oil." Chew had been on deck contemplating the fleet of canoes and regretting that he could not sketch the scene with sun pouring down upon bare backs and many holding up large green leaves that made splendid umbrellas.

The chief departed in the best of spirits, inviting all ashore with a hearty welcome. During the day, the ship received quantities of coconuts, pineapples, pigs, chickens, bananas, and plantains and gave tobacco in pay. Some crewmen were allowed ashore and came off sober because they could find no liquor. But what was ridiculous in the eyes of the Americans would have greatly pleased the chief. He was the *Nahnmwarki* of Madolenihmw, one of four principal chiefs and leader of one of the most powerful clans. His royal reception and tour of *Shenandoah*—a privilege that whalers and traders did not extend— brought the vessel within appropriate Pohnpeian categories, accomplishing an emblematic assertion of suzerainty over the warship, her officers, and crew; the tour was a significant enhancement of his prestige. Gifts and promise of loot from the whalers were especially effective as confirmation of his authority.

The chiefs dominated society. Their status was the central organizing concept linking the people with the land, with their past, and with their gods; Pohnpeians viewed themselves through this network of relationships. Chiefs were protected by the gods and spirits; they were the physical embodiment of the whole system, and all things belonged in principle to them. Land, sea, and forest provided abundantly as long as chiefs and gods were properly honored. The islanders' possessions—clothing, adornments, tools, and structures—were ephemeral objects mostly of wood and plant material, the products of loving craftsmanship. Everything was communal; the natives gave freely and spontaneously within lifelong relationships of mutual obligation and a strict hierarchy of social rank. Gifts from the chief symbolized recognition, respect, and obligation; tithes, honors, and obedience to him freed the wealth of the land for the people's benefit. Rituals of welcome and feasting and, when they failed, occasional violence maintained the order of society.[12]

These principles extended to vessels in the harbor. They and everything on them were the chief's to share with his people as he saw fit. Islanders did not possess or need durable goods or precious metals in any quantity; they did not use such articles as mediums of exchange and did not accumulate them as expressions of individual wealth and power. Direct trade of items of equal value and the use of money were not part of their economics and had no meaning. They bored holes in coins and wore them around their necks as adornment; copper was valued over gold for its color. To Pohnpeians, the vessels were floating islands containing many and varied items of material goods. They appreciated the benefits and readily adapted the articles to their use, as they had when previous immigrants brought new plants, animals, and ideas.

But the chiefs learned from experience that they could not enforce island ways on foreigners who tended to come and go as they pleased and to insist, even violently, on property rights alien to the culture. Ship captains acted like independent sovereigns jealously guarding their domains. All this wealth in alien hands represented a threat to order, and so Pohnpeians felt obligated to appropriate anything they could get away with, much to the frustration of their visitors. Theft liberated what was rightfully theirs, expressed protest against perceived injustice, and was good fun. It was a way of enforcing the islanders' will and of asserting proper power relationships. Among Westerners, the Pohnpeians (and Pacific Islanders generally) were well-known thieves. "[The] Natives are a graceless set of scamps," complained a visiting captain. "They did not steal the main mast or the anchor for the simple reason that they could not carry them off."[13]

With considerable guile, the chiefs marginalized the aliens and managed their actions, at least symbolically if not in fact. Each side patronized the other as is to be expected, but Confederates and islanders had more in common than they understood. Both peoples stressed structured interaction within an ordered hierarchy with well-developed rules of etiquette to lubricate the gears of society (a process intended to maintain a social order that Yankees refused to comprehend). Like Southerners, Pohnpeians placed more value in land (although held communally) and in inherited social position and power than in accumulated material wealth. Communal rituals of hospitality and feasting with strict obligations of superior and subordinate differed in content but not in purpose, and violence, when called for by individual or tribal honor, would look very similar.

Meanwhile, information in newspapers found on the victims tempered the elation on board *Shenandoah*: Sherman had traversed the entire state of Georgia and taken Savannah on 21 December; Confederate troops evacuated the city, leaving Charleston open for attack in the rear; John Bell Hood's defeat by Thomas at Franklin and Nashville (16 December 1864) lost all ground gained in east Tennessee; and Admiral Porter took Fort Fisher on the Cape Fear River (15 January 1865), closing the last blockade-running port at Wilmington and all portals to the world.

Whittle wished to discount the news coming as it did via California and therefore known to be unreliable: "If [the papers] all be true, it is terrible. In God's hand I resign all, and in His Devine will, is my trust. I can never think that an Almighty and merciful & all powerful God will allow such a people as ours to suffer subjugation. God grant us his blessing I pray." Mason could not believe them either: "For that reason I did not look at the papers, nor read any of the 'official' reports. May it be all a falsehood."

Chapter 14

The World on Fire

In the cool dusk of Sunday, 2 April 1865, Abraham Lincoln sat with Rear Admiral David Porter on the upper deck of the USS *Malvern* at City Point, the huge Union supply base on the James River near Petersburg, listening to the distant boom of artillery and rattle of musket fire. "Can't the Navy do something at this particular moment to make history?" asked the president. "The Navy is doing its best just now," replied Porter, "holding the enemy's four [three] heavy ironclads in utter uselessness. If those vessels could reach City Point they would commit great havoc." Under command of Admiral Raphael Semmes, the iron monsters *Virginia No. 2*, *Fredericksburg*, and *Richmond* defended the Confederate capital.[1]

At about the same time—Monday morning, 3 April in Pohnpei—Captain Waddell ordered *Pearl*, *Hector*, and *Edward Carey* destroyed, saving *Harvest* for later. But first, the natives were turned loose: they took every removable plank, spar, and bulkhead ashore for flooring; they stripped sails from yards and cut them to pieces for tents and canoes. Midshipman Mason was amused at one poor fellow who clambered up on the royal yard and in his haste cut away the lift, which cockbilled (tilted) the yard, leaving him "swinging about between wind and water much to his astonishment & discomfiture." As the vessels floated higher, the natives peeled copper sheets from the bottoms of the ships to use for pointing spears and arrows, for breastplates and shields, and for trade with neighboring tribes.

"All day long they swarmed over the vessels like driver ants upon a dead carcass," recalled Master's Mate Hunt. Canoes passed to and fro, laden with bread, tobacco, bits of iron, harpoons and whaling lines, and all sorts of odds and ends "until they were fairly surfeited with plundering." Waddell remarked, "The canoes surrounding them were handled more beautifully and skillfully than I had ever seen man handle boats." Rather than rigging tackle to hoist out casks of flour, meat, sugar, and molasses, the natives broke them open in the hold, losing half and making a horrible mess. Once the bones were picked clean, Lieutenant Lee and his boat crew boarded *Pearl*, slipped her anchors, ran her up on a shoal in front of the chief's residence, and finally, after two tries, set her aflame—everything had been soaked from incessant rain and no whale oil was on board. By evening she was burning beautifully, lighting the entire harbor despite enveloping darkness. Lieutenant Chew noted that one could read on deck at the distance of a mile.[2]

It was now early morning in Richmond, Virginia, as defenses crumbled in front of Grant's rapidly advancing troops. Secretary of the navy Mallory ordered the river squadron destroyed, directing its officers and men to join Lee's army retreating toward Danville in the wake of President Davis and cabinet. Admiral Semmes set the ironclads alight and adrift on the river. At about 3 a.m., he recalled, "An explosion, like the shock of an earthquake, took place, and the air was filled with missiles. . . . The spectacle was grand beyond description." Magazines erupted, flinging loaded shells with fuses of different lengths high in the air, which burst by twos and threes and by the dozen. "The explosion shook the homes in Richmond, and must have wakened the echoes of the night for forty miles around."[3]

Along the riverbanks, fleeing Confederates set the torch to magazines and cotton and tobacco warehouses; exploding projectiles dropped over the town, setting fire to a wide swath of the business district. "Morning broke on a scene never to be forgotten," wrote one observer. "The smoke and glare of fire mingled with the golden beams of the rising sun. The great warehouse on the Basin was wrapped in flames; the fire was reaching to whole blocks of buildings; and as the sun rose majestically above the horizon, it burnished the fringe of smoke with lurid and golden glory. Curious crows watched the fire. Its roar sounded in the ears; it leaped from street to street; pillagers were busy at their vocation, and in the hot breath of the fire were figures as of demons contending for prey."[4]

Yankee cavalry burst into the city while a boat appeared on the James carrying Admiral Porter, President Lincoln, his son Tad, and three aides. It was a mild spring day; birds sang in the orchards on either bank; trees were in bloom. As the party was rowed upriver, they observed a wide curtain of smoke ahead. President and company landed with a dozen marines and walked through the town to the capitol; a delighted Lincoln was surrounded by hundreds of black men, women, and children, some weeping for joy, others crying "Glory! Glory!"[5]

In the Pacific, Chew ignited piles of broken-up furniture in *Hector*'s cabins and saloon. The fires caught and spread quickly fore and aft, issuing great volumes of smoke. He remained below longer than was prudent before making an exit to the upper deck, where he began heaving empty tar barrels and oil down the hatches. Flames burst from hatch openings as he leaped into the boat. Nearby,

Carey was run up on the reef and set aflame, all in a drenching rain. By dark both ships burned furiously. The whale oil cargo shot immense flames high in air as masts came crashing down one after another. "The sight was grand & melancholy, the fruit of months of toil so soon destroyed!" wrote Chew. Hunt observed, "[The burning vessels] sent forth a lurid glare which lighted up, like the eruption of a volcano, the quiet bay whose waters were disturbed by scarce a ripple, and the tropical shore far inland, with its strange vegetation and grotesque humanity." This uniquely American conflagration flared simultaneously at opposite ends of the earth.[6]

Succeeding days on Pohnpei alternated between rain and pleasant weather. An awning was spread across the poop for protection of the officer of the deck and men on watch. Whittle kept the crew busy shifting coal and restowing the holds with pork, beef, and other stores from the prizes. He painted the ship and generally spruced up things. A total of ten men from the whalers signed on as crewmen, most of them Pacific Islanders with anglicized or Spanish names; two were Americans—James Welsh signed on as a marine private and Joseph Stevenson was a freedman enlisted as ordinary seaman. The six-month enlistments for five original crewmen expired, and Whittle reenlisted a boatswain's mate, James Brosman, for twelve months. Off-duty officers amused themselves with touring, hunting, sailing, swimming, and trading tobacco or cloth for native curios.

Chew and a party of officers pulled themselves ashore in a captured whaleboat, landing in a secluded nook out of view from the ship and almost at the door of the chief's house. Chew recorded that the houses had walls of stone four feet high and about a foot thick with no mortar, topped by wicker walls and thatched roofs. "What prevents them tumbling down, I cannot see." The structures were small but dry and comfortable, needing only to hold out rain in the mild climate. Grass mats served as beds with one rolled up for a pillow. Large boathouses sheltered canoes big and small on poles extending from wall to wall. In one of these structures, Chew encountered groups of men, women, and children sitting cross-legged on the ground, jabbering, eating, and smoking. "We spent a little time contemplating the scene. I thought, happy beings! Not a care to trouble you." Nature had provided a mild, delightful climate and placed food at their door; they had only to reach forth and pluck it. As for clothes—a great item in civilized life—a few minute pieces made up a suit to last for months.

Chew removed his coat, rolled up his sleeve, and asked an old woman to tattoo a bracelet on his wrist. She applied black ink made from the juice of a nut with a tool consisting of four or five wooden needles secured to the end of a stick. "The operation is very paining, and smarting under it, I somewhat regretted having commenced. I thought if the pricking of a small bracelet was so painful, what must it be to have the arms and legs almost covered?" A girl about five years old sat down beside the woman and held his arm. When her mother stopped to dip the needles, the girl snatched a bite of breadfruit, talking and laughing, her dark face lit up with joy. "I was much struck with her appearance, so small, so sweet, & so innocent! She had the most open & intelligent expression of countenance I have seen on the island, and such eyes! Words cannot picture them. I looked upon this poor, innocent, beautiful little savage with admiration and pity." The bracelet finished, Chew gave the mother two plugs of tobacco, which she considered very generous, bade the little girl good-bye, and returned to the ship.

Mason was delighted with the people and the flora, especially the coconuts. The natives liked to eat them green and full of milk, but he preferred the meat of a fully ripe nut. Other foods were breadfruit, plantains, yams, pumpkins, and "morning apples," which he did not fancy, along with plenty of sugarcane. The people were constantly around the ship bartering fruits, shells, and curiosities as well as pigs and chickens. Mason had no need of money; anything he wanted was available for a little tobacco or a colored handkerchief, "such as the old Negroes wear on their heads at home." He considered the natives debauched for prostituting young girls; sailors had mistresses while whaling captains and officers chose chiefs' daughters. Paradoxically, Mason noted, natives considered it a disgrace for a man to have an unfaithful wife. Waddell wrote, "The women are decidedly homely, but graceful. His majesty made me a present of the royal princess, which gift I was rude enough to decline; I told him I was married."

To missionaries and religiously inclined officers, sexual commerce was scandalous. The missionary referred to visiting ships as "the most disgusting of moral pesthouses," with vices like Sodom and Gomorrah. Most Pohnpeians looked with disdain on sexual commerce, regarding it as an aberration unrepresentative of their culture just as Americans considered prostitution, however widely practiced in port towns, to be unrepresentative of theirs.[7]

Sunday, 9 April 1865, was another day of rest. Whittle let the port watch go ashore on liberty in the forenoon and the starboard watch in the afternoon, each armed with two plugs of tobacco for barter. Lining rowed up the river with the captain and Blacker, and afterward visited the chief.

———

As day departed the Pacific, leaving these wayward Southerners asleep under tropic stars, far away in the blooming Virginia countryside the sun rose to a calm spring morning. A cold rain wept on smoky breakfast fires and the quiet conversation of masses of waking men. The guns were silent. Lieutenant Lee's uncle donned a new full-dress uniform and rode to a meeting at the small crossroads town of Appomattox Court House. Included in the surrender, Admiral Semmes—now also with the rank of general—and his naval brigade from the James River Squadron rested in their defenses around Danville. Jefferson Davis fled on south with remnants of his government, among them secretary of the navy Mallory and what was left of the treasury.

———

Monday morning in the Pacific, *Harvest* was hauled alongside *Shenandoah* to transfer stores and supplies. Mason spent one day supervising this work and another stowing the after hold. Perspiration saturated shirt, drawers, pants, socks, even shoes. "The hold [was] as close as forty thieves. I thought I would certainly melt away and if not the hardest it was the most disagreeable work I ever had to do." They now had rations for eleven months and bread for over two years; and with everything properly stowed, there should be no more breaking out of coal and transferring it to bunkers at sea. Later in the evening *Harvest* was cast off, run across the harbor, and grounded near *Hector*'s wreck where she too was set on fire and abandoned.

Chew recorded an excursion to visit some famous ruins. Natives paddled canoes carrying eight officers along the shallow reef, entering a small arm extending inland. The passage gradually narrowed to a small, tortuous channel; there the canoes were pushed along by poles, trees merged overhead forming a natural bower hung with luxuriant orchids and ferns that hid the banks. Bird songs were the only sounds.

They came to an islet and, jumping from the canoes, confronted a twenty-five-foot-high wall of "black flint" stone blocks, each five feet long and a foot thick with mounds of stones at the base indicating the structure was once higher. Passing through an opening, they found two concentric squares of similar walls, the largest one hundred feet long with a platform in the middle. No mortar had been used, and Chew could not imagine how natives cut the massive stones, moved them, and piled them up this way.[8]

"These ruins are indeed wonderful. It is impossible to say what they once were or by whom built. The natives know nothing of them." The edifice must have been constructed many years ago when the island was more populous, Chew concluded, before the people were decimated by outside diseases introduced by whalers, along with other vices of "civilized life"—smoking, rum drinking, stealing, and the like. "From various causes, they have become weak and effeminate, lazy (and immoral)." Judging from the number of sickly children he observed, succeeding generations would be even worse. "At one time . . . they may have been a fine race, but now I think them inferior to our Indians in every respect."

Chew's perspective was typical but mistaken. Europeans and Americans did bring syphilis and other sexually transmitted diseases and smallpox, which along with a low birthrate led to drastic population decline in midcentury. Influenza and measles took a toll on both natives and sailors. But the Pohnpeians, a courageous and resourceful people, weathered these vicissitudes without serious damage to their way of life—a characteristic the Southerners would have appreciated and respected. The islanders confined the aliens to the periphery of both the island and the society while traditional work, feasting, and war continued. They utilized foreign goods to serve traditional goals and values. But visitors, looking from shore inward, observed only the vice; they could not see to the complex physical or cultural heart of the island.[9]

Contrary to outsiders' assumptions, the islanders knew very well the origin of the ruins, which were used still for ceremonies to the gods. A succession of immigrant tyrant kings known as the Saudeleurs created the massive complex of Nan Madol, probably between the tenth and twelfth centuries. It consists of ninety-two artificial islets in a labyrinth of manmade canals covering a fifth of a square mile, built upon coral fill and enclosed by large rectangular columns of basalt. Additional ruins stretch over eleven square miles. The Saudeleurs administered a brutal, dictatorial police state until the island exploded in bloody rebellion. Another new arrival, semidivine war chief and hero Isohkelekel, led the people to freedom, instituting a new order of chiefdoms that exists to this day. The Saudeleur era is vividly alive in the minds of the islanders, as is the Civil War in the minds of generations of Americans. War on a smaller scale frequently accompanied political maneuvering in individual and clan rivalries for power and resources. For the males, battle was one of life's most meaningful activities, validating honor, courage, and status. To the degree the natives understood what the men of *Shenandoah* were saying about their own struggles, the Pohnpeians would have respected fellow warriors and sympathized with rebels against a tyrannical regime. Isohkelekel would have been their Robert E. Lee.[10]

Tuesday was a most beautiful day. Chew and a party of officers rowed up a small creek for the luxury of a freshwater bath in a pool shaded by trees. "For myself, I have become tired of salt water. . . . We were in the water about two hours and such a swim I have not had since leaving Missouri."

Everything on board was being made shipshape for departure. Dr. Lining went ashore once more to acquire green coconuts for wardroom stores. Captain Waddell paid a final courtesy visit to the chief at his home, relating the experience postwar with quotes presumably based on what the pilot/interpreter said. Pilings elevated the structure above tide and river flood levels with access by a pair of rickety wooden steps. The royal family slept, ate, and received visitors in one six-by-eight-foot room; two upright poles supported the roof, between them were piled fruit and other eatables. Furniture consisted of two wooden chairs, a box, and an old trunk.

His majesty sat on a mat; the queen sat near him with her hands and chin resting on her knees. "The queen was downright ugly." In accordance with etiquette, she did not in any way acknowledge the visitor's presence. The chief beckoned the captain to a seat on the trunk, which being soft on top, he supposed was the seat of honor on state occasions. The chief asked when the steamer would depart and what Waddell intended to do with the prisoners, assuming they would be put to death as was fitting for enemies. Waddell informed him that they would be unharmed, that in civilized warfare only men in armed resistance were destroyed. "But," said the chief, "war cannot be considered civilized, and people who make war on an unoffending people are bad people and do not deserve protection." Waddell: "I consider that pretty good for a savage. He said the above because he feared the prisoners whom I should leave behind."

Waddell related that they would sail the following day, 13 April, and that he would convey to his president the kindness shown *Shenandoah* and the respect paid the flag. The chief responded: "[Tell] Jeff Davis he is my brother and a great warrior, and that I am very poor, and that our tribes are friends, and if he will send your vessel for me I will go to see him in his country. I send these two chickens to Jeff Davis and some coconuts, which he will find very good." The captain presented the chief a silk scarf, which he admired, and received in turn a woven belt of coconut fibers interwoven with wool, "artfully done and tasteful in the blending of colors."

Concluded Waddell, "The king was always cold and reserved in manner. He was a selfish old beggar until the schnapps and pipe warmed him, and he did not consider it undignified or unselfish to ask for whatever he fancied and show displeasure if refused. He is, however, not unlike his brother sovereigns of this world in that particular. . . . He sent on board several times fruit and a few fish, and visited me every day, when he took his schnapps, of which he was too fond." Waddell preserved the coconut belt as a memento from "the only sovereign who had an independence of character and fearlessness of disposition to perform a common duty toward a righteous people and just cause." It could be noted that the Confederacy had finally—through the men of *Shenandoah* and three days after Appomattox—achieved its primary foreign policy objective: recognition and offer of assistance by a foreign power.

They had been twelve days at the island. Waddell enlisted eleven sailors and paroled the rest, leaving them ashore. When the men protested a lack of subsisting provisions, the first lieutenant informed them that natives did very well on breadfruit, yams, and coconuts and so could they. *Harvest*, burned to the water's edge, still smoldered on the reef that was her grave. They unmoored, got up steam, and at 8 a.m. weighed anchor and stood to sea. Thomas Harrocke piloted them out again and was rewarded with a Yankee whaleboat as well as pay. Waddell wrote, "That harbor will always be one of interest to the Yankee whaler, and tradition will point out the exact shoals on which the prizes were burned, the management of the affair, and where the *Shenandoah* lay calmly at anchor amid that scene of vengeance and destruction."

By four o'clock in the evening land was out of sight. The engine was stopped, screw hoisted, fires drawn, smokestack lowered, anchor cables unbent and stowed, and anchors secured for sea. The ship was put under all plain sail. Mason went aft to heave the log. "Everything seemed as natural & sea like & the old ship glided along smoothly with a ten knot breeze as if we had not been in harbour for a month." They headed north, leaving to westward the Ladrones Islands, which include Guam.

"In all the course of my sea life I never enjoyed more charming weather," recalled Waddell. "The sun shone with a brilliancy, and the moon shed her peculiar luster from a dark-blue vaulted sky, while the vast mirror below reflected each heavenly body and flashed with sprightliness as the great ocean plow tore the waters asunder, and for ten consecutive days I would stand for hours on her deck gazing on that wonderful creation, that deep liquid world."

Shenandoah was in better trim and order than ever, wrote Whittle, steering beautifully and averaging nine knots in brisk northeast trades with moderate seas. His friend Jack Grimball suffered with a fever, at times delirious and talking constantly as Whittle affectionately nursed him. Many of the men were sick also but with only slight complaints. "I am delighted to be once more at sea, and hope to remain so until our work is done. I am a hater of port." They cruised for days without touching a brace or trimming a sail.

Mason immersed himself in duties and in reading when he could manage evening time in his bunk or at the small table, especially Charles Dickens. He enjoyed *Nicholas Nickleby*, moving on to *Martin Chuzzlewit*, and *Dombey and Son*. The midshipman perused a history of the French and English navies (in French) and consumed Raphael Semmes' *The Cruise of the* Alabama *and the* Sumter, a work that must have inspired them all. On one black, boring, and sleepy midwatch (midnight to 4 a.m.), he and Lieutenant Scales sang French and English songs to stay awake. Mason recited from memory Poe's "The Raven" along with portions of Shakespeare and whatever he could think of. In the morning, he turned out of his bunk at seven bells (7:30 a.m.) to supervise the issue of grog to the crew. "Of course I had a big growl at not being able to sleep an hour longer & vented my spleen on the captain of the hold & Purser's steward." But regaining his humor, he dressed and ate breakfast as usual, oversaw the dinner issue grog, and stood the afternoon watch (noon to 4 p.m.). Another long sea day.

One evening the captain, as a training exercise, charged Mason with the routine but complex operation of wearing—turning the ship away from the wind, hauling braces to swing the yards, and trimming sails with sheets and tacks—to bring her around with the wind on the other side on a new course. Mason completed his first attempt at the long string of precisely worded and timed orders "in rather a bungling manner" with little or no wind. He hoped to do better next time; wearing and tacking were required skills. Another afternoon, the midshipman was ordered to locate a cask of cheese in the after hold, but everything was "six ways from Sunday." He donned old clothes and went "hunting, rummaging & turning things upside down" in fruitless search. He occupied another day, when not on watch or drilling at the guns, sewing a new pair of flannel pants to replace those his steward lost overboard and those worn out working in the hold; the new pants fit tolerably well.

Easter, 16 April, was fine, bright, and sunshiny, but they were unable to celebrate it properly, noted Mason, having brought no eggs from Ascension. They could say prayers and sing hymns and "do various & sundry other things appropriate to the occasion." Spring was setting in at home along with the campaigns, but many a long month would pass before they heard anything about that. He read the service in his prayer book, spent the rest of the morning reading novels, caught a rare nap in the afternoon, and then occupied a half hour at the masthead with a spyglass in another futile search for a prize. Chew was disappointed that no one would formally read the service and offer prayers. He thought nothing more beautiful than the Episcopal service, taking him back with "softened and more vivid remembrance" to a little church in Lexington, Missouri.

For over a week, they hovered around 19° and 20° north, 150° east, just under the Tropic of Cancer and northeast of the Mariana Islands, in the trade route between America and Hong Kong according to Maury's charts. Waddell kept her under short sail in brisk squalls, close hauled, beating northward on the starboard tack then south and eastward on the port tack, with all eyes alert for a fine Yankee clipper loaded with China silks and curios or perhaps silver. *Shenandoah* could outsail all but the fastest clippers, noted Whittle, and in light winds the engine would assist, but they had to be cautious. Clipper masters were adept in deriving every knot of speed in all conditions; they carried large crews with abundant replacement spars and sails, making shorter voyages in well-traveled routes. None of this applied to *Shenandoah*, and risks were not acceptable.

Grimball had his twenty-fifth birthday on 18 April. On the same day, with the weather much cooler, Lining was sleeping delightfully. He looked back one year, recalling with pleasure his arrival in Paris—scenes he never expected to see again. "How much does my life differ now, from what it did then!, when I spent my time in visiting from house to house & seeing sweet young ladies & kind faces. Now here I am in the broad Pacific!!!!!! Well! What difference does it make so long as you are happy!"

The northeast winds freshened, a sign of bad weather. They were well prepared, noted Whittle, but "I am not so romantic as to be able to see the grandeur of a gale. If I ever was, I have seen so many as to drive all such foolish admiration out of my head." A clipper from the west coast might bring bad news or good as God wills, but "let the news be ever so bad, our course & duty is clear, and every new disaster to our heroic armies at home should nerve us anew to do our duty like men. We will do it. God preserve and protect our dear country." He wasn't feeling well; he longed for dear Pattie and was homesick, but he was able to read and enjoy Thackeray's *Adventures of Philip*.

Not a sail dented the azure horizon, so Waddell finally turned the ship's head north to find whalers. But the delay looking for clippers had allowed the boatswain to prepare the vessel for "hard knocks" and hard knocks there would be where they were going. Trade winds gently ushered *Shenandoah* northward through the temperate zone and across the Tropic of Cancer but faded into light southwest breezes and calms, an effect of the China Sea monsoon. "This has been one of the loveliest days I ever beheld," noted Whittle. "The temperature is delightful." He kept the crew busy as usual: the boatswain supervised tarring down the rigging while carpenter's men painted yards and masts. Sailmakers plied their trade; gun crews drilled on the big guns. Others scrubbed the berth deck and the paintwork and holystoned the spar deck.

"The ship now looks very well alow and aloft," wrote Chew. "The decks begin to resemble those of a man-of-war for the first time." On a day with all sails set to the royals: "How beautiful the old ship appeared under her cloud of canvas! I greet it with pleasure." But Chew was not making progress with his French exercises in the evenings. Lining decided to learn a bit of navigation, which might be useful at some time. One night he sat up until midnight in the wardroom talking with Bulloch who again was suffering with rheumatism, this time in his knee.

On the last day of April 1865, recorded Mason, they were seven months from England and it was two years since he left Virginia. "For all I can tell two years from now I shall be as far from home as ever; perhaps I shall never see again all those dear faces. Even now while I write some of those dearest to me may be in heaven. I am not given to 'homesickness' or 'blues.' Indeed generally speaking, I see always the brighter side of the picture, but it must be acknowledged that the prospect is by no means cheering." His last letters were ten months old. The cruise probably would last another year, he thought, with no prospect of hearing from home, but what a fine time he would have when new letters did arrive. Or if the war should have ended, "what a blessed thing it would be!" How pleasant it would be to steam into a Confederate port in *Shenandoah.* "But I am building 'des Chateaux en Espaigne' & must come down to the stern reality of life again." The ship had been taken aback twice in frequent rain squalls, the first storms experienced since leaving Ascension. Only shortening and making sail varied the monotony.

Tranquil weather gave way to clouds, high winds, and additional sudden squalls from the northwest. "May Day and a gale of wind! What a contrast!" wrote Chew. He had been awakened by the rolling of the ship and seas striking the hull alongside his bunk. This was the first gale Lining had seen with perfectly clear sky and bright sun: "The month opened like a lion." Whittle thought the ship would "ride the waves like a duck" with sail properly set and helm half down, but the captain insisted on keeping the helm amidships, which threw her into the trough of the sea, causing *Shenandoah* to labor much more than was safe, comfortable, or necessary. "In these things he is stubborn as a mule, and I fear that his stubbornness will someday do us harm." They wore ship and stood to the southeast to clear the storm, then turned back north in the morning.

The thermometer dropped to 60° Fahrenheit; Whittle thought the chilly winds must be flowing off the snow-clad cliffs of distant Japan. Woolen underclothing, heavy pea jackets, and overcoats emerged from clothing bags. Mason agreed that neither the weather nor their celebrations were anything like May Days at home despite *Shenandoah* being on the latitude of Virginia; he bundled himself up for the midwatch and still felt cold. Chew managed to keep up his circulation by walking the deck—if he stopped, piercing wind penetrated to the core. It was becoming uncomfortable in officers' quarters, but the crew seemed warm and cozy around the cooking stove on the berth deck.

Some days saw moderate weather and seas with cool, bracing atmosphere and beautiful, moonlit nights. They could set the foresail and shake a few reefs out of the topsails. Lining reported the antics of the young lieutenants as they entertained themselves at a pitching and rolling table in the cramped wardroom with little headroom and closed doors. They kidded each other, told funny stories, played chess or backgammon, and even engaged in impromptu dances or wrestling matches. Whittle saw a large albatross, something he had never seen north of the equator. "Our time passes monotonously," he wrote, "but there are so many of us and all so cheerful that we manage to drive a good deal of care away." He expected to catch a good many Yanks at their destination. "I trust it may be so—but Patience!!" The captain continued cautiously, reefing down at the first sign of rising wind and in no hurry to reach the Sea of Okhotsk before ice cleared in June. He also fretted about that old Indian Ocean problem: a certain rattling noise accompanied by an uneasy motion about the rudder head and chains.

On 5 May the USS *Jamestown* reached Macao. Captain Price reported to Secretary Welles that nothing more had been heard there of *Shenandoah* since she left Melbourne although rumor had her all over the China Sea, "to the delight of English interests." He thought, however, that British authorities did not desire to see her in their ports, "for they realize more and more the responsibility of giving hospitality to such pirates as she and the *Alabama*." Two days later, Captain Russell of the USS *Cyane* (on which Dr. Lining had served before the war) reported from Panama that he had received a communication from the U.S. consul in Chile—based on the word of a recent arrival from Melbourne—that *Shenandoah* could soon be expected in nearby waters. "American whaling and merchant vessels trading at the south Pacific ports will be in imminent danger," stated the consul; he was anxious that a vessel of the Pacific Squadron be detached for service on that unprotected coast. Copies of this communique went to San Francisco for the squadron commander, Admiral Pearson, and to Commodore Poor at Acapulco. The USS *Wateree* patrolled the Panama coast looking out for rebels reportedly crossing the isthmus to seize American steamers in the Pacific.[11]

Chapter 15

Invading the North

Coming on deck at 8:30 a.m., Chew found it almost calm with an ugly cross sea running and thick overcast piled up on the northeast horizon, heavy and threatening. The barometer plunged, signaling atmospheric convulsions to come. Suddenly the towering rampart of billowing black cloud was rushing at them, resting so close upon the surface of the water, recalled Waddell, "that it seemed determined to smother and blot out of existence forever the little vessel." Chew started to wear ship under topsails, but in the light airs, it was taking time to get her around. The wind abruptly shifted and strengthened, taking sails aback with a thunder of thrashing canvas. Men scrambled aloft to furl the mizzen topsail and to close-reef the fore and main topsails. The ship had just enough headway to continue turning onto the other tack when a wall of wind slammed her abeam. The very air turned liquid, blinding them in mist and cold, driving rain. The thermometer dropped in minutes from 46° to 39° Fahrenheit. Chew had never seen a gale come up so suddenly and blow with such terrific force. Had the topgallants been set, he thought, *Shenandoah* would have gone over on her side and filled; spars, sails, and other debris would have told the mournful story of foundered at sea.

Waddell noted, "She started like the affrighted stag from his lair, bounding off before the awful pressure. Squall after squall struck her, flash after flash surrounded her, and thunder rolled in her wake, while every timber retorted to the shakings of the heavens. It was a typhoon; the ocean was as white as the snowdrift." The main topsail exploded into shreds. In a gut-wrenchingly tilted world of screaming winds, they repaired lines, struggled aloft a giant roll of new topsail, secured it on the yard, reset it, and regained control. She scudded to the southeast before the tempest.

Mason had been sewing in his dark steerage cubbyhole. The ventilator that pierced the hull just over their bunks was nice in hot weather but it was "indescribably disagreeable" in cold, wet weather like this. As squalls hit, water blew through the vent, soaking beds, floor, shoes, boots, and everything. "A wet bed was by no means a pleasant thing." Every lee roll tumbled his candlestick off the table onto the bunk, greasing the blankets and damaging his new pants. Patience exhausted, the midshipman was interrupted by noise of the shredded topsail flapping about, so he jumped on deck to witness seas worse than those in the Indian Ocean. He struggled onto the forecastle to help set a storm staysail and, glancing aft, saw waves behind looming above the mizzen topsail yard.

Shenandoah surged through the water at a fearful rate as the sea—dark, gloomy, and mournful—made an awful noise boiling up to the rail on either side, cresting over the bulwarks, and flooding the deck in foaming, hissing fury. The hull creaked and groaned and complained in every part as she lunged headlong into the abyss, or was thrown high in air. "Ah! what a grand, what a sublime, what an awful scene!" wrote Chew. "She seemed an insignificant toy in this wild strife of the elements." The storm finally eased in the afternoon, shifting to northwest. They hauled up to northeast and lay to. Coming up into the wind, another mountainous wave poured over her. "She stopped, trembled like a leaf and seemed overwhelmed."

"Aeolus soon emptied his wrath upon the bosom of Neptune," wrote Waddell. In ten hours they were making northing again, but that night the old ship rolled like a log. Chew was knocked about from one side of his bunk to the other. Lining had one of the most uncomfortable nights ever; he remained in the bunk to keep warm but sleep was impossible. Mason found it amusing to ask old sailors, Is this ship considered dry or wet in a gale? Is she a good "sea boat" or not? No two would tell him the same thing. Although some ships are more disagreeable than others, he concluded, none could be dry or comfortable under such circumstances. "On this point I am like the lover of whiskey, who said that some whiskey was better than others but that he never saw any that was bad."

The next few days saw light breezes with almost continual rain and thick mist, the sea smooth as a pond, and the ship gently rising and sinking to long, easy swells. Coming off watch, Chew occupied himself by wrapping in protective paper the seashells he had gathered on the island. He installed clothing hooks in his room and tacked canvas over planking seams on the bulkheads to block cold air blowing through. Another squall struck but was easier and shorter. The captain couldn't relax; they would never make progress. Bad weather was to be expected in all seasons between 40° and 45° north, but this past week appeared to have been "more replete with desperate trials of wind and weather . . . than all my former experience or imagination could fortify me to meet."

Wind and seas continued calm as the temperature declined; clear skies alternated with clouds from the west and cold rain. "Not one of your rearing, tearing, pitching showers, but a good old fashioned drizzle-drazzle," wrote Mason. A piece of gear falling from aloft cut Bulloch's head open—one of the few calls for Dr. Lining's skills. Otherwise the doctor enjoyed walking the deck—for nearly two hours one night—and observing new sights of the marine world. On one nearly calm day, the ship sliced through a group of large Portuguese man-of-war, and two days later Lining observed a large sunfish—an ugly thing looking more like a turtle. Meanwhile, Whittle lamented, "No sails in sight." "Oh! how I wish we could capture something."

A few days of light southerly breezes and cloudless skies dried sails and decks as they made sail to the royals and flying jib. Lining found it warm enough to sit on deck and luxuriate in the sunshine. Whittle witnessed a peculiar sign: a bright, distinct ring around the sun, which he hoped indicated good weather. "I have had a strange presentiment that when we get back we will find the war over. I humbly pray to God that it may be true." It was middle May, and Chew didn't see any flowers and green grass—just the same view of sea and sky—"nothing to recall the beautiful spring, and the singing of birds." Heavy fog and rain descended, icing up on deck, portending the proximity of icebergs. As wind hauled to the southwest and evening descended, Whittle hove to on the starboard tack under short sail so as not to run into ice. He thought the ship was ready for bad weather but worried that a piercing northeast gale with freezing temperatures would be trouble. They celebrated Bulloch's twenty-third birthday, 18 May 1865.

Dawn light suffused outward in light snow as fog slowly lifted, revealing barren volcanic cones frosted in white bearing northwest by west about thirty-five miles across calm gray water. *Shenandoah* approached Onekotan Island, one of the northernmost of the Kuril Islands, on course to pass between it and Paramushir Island near the tip of the Kamchatka Peninsula at the edge of Asia. "The island appeared the most desolate and uninviting piece of terra firma I have ever seen," wrote Chew, "no vegetation, consequently no inhabitants." No one came there but whalemen. With the wind against them, they waited for the next morning and then proceeded under steam and fore-and-aft sails. Snowy peaks shone in the early sun with bitter cold winds rushing off the slopes and high seas running. Once safely through the narrow passage, the propeller was hoisted and sail set to make a good offing from the coast. Without steam, noted Whittle, they would never have made it through. The Sea of Okhotsk is an enclosed, shallow arm of the northwestern Pacific Ocean lying behind the Kamchatka Peninsula. Ice floes generally lock it up in winter and are a menace all year.

When Chew came on deck the next morning, he found snow falling fast. "It reminded me of old times and I took pleasure in looking at it." Snow sparrows and robins, much like those at home, flew around the ship from islands on the port beam. Mason had a bad case of the "chillblains" from wet, cold feet; he applied cold salt water and felt better. High land could be seen forty miles off, hills and mountains covered with white. "They look terribly cold & make one shiver at the thoughts of what we are going to find farther north. I feel this weather much more than I expected."

Beautiful days with crystal sunshine, smooth sea, little wind, and comparatively warm temperatures in the thirties—which dried sails, decks, and clothing—alternated with fog, drizzle, and steady, cold rain or snow, punctuated by the occasional gale. Waddell issued an order forbidding unnecessary exposure and kept the vessel under easy sail. Dr. Lining required all to clothe themselves warmly and keep themselves dry. Extra rations of grog and hot coffee were served at regular hours while the surgeon's assistant, Dr. McNulty, inspected the food before and after preparation. The crew suffered only "catarrhs" or head colds from which they soon recovered. Waddell complimented the medical gentlemen for their "excellent discretion in preserving the sanitary condition of the vessel."

Shenandoah sailed northward along Kamchatka's western shore during the day and lay to at night out of respect for the ice. Lining carped about Waddell's cautionary progress as well as his practice of straying too far from the coast where whales feed and whalers hunt them. "Will we ever learn by experience?" He wished he had something to write about except the everlasting weather. A stove had been installed in the officers' quarters, giving the doctor his first really comfortable night since arriving in the north, but it did look queer in a wardroom. "Can I really call this a man-of-war?"

Chew came down after watch and sat reading by the warm stove, listening to the wind whistling and the rain pattering on the deck overhead. Along with novels, he was working on the four-volume history of the French Revolution captured at Ascension. But when it came on to blow with heavy seas running, the lieutenant felt uneasy in the stomach. He was seasick, which surprised him after so long afloat and so many gales. "It was caused, I think, by tobacco and sitting over the fire." (Shorter and choppier waves in a relatively shallow and enclosed sea could have caused different motion.) Scales also became sick and the captain stood his duty. The doctor wondered at a captain keeping watch when there were two other lieutenants, Whittle and Chew, who could do so. "But as he says he is crazy & there is no doubt about it."

On 27 May the sun burned through morning fog, flashing off a blue-white expanse of floe ice stretching away westward to merge with an azure sky; numerous seals reposed on the ice. A whaling ship appeared nearby. Dr. Lining climbed to the fore topsail yard to survey the scene as the two vessels approached each other around a narrow point of ice. *Shenandoah* raised the Russian banner; the stranger hoisted the Stars and Stripes. She was the fifty-five-year-old blubber-hunting bark *Abigail* of New Bedford, Captain Ebenezer Nye, thirty-three months out with twenty barrels of oil on board. Most of the previous take had been sent home via Hawaii. Nye had been in the Arctic every season for the past twenty years and owned two-thirds of the vessel. As intended, he had mistaken *Shenandoah* for the biannual provisioning vessel to the settlement of Okhotsk. Chew wrote, "I believe he is rich and well able to afford to lose his ship, much used by age." Captain Nye was heard repeatedly to say in his native twang, "In New England we can make a substitute for ile, but we must 'ave bone."

Abigail was last from Yokohama and had curios, fancy articles, and silk dresses on board. Mason, Chew, and Scales appropriated glove boxes among other souvenirs. Four or five bags of Irish potatoes and boxes of canned meats elicited surprise and gratification from the officers' mess. Other provisions recovered included salt meat, three live hogs, and three just butchered. But that wasn't all: twenty-five barrels of trading stock whiskey, brandy, and rum were removed to *Shenandoah*, and in the confusion of transfer, not a little of this bounty found its way into the sailors' hands to be consumed immediately or squirreled away for later.

Numerous crewmen and two warrant officers got roaring drunk. Whittle put them in irons, gagged them, and triced them all around. This was the first major debauch on board and he was determined that it not be repeated. On the way back to the ship, one inebriated sailor jumped out of the boat into freezing water, was hauled bodily back in, and lashed in the bottom. "Hell to pay generally," complained Mason. Those involved included the youngest engineer, McGuffney, an Irishman (the midshipman judged him to be of mean birth and a "low blackguard"), as well as Carpenter Lynch and Boatswain Harwood, both Englishmen. Lynch was confined in irons and finally triced up and gagged in the propeller well, an everlasting disgrace for a warrant officer. Such men as these, concluded Mason, had no pride, principles, or honor; they joined for mercenary motives not for the cause. He had no patience for such "canaille" (riffraff) who were most emphatically a disgrace to the uniform. Whittle paroled thirty-five *Abigail* crewmen, leaving them free of irons, and then set her alight. This fourteenth prize was valued at $16,705.

On this same day, 27 May, the *San Francisco Bulletin* reported in its Finance and Trade section considerable speculation among ship owners and underwriters as to the course of *Shenandoah*. Popular belief held she would be next heard from along the west coast of South America. "Those having vessels in the South Pacific very naturally feel a little nervous, and there is decidedly more inclination to affect insurance against war risks." The captain of the USS *St. Mary's*, a 20-gun sloop-of-war, reported from Callao Bay, Peru, that he heard rumors and was on the lookout. "Should she come will do all that can be done with a sailing vessel to prevent her doing injury to our commerce." He supposed that the pirate would visit the Chincha Islands and, as soon as wind permitted, proceeded there himself to find thirty American ships loading guano.[1]

The next morning through late evening a moderate gale and heavy snow engulfed *Shenandoah*, whitening everything aloft and every little nook about the decks; snow tumbled down as the yards swung while wearing ship. A piece of canvas was secured in the weather mizzen rigging to shelter the quarter-deck. Booze flowed on for days. "Worse & worse do things go," moaned Lining, "and many are the changes that take place." Carpenter Lynch was again drunk and insolent, put back in irons and gagged. Both the officers' steward and cook were "in the state" as were additional crewmen; a boatswain's mate was disrated back to seaman. The captain suspended Scales from duty for keeping liquor in his room for private use and for sharing it with Blacker. He then issued a written order that nothing should be taken out of a prize for personal use without permission of the first lieutenant and the paymaster.

The weather turned again: bright sky, smooth sea with the sun over seventeen hours above the horizon and the remainder of the day in twilight. As *Shenandoah* approached the northeast bay of the Sea of Okhotsk, Kamchatka was visible on the starboard bow and Siberia on the port—"that desolate, dreary land, the home of the unfortunate Russian exile," wrote Chew—all covered with snow and distant about eighty miles. Whittle learned from an *Abigail* prisoner that the whalers were at St. Jonah's Island to the west, probably locked in ice, but they would come east as the ice receded. Taking advantage of the fine weather, the first lieutenant restowed the boats to lower the center of gravity and reduce wind exposure; and on a perfectly calm day, he lowered a boat and had them scrubbing the hull. Scales was restored to duty and things settled down to their own old course. Noted the doctor: "Reading newspapers &c. are our only occupation. The weather is fair & delightful."

They poked around to the north, northeast, and northwest for a week—bumping into ice everywhere and looking into one particularly large bay whose name contained such a succession of consonants as to be unpronounceable. Land could be seen distinctly at a great distance with peaks clearly visible from sixty-five miles on a clear day. Through a telescope, outlines and inequalities of mountain sides could be traced as distinctly as if they had been within eight or ten miles. But no whalers appeared. Even if they had, the captain's international law books said he could not take them in bays and rivers belonging to a neutral nation.

The paroled *Abigail* prisoners appeared comfortable and contented. Captain Nye, his mates, and harpooneers were on the berth deck in a portion partitioned off by a canvas screen; the hands, all Hawaiians, were quartered under the forecastle. The Kanakas, noted Mason, have nothing to do but eat and sleep, their favorite pastimes. He often went forward in the evenings to watch one or two who were beautiful dancers. The midshipman also reported on his reading, having finished *Dombey & Son*, thinking it one of Dickens' finest, and now on the *Christmas Stories* with two or three Dickens yet to read; he was progressing well with *Les Misérables*.

On 1 June Chew reported not a capful of wind in warm and pleasant sunshine; *Shenandoah* lay "like a painted ship upon a painted ocean." He had never seen a more beautiful day. Within sight of snow-clad mountains, they were comfortable on deck without overcoats. The officers amused themselves by shooting pistols at gulls that flocked about the ship and throwing pieces of bread for the birds to fight over. They observed a gorgeous mirage, an exact inverted replication high in crystalline air of a mountain scene below, forming fantastic shifting shapes, disappearing and reappearing. Perfectly inverted shimmering summits descended to touch tips with real ones; ethereal slices of a mountain's lower slopes were duplicated higher up the peak, forming a perfect cross. The sun rose at 3 a.m. and did not set until 9 p.m.; even then one could read by twilight until 10:30. "What a beautiful sun-set today's was!" wrote Lining. "The horizon shaded from red through pink to the dark blue of seaward, while the nearly smooth sea, without a ripple on it, was tinted from gorgeous crimson to light green, and again to the dark blue sea. Everybody in a good humor & happy today. And so to end these twenty four hours."

A lone vessel was spotted up to windward but appeared to be a brig. American whalers were known to be three-masted ships or barks, so they supposed she was a Dutchman and did not pursue. Waddell sought advice from Master's Mate Minor, who had not only sailed on *Alabama* but had been whaling in these waters on several cruises. Minor pronounced that the vessel had only two masts, but Mason felt they were not close enough to positively determine her rig. "My candid opinion is that we lost a prize which we might have had with ease—but enough of this."

Shenandoah ranged as far north as the 58th parallel when ice appeared ahead and on both bows, threatening to surround the ship while rain returned with a vengeance. This far north summer gales were frequent and of few hours' duration, moving with excessive velocity, recalled Waddell, "testing the forbearance of every object within its path." The ship was to windward of a twenty-mile ice floe when a storm hit, and being blown downwind faster than the ice, she soon would be pushed right up on it and destroyed. They steamed slowly along the edge until a narrow passage was seen from aloft, steered carefully through the ice, and lay to. On the lee side, the water was as smooth as a mill pond while seas broke furiously on the farther edge of the floe, throwing sheets of water twenty feet high. "It was a majestic sight," wrote Waddell, "resembling an infuriated ocean wasting itself against an iron-bound coast."

Bitter cold wind froze the rain hard, which formed a crust wherever it struck. Ice from a half inch to two inches thick thoroughly coated braces, blocks, yards, sails, and running rigging, transforming the ship to glass; huge icicles hung everywhere. Numerous land birds exhausted by the storm rested about the ship and several were caught by hand. Whittle: "The sight was certainly beautiful & grand but was most severe." The roomy ship with galley on the berth deck and little stove in the wardroom kept those below decks cozy while exposed officers and men on watch were dreadfully uncomfortable. "Oh! how I thank God for his numerous blessing," wrote the first lieutenant. "Oh! if I but knew that all was well with our dear country. I leave all in God's hands trusting in him as the supporter of what I consider the Just Cause. I trust we may have a good day tomorrow, for I am sure that there are sails near us." The captain remained in the wardroom near the stove most of the day.

On the midwatch that night with Lieutenant Lee, Mason watched the rain peter out, draping them in dense, damp darkness. Small ice cakes, fifteen to twenty feet in diameter, began floating serenely past the hull followed by a field of larger blocks. Whittle had felt safe when he turned in that evening, but at 3 a.m., he was shaken by heavy thumping against the hull. He and the captain jumped on deck to find that the ship had forged ahead into the middle of a heavy mass of ice. Fore and main topsails were still drawing and could not be taken in; braces, clew lines, bunt lines, and sheets were frozen solid, the sails hard as boards. In dawn twilight Lee had men aloft and on deck beating lines and blocks with belaying pins and capstan bars. Fortunately the sea was smooth and the ice well broken up, and they were only going about three knots, so the shock of impact was not great. Had there been a sea on, they would have been in great danger, for thin sides could not have resisted large pieces of ice thrown against them by high waves. The breeze drifted *Shenandoah* slowly through ice to the westward.

It was three hours before the men could "by main force and stupidity" and extra tackles haul frozen braces through squealing blocks and force groaning yards around enough to take the sails aback and start reversing out of the ice. But now ice was behind them and reverse motion brought such a strain on the rudder that it could have hit and split. The yards were swung back again and the sails filled ahead as the ship thrust deeper into ice made up of many thick pieces, some thirty feet deep and fifteen yards square. Mason noted, "Some of them looked very formidable & crunched against the frail sides of our ship in a manner that was by no means calculated to make one feel easy." The sails were taken in. As morning fog cleared, nothing could be seen to the horizon but ice ahead and on both sides. Mats made up of old line were lowered in front of the stem to keep the ice from ripping off copper and stoving in the bow. Just when it seemed they were locked in, an open patch appeared with a narrow path to the northeast. The men struggled to hoist the fore topmast staysail and fore topsail, providing leverage to wear the ship around. Very slowly she started pushing out.

When Lining awoke that morning and looked out his cabin port, to his surprise he saw nothing but ice. "How we got there I could not tell, but that *Hot Rum punch*, in which I drank 'Sweethearts & Wives' last night must have been very potent to have made me sleep through all the noise." Toward noon, clouds began to clear away and ice to melt; the sun came out bright and warm. "What a beautiful sight our ship presented!" wrote Chew. Masts, yards, and lines glittered like diamonds. But the scene was soon destroyed when the watch was sent aloft to clear the rigging, striking each rope with hand spikes, billets of wood, or belaying pins. Great chunks of clear, beautiful ice crashed down, endangering men below, shattering into a thousand pieces and blanketing the deck. Water tanks, casks, and every available vessel were filled for fresh drinking and washing water. Whittle wrote, "I never did see anything like it nor never wish to." A party of officers went forward and engaged in a schoolboy snowball fight. By evening they were clear of the ice with no damage as fog returned and it began again to snow.

Heavy ice reappeared that night, but they cleared it safely. Lining once again missed the fun—hot whiskey punch this time. Whittle was utterly opposed to going further into the ice after whalers, for fear of scraping copper off the hull and ruining *Shenandoah's* sailing qualities if not endangering the safety of ship and hands. He was convinced that one ordinary merchant vessel was worth three or four whalers, so they "should risk nothing for the uncertain destruction of the latter to unfit our vessel's cruise against the former." The captain called a conference of officers. Lieutenants Lee, Chew, and Scales agreed that they should keep out of the ice; Lieutenant Grimball and Sailing Master Bulloch believed that they could go in. "He (the Capt.) will act by his own opinion & that of the majority," concluded Whittle.

Early June—the days turned gentle with light breeze from the northeast—fine weather for drying damp clothes and wet sails, scrubbing the berth deck, and airing bedding. Lining took his chair out on deck and sunned himself. *Shenandoah* edged up within thirty miles and full sight of Tausk Bay on the southern coast of Siberia. Barren land and ice almost surrounded them; the ice grew thicker and more dangerous toward the west where the Yankees were thought to be. "A woman's temper," noted Hunt, "is not more capricious than the movement of ice in these Northern Seas." Waddell decided to turn southward and leave the Sea of Okhotsk.[2]

Whittle regretted having taken only one prize. He suggested they capture another whaler, commission it as a raider, and then take it into the ice after more prizes, but Waddell thought that would take too much time even if successful. The captain had it on good authority—perhaps more advice from Master's Mate Minor or from one of *Abigail*'s men—that there were only twelve whalers in the Okhotsk and sixty to eighty in the Arctic Sea and Bering Sea. "Whatever he decides upon I will do all I can to assist in carrying it out," concluded Whittle. "So here we go for Bering Sea, I trust with good luck ahead. As to a commanding officer pleasing all hands, it is impossible. . . . We saw today the snow clad mounts of Kamchatka distant 76 *miles!!*"

Chew selected a large, flat whale tooth from the booty, filed and polished it smooth, and engaged an *Abigail* crewman to carve or "scrimshaw" it. On a day of dense fog with little to do, Whittle read newspapers from the whaler and was deeply affected by the reported death of his uncle Captain Arthur Sinclair (whose old friend Whittle had met in Melbourne), drowned near Liverpool. He was further saddened to learn of the fall of Savannah and Wilmington, but as usual took the news as incentive to greater exertion in fulfillment of his duty: "Our cruise thus far has been commenced & vigorously prosecuted amid unprecedented difficulties and we are certain, with a proper degree of energy, to come out with flying colors. God aid us, I pray." Lining declared, "We have succeeded in capturing one poor whaler. . . . Sic transit Gloria mundi!" Mason was incensed: "Now it stands to reason that if we go away after the capture of one miserable old coffin, the meanest ship in the whole sea, we have failed in the object of our cruise, the authorities at home will be disappointed, and the Yankees will laugh at our stupidity & crow over their escape." Chew recorded, "All of us are much disappointed in the results here."

Shenandoah worked her way back southward through light, baffling airs, and thick fog. On a dead flat morning, the crew crowded the rail to watch two large finback whales—about sixty feet long and six to eight feet through the body—cavorting around the ship in clear water. The whalemen itched to be in boats with their irons. Chew was so engrossed that he knocked his last cap overboard; a boat was lowered to retrieve it. It was the first time Dr. Lining had seen him angry. (Chew did not mention the incident in his journal.) As the sky cleared and brilliant sun returned, whale spouts could be seen at great distances like sails or plumes of smoke. On Trinity Sunday, 11 June, Whittle again rested in his cabin rereading the services and the letters from home and Pattie: "It seems to me that I love her more and more every day. God protect her I pray. My great effort is to make myself worthy of her love. . . . Oh for but a line."

Ten *Abigail* crewmen—all Hawaiians—enlisted despite the efforts of Captain Nye to discourage them. Whittle had never seen such strange names, among them Jim California and John Boy; one tall fellow called "Long Joe" put himself down as Joe Long. "They are a poor looking set but they can haul on the ropes." Dr. Lining examined the men and rejected two. "I do hate to see our ship's company filled up with such men as these, for won't we look beautifully while going into port with a crew made up with such people." Mason considered them more civilized and less thinly clad than the Ascension Islanders but still a confounded nuisance. After the grinding labor of a whaler, the poor devils considered this a sort of paradise with grog twice a day, coffee four times, and tea once while standing four-hour watches. They were accustomed to laboring all day every day, especially with a dead whale alongside, and standing watches at night. The midshipman had a terrible time teaching the Kanakas their stations and duties at the guns. It seemed impossible for them to pronounce English. "I hope however with patience & perseverance to beat it into their heads, one thing is certain, they are very 'willing.'" An Englishman, a Prussian, and a Portuguese from *Abigail* joined as marines. This was more enlistments than they had garnered from the last thirteen prizes.

Abigail's second mate, Baltimorean Thomas S. Manning, declared Confederate sympathies and signed as an experienced seaman; the captain rated him ship's corporal. Whittle was glad to have him—the more Southerners the better—and he was an old hand at Arctic whaling as well as "a fine looking fellow." Manning offered to pilot *Shenandoah* to a place where many whalers could be found, and as a reward was promoted to master's mate. *Abigail*'s fourth mate also joined, a New Bedford man who, wrote Mason, "wears striped pants & looks Yankee all over. . . . He says he has not been home for ten years now & don't care one way or the other."

The midshipman reported a contretemps in the steerage between two master's mates, Minor and Colton. Minor tended to bully his smaller colleague until Colton finally reacted and challenged him, so they both jumped up and went for their "toothpicks," facing off "en garde" with naked blades. Their messmates noted fear and reluctance in both parties, concluded no blood would be spilt, and didn't intervene. After a few harmless demonstrations, the combatants separated by mutual consent. "I don't think I ever saw a more absurd spectacle in my life," concluded Mason.

Skies continued clear and bright following morning fog. Captain Nye said he had never seen such a long spell of fine weather in twenty years in the Arctic. True to his sunny disposition and despite the lack of prizes, Chew considered their time in the Okhotsk as the most pleasant they had yet experienced, even including being jammed in the ice with every rope stiffly frozen and no clear water in sight. "No doubt that when sitting by a good fire, enjoying all the comforts of the land, the remembrance of that day will give great pleasure; in fact I now recur with satisfaction to all our gales, bad weather, etc."

Chapter 16

High Tide of the Confederacy

Shenandoah passed back through the Kuril Islands into the Pacific and turned northeast with the peaks of Kamchatka looming above the fog on the port bow and Shrinsky and Borunsky isles in plain sight ahead. Then the wind hauled to the south and southeast, producing a condensation that terminated in thick, black, impenetrable fog. Whittle organized another gun crew; all guns on a side could now be manned. He cleared additional coal out of the after berth deck to bunkers and cleaned the space for use of prisoners. Good topgallant breezes pushed them along at eight to eleven knots through occasional light rain or "Scotch mist." Dumbbells and gymnastics had taken the place of chess, reported Lining. "Such an amount of good, hard exercise was perhaps never taken in the Ward Room of an American ship." Whittle continued to fret about ice.

Three days elapsed without a sun observation when a sudden parting of the gray drapery revealed land ahead on both bows not six miles off. They immediately tacked ship and stood to the southeast under steam. Had the fog not lifted, noted Whittle, the ship's ribs would have rested forever on an uninhabited island. "Surely God is with us." The barometer was low, indicating either a gale or westerly winds; he hoped for the latter, which would mean clear weather. The sky finally opened up the next day, allowing noon sun sights and a calculated position. Northwest currents from the Sea of Japan apparently had pushed them thirty miles closer to the islands of Bering and Cooper (Mednyy) at the entrance to the Bering Sea than their dead reckoning showed. The first lieutenant was exhausted by anxiety as well as by continuing noises from the rudder. Mason estimated that a fair wind and eight knot breeze would bring them to the Bering Strait in a week. "May Aeolus smile on our enterprise!"

They ran a thousand miles north and east across the Bering Sea past the jutting capes of Siberia—more fog and rain, some sun, and generally good wind assisted by favorable currents. One cry of "sail ho" turned out to be a "sail rock." As anxious as he was to take prizes, Whittle did not expect to see Yankees until they reached the straits, but they could not run too fast for fear of ice. "This ship should never go into ice—she is too frail." Whalers, he noted, not only had copper sheathing on the hulls, but usually iron sheathing on the stem and double planking. "Higher north than I ever was before, or ever want to be again," wrote Lining, "& yet northward still we go & will be going for some time." Waddell invited Lining and Bulloch into his cabin one evening for a feast on sardines and port wine that went on past midnight.

Pieces of whale blubber floated by—a sure sign their prey was not far off—and shortly after midnight in the Arctic twilight, the horizon was smudged by smoke from a whaler's tryworks. Around 9 a.m. on 22 June, New Bedford whalers *Euphrates* and *William Thompson* hove into view and became the next prizes. The latter was said to be the largest ship in the whaling fleet with upper and lower topsail yards on all three masts. Lining went over to *Thompson* for medicines and found her the cleanest, nicest-looking vessel he had seen, but spent most of his time trying to keep Warrant Officer Lynch and the sailors from getting at the liquor. In the meantime, *Euphrates* made a feeble attempt to flee, was quickly caught, and went up in smoke immediately.

Another sail was spotted and chased, but proved to be *Robert Towns* of Sydney with Australian register. When her captain, Frederick Barker, hailed to ask what ship, Waddell ran up the Russian flag and responded with the name *Petropavlovski*. But Barker, a Nantucketer himself, had been around Australia earlier in the year, probably had a description of *Shenandoah*, and was not fooled. He set out at once to warn those farther north. *Shenandoah* lay alongside *Thompson* through the night in heavy fog, transferring beef, pork, and other stores. Five one-thousand-gallon casks of freshwater were swung on board to save coal, and she too was burned.[1]

From *Thompson*'s Captain F. C. Smith they learned of the 14 April assassination of President Lincoln and the attempt on Secretary of State Seward. "I am certain that it was not done by anyone from our side," wrote Whittle, but he feared that Confederates would be blamed anyway. Newspapers from San Francisco via Hawaii provided additional discouragement. The first lieutenant had anticipated the loss of Charleston and Savannah, and even the evacuation of Richmond once Wilmington was gone, but not Lee's reported surrender at Appomattox on 9 April. "All this last I put down as false. . . . I do not believe one single word." Lining wrote, "I was knocked flat aback. Can I believe it? And after the official letters which are published as being written by Grant & Lee, can I help believing it?"

Mason concluded that there must be some truth to it: "I am very uneasy about Mother, Aunt E. & the girls, as well as Tom, who no doubt has been in all these battles." Chew avoided the subject altogether. One might think from reading these newspapers, wrote Whittle, that the Confederate States were subjugated, but considering the enemy's propensities for falsehood, he would place no confidence in them. Still, the news was very bad. "My heart is heavy! heavy!! heavy!!!" God alone knew what would become of his darling sisters if, with no means of support in a country devastated by invasion, their dear old state should be given up to cruel and relentless foes. "God help us I pray. Oh! God protect us." (Waddell's decision to continue operating after reading of Lee's surrender would be excoriated by U.S. authorities.)

———

On this same day in London, the secretary of state for foreign affairs consented to a request by Confederate representative James Mason (distant uncle to Midshipman Mason) to forward sealed letters to *Shenandoah* through consular channels in Nagasaki, Shanghai, and the Sandwich Islands should she appear in those ports, directing that Captain Waddell desist immediately from offensive operations. Copies would also be forwarded to colonial governors and to Her Majesty's ships and vessels on foreign stations. The letter had been suggested and written by James Bulloch, who felt responsibility for his last raider. He had little confidence that the missive would reach its addressee (and indeed it did not), but thought it necessary to put the attempt on record. The letter summarized the collapse of Confederate armies and capture of President Davis, noting that hostilities had formally ended and Southern ports opened to trade.[2]

Bulloch went on to define *Shenandoah*'s status and instruct Waddell: European powers had withdrawn recognition of belligerent rights and forbidden vessels bearing the Confederate flag entry into their ports, except for the sole purpose of disarming and dismantling. Under such circumstances, the officers would enjoy protection and safety of local laws. Waddell's first duty was to take care of his personnel, to pay off and discharge the crew with due regard to their safety. He was to take receipts from each man, expressly waiving all further claims against himself or any representative of the Confederate States. If sufficient funds were not available to pay in full, Waddell was to provide each man an order on Bulloch's name, payable in Liverpool, for the balance and return there to settle accounts. Finally, concluded Bulloch, "[The terms of the president's proclamation] are such as to exclude most of the officers of your command from the privilege of returning at once to their original homes." He advised them to come to Europe or to await developments elsewhere. Bulloch would remain in Liverpool indefinitely and could be contacted at his usual address.[3]

———

Meanwhile *Shenandoah*, passing herself off as a Russian or American man-of-war, struck back with a vengeance. In the next week, she would take a total of twenty-four prizes—an unprecedented accomplishment that a few months before would have been greeted with jubilation in the South and despair in the North. The unfamiliar boom of cannon echoed across frigid waters; a wholly unexpected flag appeared; boats scuttled like beetles; whale carcasses floated loose; sails flapped (when there was wind) in frantic attempts at escape through ice and fog or into Russian waters. Under steam or sail, the rebels devoured each victim individually or in groups and rushed on to the next. They ordered some to follow as they chased others. Giant pillars of black smoke smudged the crystal air. Towers of flame glowed through fog or illuminated midnight dusk. Eighteen whalers were out of New Bedford and one from Fairhaven, three hailed from New London, another was a Rhode Islander, and one was home ported in San Francisco. Four of the oldest and slowest were bonded and sent off to San Francisco crammed with almost eight hundred prisoners of war; there were no casualties. A number of captured sailors joined the Confederates.

After destroying *Euphrates* and *William Thompson*, *Shenandoah* crossed the 180th meridian, logging a second Thursday that week, and culled three Yankees from a group of nine sail that included a Frenchman and a couple of Hawaiians. Captain Jonathan C. Hawes of *Milo*, conversing in Waddell's cabin, said he had heard of *Shenandoah* being near Australia and was astonished to find her here, initially assuming she was a Russian vessel sent to make preparations for laying telegraph cable under the straits. They agreed that the war was deplorable, and Waddell assured his prisoner that the issue was not personal. Hawes said the war was over but could not produce documentary evidence. He described Waddell as "pleasant spoken, and polite and gentlemanly in his demeanor." With Hawes' wife and daughter on board, Waddell bonded *Milo* and loaded two hundred prisoners.[4]

Anxious to be off after other prizes, Waddell instructed the boarding party on *Sophia Thornton* to return immediately after they cut down her masts so she couldn't run and to leave orders for the whalemen to set fire to their own ship and row over to *Milo* with whatever provisions they could carry. Hunt observed the disabled vessel with her masts dragging alongside and the boats pulling away as a bright tongue of fire shot skyward. When necessity compels a sailor to torch the ship he has learned to love, Hunt recalled, "he has good grounds for complaints against the fates." Captain Tucker of *Sophia Thornton* had asked to retain some of his $90 cash to see him through at San Francisco. "No sir," replied Waddell, "your people have beggared me and my family and taken away all our property, and I can't see any reason for accommodating you."

The aptly named *Jireh Swift*—reportedly the fastest whaler in the fleet—tried to get within Russian territorial waters along the Siberian coast, but was caught after a three-hour chase in light breezes. When Lieutenant Lee boarded, he found captain and crew with their personal effects packed and ready to leave; the bark was in flames twenty minutes later. Mason thought they should have captured at least three more of the pack as they scattered into and around drift ice.[5]

Captain Williams of *Jireh Swift* told Waddell that he did not believe the war was over but that the South would yield eventually. He also said the South should have sent a cruiser to the Arctic two years before; the destruction of the New England whaling fleet "would have more seriously affected the Northern mind than a dozen battles in Virginia." To Waddell, this remark revealed "the genuine philosophy and morality of his countrymen." They waged war only for money. High tariffs taxed the people while politicians fed on fat contracts and government expenditures, and manufacturers realized fortunes. Newspapers related gory battles, increased circulation, and enriched their proprietors. The government stimulated business by issuing paper and creating a debt that the South would eventually pay. "[The war] was only to be stopped on the mercenary principle of showing that it would no longer pay to keep it up."

While *Sophia Thornton* and *Jireh Swift* burned, the whaler *Gustave* lay two miles away flying the French tricolor, with New Bedford bark *William Gifford* secured alongside. From a distance, the two lead-gray ships were indistinguishable, so the lucky Yankee went undetected. As soon as *Shenandoah* moved on, they separated. Captain Vaulpré took *Gustave* north to warn others while *William Gifford* headed south out of danger. Hawaiian vessels *Hae Hawaii* and *Kohola*, captained by, respectively, Australian American John Heppingstone and Irish American Barney Cogan, also witnessed the action and sailed ahead to warn the fleet. Ebenezer Nye of *Abigail* (captured 17 May in the Okhotsk Sea) transferred to *Milo* with other prisoners. But rather than departing for San Francisco, Nye and his first mate manned two whaleboats and set out for Cape Bering two hundred miles away to warn compatriots there. Not only was this a risky passage in open boats through ice, it broke their parole, which promised in exchange for freedom that former prisoners engage in no activity to the detriment of the Confederate States. If caught, repercussions could be severe.[6]

The weather continued to worry Whittle. When it was clear enough to see any distance, they steamed on but had to stop frequently for fear of ice. Light fogs with calm or light breezes were to their advantage; impenetrable fogs quite the reverse. They brought out foghorns and blew lustily in the hope that potential victims would respond but had no success. Several more prizes were lost in the murk.

On 23 June, brigantine *Susan Abigail* was taken. She was a trader straight from San Francisco with an immense quantity of liquor, gunpowder, and guns to trade for native fur and ivory. Captain Redfield expressed uncertainty about the outcome of the war but said he was having a good season and did not want his ship burned, which Dr. Lining considered the best reason for doing so. Newspapers up to 17 April stated that the Southern government had fled

Richmond and that Lee had surrendered, but others reported that Lee had joined General Johnston in North Carolina for an indecisive battle against General Sherman.

Two *Susan Abigail* men joined *Shenandoah*, telling Whittle that they put little confidence in the dire news and that very little of it was to be believed. The men said that riots were erupting all through the North and the public mind there was "most feverish." The papers carried a dramatic proclamation by President Jefferson Davis, issued from Danville, announcing that the war would be carried on with renewed vigor and exhorting his people to bear up heroically. This futile promulgation received little circulation and was widely ignored by those who did see it, but half a world away and months later, *Shenandoah* rebels took it to heart. Off the port bow, they sighted St. Lawrence Island, the westernmost chunk of Alaska lying at the entrance to the Bering Strait eighty miles from the Siberian coast.

———————

On that same date, 23 June 1865, in Oklahoma Indian Territory, Cherokee chief and Confederate general Stand Watie surrendered the last rebel forces—his battalion of Cherokee, Seminole, and Osage warriors. Of the occasion, Jefferson Davis recalled in his memoirs: "the Confederate flag no longer floated on land, but one gallant sailor still unfurled [it] on the Pacific."[7]

———————

It was a beautiful Sunday, 25 June, when the ship *General Williams* of New London was captured while cutting in a whale near a large ice floe. "Her Captain was a miserable old whine of a Yankee," wrote Mason, "& cried like a child when we told him his ship was to be burnt." Waddell noted that Captain Benjamin was certainly a Jew. Waddell thought that he "was a dirty old dog." While stores were transferred, a few Eskimo boats came alongside from St. Lawrence Island to trade furs and walrus tusks. Whittle wrote that the boats, made of a light, stout wooden frame covered with walrus hides, were easily managed and good sea-boats. He thought the natives were a miserable looking race of light copper color with straight black hair, but well formed, muscular, and dressed from head to foot in the thickest skins. They lived on fish and whale blubber "and are known to be no more choice in their diet than are buzzards." Lining considered them fat and healthy looking, the women much fairer than the men, "but whew, how they did smell!" Large chunks of raw whale blubber from which they feasted were tied to and floated alongside the boats. The doctor bought a dog skin for two plugs of tobacco. They spotted another Hawaiian and a Frenchman; both might have proceeded on to warn others.

In his small boat, Ebenezer Nye intercepted and warned four other American whalers; they all fled westward hoping to keep out of sight. After leaving *Shenandoah* behind, Captain Vaulpré in *Gustave* caught up with the bark

Minerva. Captain Edward Penniman of *Minerva* had his boats in the water off looking for whales in light airs. He hauled an old cannon up from below decks and lashed it down on the gangway thinking to get his boats' attention. When fired, the thing leaped up in the air and smashed down, gouging a gaping hole in the deck and blowing out glass in the cabin skylight. "Everybody was scared out of their wits," wrote Penniman, especially Mrs. Penniman who had just gone below to breakfast. Vaulpré also alerted Captain E. R. Ashley of *Governor Troup*, but he did not initially believe the warning: "It is a damned French trick to get north of us and best us in whaling." The next day, however, Ashley saw ships burning in the northeast; he hightailed it too.[8]

The sun did not set until nearly eleven o'clock and stayed just below the horizon, giving the clouds a twilight crimson hue. They captured *William C. Nye*, *Nimrod*, and *Catherine*. James Clark of *Nimrod* had previously commanded *Ocean Rover*, which *Alabama* had captured in the North Atlantic in September 1862. According to Waddell, one of the mates said of his captain, "You are more fortunate in picking up Confederate cruisers than whales. I will never go with you again, for if there is a cruiser out you will find her."[9]

The sun rose at 1 a.m. at a point west of north by the magnetic compass; dawn was clear and pleasant in near calm as the three ships burned. Prisoners and belongings were dumped into their own boats and towed in a line behind *Shenandoah* while she pursued others in sight. Before noon *General Pike*, *Isabella*, and *Gypsey* were caught. Waddell bonded *General Pike* and loaded three hundred prisoners. Another whaler, *Benjamin Cummings*, was let go— crewmen reportedly had smallpox. All night and the next day were occupied repairing *Shenandoah*'s engine and getting provisions and water out of *Isabella*. Just after midnight, they cast off, set her alight, and proceeded as far as fog would allow. Within forty-eight hours, *Shenandoah* destroyed and ransomed property estimated at $233,500, more than $200,000 of which was destroyed.

─────────

"The Confederate Pirate 'Shenandoah'—Where Is She?" inquired the *San Francisco Bulletin* on 26 June, citing a *Panama Star and Herald* article about an English report of a 1 May telegram from Ceylon that stated a Confederate cruiser was departing that island for Manila. *Shenandoah*'s identity was then considered confirmed by an earlier dispatch about a strange vessel observed 11 March, hovering off Adelaide, Australia, west of Melbourne, then disappearing before it could be identified.

─────────

On Tuesday, after passing through a great deal of ice, *Shenandoah* sighted seven or eight sail far to windward beating up in the first fresh breeze encountered in a while. If *Shenandoah* revealed herself too soon while the wind blew, and if one of the frequent fogs came up, some or all of them would be lost. Waddell banked boiler fires, hoisted the propeller, lowered the smokestack, and made sail. He continued in the rear of the whalers, keeping a luff, and retarding progress so as to arouse no suspicions. A crow's nest—a boxlike frame covered with canvas to protect lookouts on whalers—was built in the fore topmast crosstrees. The contraption "gave us quite an 'oily' appearance," noted Mason. All day and night they worked northward, rapidly gaining on the targets due to superior sailing qualities and waiting for a calm to bag the whole bunch.

"What a day's work we have had today," wrote Whittle the next evening. Eleven weeks after Appomattox in a conflict replete with irony, the Confederate banner reached its northernmost advance just below the Arctic Circle. The rebel navy fired the last gun of the Civil War on 28 June 1865 and achieved—if not quite victory—at least one of the greatest accomplishments for a country that no longer existed.

As dawn brightened, banks of fog rolled leisurely across tranquil waters turning sunlight from brilliant to misty opaque and back. *Shenandoah* approached the narrowest part of the Bering Strait and at 6:30 a.m. sighted the rocky tabletops of Big Diomede Island and Little Diomede Island north-northeast about twelve miles, smack in the middle of the fifty-eight-mile-wide waterway. Summits along the Russian coast appeared off the port bow. The easternmost cape of Siberia (Cape Dezhnev) was a high, bold, desolate headland, devoid of vegetation except in a few sheltered areas showing stunted shrubbery. Alaska's western tip (Cape Prince of Wales) rose to starboard. Ice floated all in between. The islands and the ice seemed to connect Asia and America, wrote Lining, "so we could see two continents at the same time, what very few have seen."

Ahead and to windward lay ten sets of masts in a cluster below the cape, apparently anchored or unmoving; another lone sail was sighted to the south. With the upwind vessels trapped against the cape by light airs, Waddell turned southward under steam and caught the bark *Waverly* of New Bedford, removed prisoners, and set her alight. Then heading first west around the ice, he turned north and approached the stationary flotilla, alternately revealed and obscured in the murk. "The *Shenandoah* came plowing the Arctic waters under the American flag with a fine pressure of steam on," recalled the captain. Every vessel hoisted the Stars and Stripes. One of them was lying over on her side with the ensign upside down at half-mast, a universal call for help. *Brunswick* had been stove by ice the night before, already a loss. The other whalers were anchored nearby providing assistance and purchasing equipment, stores, and oil from her.

All five *Shenandoah* boats were called away manned by armed sailors. The signal gun boomed as the Confederate banner replaced Stars and Stripes. Boarded in succession were the ships *Hillman, James Maury, Nassau, Brunswick*, and *Isaac Howland* and barks *Martha* (Second) and *Congress*—all of New Bedford—along with the ship *Nile* of New London and barks *Favorite* of Fairhaven, Massachusetts, and *Covington* of Warren, Rhode Island. Yankees rushed about their decks in confusion and consternation, scrambling to recover anchors and sheeting home sails, all to the amusement of the rebels. Several slipped their cables and attempted to flee in the mist. Imbibing liberally, some officers swore sympathy for the South while others spoke incoherently of cruisers, fires, and insurance. "A drunken and brutal class of men I found the whaling captains and mates of New England," recalled Waddell. "What an excitement!" wrote Chew.

When a boat in command of Warrant Officer Alcott came alongside *Nile*, Captain George Destin threatened to shoot him. "Shoot & be damned," Alcott replied as he climbed the side; Destin gave up and began to cry. Thomas G. Young, *Favorite*'s master and nearing seventy, armed his crew with muskets, climbed on top of the deckhouse, pointed a whale bomb gun at Lieutenant Scales' boat, and swore he would fire if approached. Waddell eased *Shenandoah* up with cannon run out. The whalemen immediately began lowering boats and scrambling into them while Captain Young walked up and down the poop. When ordered to haul down his flag, he shouted: "I'll see you damned first. Come & haul it down yourself." A loud order on *Shenandoah* to prepare to fire brought forth from Young: "Shoot away & you better aim at me!" He was plainly drunk or crazy. Whittle snatched a loaded rifle from a marine, jumped into the boat, climbed on board, and leveled the cocked weapon at the recalcitrant Yankee. He gave up with a growl: "You are darned lucky not to be shot, for if my officers & men had stuck by me I would have shot you sure!"

On boarding *James Maury*, it was discovered that the master was dead, preserved below decks in a whiskey barrel; his grieving widow was on board with two children. Waddell sent a message to the unhappy woman: no harm would come to her or the ship. Men of the South never made war on helpless women and children, and despite numerous examples to the contrary by the enemy, Waddell "preferred the nobler instincts of human nature." *James Maury* was bonded for $37,000 and loaded with 222 prisoners. The remaining 190 captives were sent to the oldest and slowest vessel, the *Nile* ($41,600 bond). Both *James Maury* and *Nile* prepared to depart for San Francisco.

With the flaming *Waverly* still in sight to the south, the rest went up at once. Explosions of gunpowder and other combustibles resembled distant artillery, recalled Waddell, as liquid flame pursued inflammable substance down the sides to the water. "The heavens were illuminated with the red glare, presenting a picture of indescribable grandeur, while the water was covered with black smoke commingling with fiery sparks." Whittle: "It is a gloomy sight to see the magnificent and valuable works of man so summarily destroyed. . . . This will cause an excitement. I trust it will do our hearts good by encouraging our noble people." Chew: "A burning ship at sea is a grand sight, but what is it when ten occupy the picture?" Mason considered it a good day's effort, but the problem with whalers was that they had such large crews—thirty to forty men, as opposed to ten or twelve in a merchantman—and so it was necessary to bond one out of every five or six captures to carry off prisoners. "I am tired to death after today's work having boarded & burnt three ships. . . . I am happy to say that I have all night in & expect to enjoy it to the utmost."

Waddell signed on another nine prisoners as marine privates—all intelligent soldiers, trained to use the Enfield rifle and to respect military discipline. Obviously, these men did not accept the Confederacy's collapse; they would not have joined a lost cause. "No, the failure of the South to establish herself was not known to any person who fell into my hands, or even believed by such persons," Waddell wrote later. It was simply impossible for authentic tidings of the war to reach so remote a place. "Individuals may lie, but facts cannot." One of the captive captains was a brother of *Abigail*'s fourth mate, the down-easter who had enlisted after capture in the Okhotsk Sea. The two men met on the deck of *Shenandoah*. The whaler captain was at first indignant of his brother's defection, but then accepted his right to make an honest living however he could, once again confirming Waddell's belief that "metallic virtue is the worship of [the Yankee] soul."

By this time, most of the remaining sixty or so whalers had scattered like pigeons seeking protection in harbors, bays, and sounds, or behind ice, islands, or capes—some for several weeks. Word continued to spread long after *Shenandoah* departed the Arctic, and few ships returned to the whaling grounds before late July. Many headed south toward the Aleutians or simply abandoned their cruise and returned to Hawaii, all costing the Yankees a great deal more lost effort and income. The bark *Gratitude* would be stove and sunk trying to get into the ice; the ship *Louisiana* would run aground and be wrecked coming to anchor. They were, indirectly, final victims of *Shenandoah*.[10]

The mist parted only enough that night to see the length of the deck as *Shenandoah* steamed slowly through the Bering Strait. It cleared about 6 a.m., revealing a most beautiful day—pure, bracing atmosphere and perfectly still sea with numerous seal and walrus sporting about. It was the warmest they had encountered for a long time. At 10 a.m., engines were stopped to examine the situation. On either hand and as far ahead as glasses could reach in the mist, one continuous line of ice sparkled—rising in places twenty feet above the water, thick and solid despite looking rotten; even small cakes of ice stopped the ship completely. Whittle again put mats down over the bow and credited them with saving the copper sheathing. The hull struck twice, going so slowly that no damage was done, but they had no desire to hit any more, and they looked in vain for a clear space beyond. "We went inside of the Arctic Circle," noted Whittle, "as was shown by our bearings. . . . I suppose Yankeedom will be astonished at our coming away [up] here after them."

A French ship and the Hawaiian brig *Kohola* were encountered but had no news (so they said) of other Yankee vessels. Waddell concluded that it was time to take the steamer out of these cramped waters. He would claim to have been concerned about ice and about the possibility of being trapped by an enemy man-of-war. However, news of their presence in the Arctic could not have reached the American coast, and it was known that the few Union warships in the Eastern Pacific guarded San Francisco and supply lines to the Panama railroad. Perhaps accumulated war news finally made him nervous about continuing without confirmation of their status. At 10:30 a.m., 29 June 1865, the prow of *Shenandoah* turned southward. "Our stay in the Arctic was short indeed," wrote Chew, "yet it has seen our flag."[11]

Chapter 17

"The Darkest Day"

"*Fairly homeward bound*," enthused Lining, "for every mile we go now, no matter where we go, must carry us nearer." Midshipman Mason was disappointed; they could have gone around the ice rather than turning about after no more than eight or ten hours in the Arctic Ocean and capturing nothing: "I wanted to see the work well done after such a good beginning." Thomas Manning (former *Abigail* second mate) informed Mason that there should be more than twenty ships in the vicinity and had it been a clearer day, they could have seen them. As usual Chew concerned himself less with the mission and more with the experience. He regretted that they did not remain to witness the midnight sun, a night when the sun did not disappear at all but just slowly circled the horizon. A few hours later, they came again in sight of stove boats, casks, and debris from the late prizes. Dense columns of smoke rose here and there out of burning hulks. Two other sail proved to be French and German.

Saturday night, 1 July, Whittle was dreaming about being again locked in ice. He awoke and went on deck about one o'clock to find the ship going along nicely at six knots under topgallants in smooth waters and dense fog. When he suggested to the officer of the watch that they were close to ice, Lieutenant Lee did not think so. The first lieutenant was returning to his room for an overcoat when he heard the cry "land ho dead ahead!" Ice had been seen materializing through the gloom less than a ship's length away. *Shenandoah* was immediately thrown up into the wind with sails thundering aback, but struck violently several times, grinding to a dead stop. Men tumbled from their bunks and hammocks, scrambling up from below thinking she had stove in the bow and was going down. "I don't know when I have been so scared," wrote Lining. Whittle supervised the lowering of mats over the bow while Lee took in sail.

Although no serious damage was apparent, the ship was deep in ice, with sails flat against the masts, going steadily astern. Whittle peered anxiously over the aft rail and saw the rudder swung to port, about to be splintered against a big piece of ice. He shouted for rudder amidships, ordering three men to hold it firm. She crunched hard again. Another inspection revealed no holes in the hull and the rudder still intact, but the chains that turned it were broken, rendering the big wheel useless. Crewmen rigged relieving tackles to the tiller, regaining control of the rudder. "The ship was in great peril," wrote Whittle. Current was sweeping the ice around—high, hard, and heavy—and enclosing them as far as the eye could see in the fog; they did not know which way to go. *Shenandoah* could be locked in and hull crushed. A boat was lowered and rowed out with a grapnel, which they embedded in a heavy cake of ice with the line run back on deck. Cranking on the line with the capstan, crewmen pulled the ship's head around, and then reset the grapnel and repeated the process until the ship was pointed back the way they came. Waddell ordered steam up and propeller lowered.

Crewmen shoved with oars and poles to fend ice clear of the slowly turning screw. The massive hull inched ahead, pushing one large block like a wedge in front and opening a channel. "At 4:30 got out of the heavy ice," recorded Whittle, "and I trust we may never see any more." Mason observed that the first lieutenant had a wholesome terror of ice and was much excited, but as soon as a little calm was restored, things went quietly enough. This ice had been larger and thicker, he thought, than even in the Arctic. After splicing the main brace, the exhausted midshipman turned in. Lining was truly thankful to be safe and went to bed hoping never again to see ice. They proceeded under steam the rest of the day, piling it on to get south, "but at an expense of how much coal?"

The rudder chains were mended. Waddell concluded that impact with the ice had bent the pintles and gudgeons (pins and brackets supporting the rudder), finally curing the worrisome thumping they had endured for so long, but he considered this a pretty severe remedy. Routine returned as *Shenandoah* continued back across the Bering Sea. On Sunday the crew mustered and was read the Articles; the first lieutenant read in his room and prayed. "We are beginning now to have night, as in days of yore. I shall be very much rejoiced when we get out on the broad Pacific once more. I shall hail it with joy." On the Fourth of July, Whittle expressed his bitterness:

> Who can celebrate [the Fourth]? Can the Northern people, who now are, and for four years have been waging an unjust, cruel, relentless & inhuman war upon us, to take from us the very independence, the declaration of which 90 years ago, made this a day to be gloried in[?] . . . I would rather see the most worthless Negro in the whole world rule over us than the Yankees, who I consider a race of cruel, fanatical scoundrels, lost alike to honor, decency, honesty & Christianity. . . . Let us free & arm our slaves; let every old man, every young woman in the South be armed, let their principle, practice & cry be to shoot dead the invader, whenever & wherever he be found, putting their trust in the justice of an Almighty all powerful & all just God.

The doctor was up past eleven o'clock treating his sick captain. Lining noted that another glorious Fourth had rolled around, finding them still struggling to get out of a cold sea and wondering where they would go. "I rather think the 'Shenanigan' is like a dog which has stolen a bone & goes off, its tail between its legs. . . . Will we ever reach Europe?"

Shenandoah pressed on south toward the Aleutian Islands—a vast and barren chain stretching westward from the Alaskan mainland over 1,200 miles and 20° of longitude. Waddell aimed for the Amukta Pass, the largest channel through this dangerous barrier. A flash of blue sky around noon provided three quick sun sights leading to approximate positions, although no two agreed. Then for forty-eight hours, black fog shut out the heavens and everything else beyond fifty yards in any direction. Waddell ran on dead reckoning and hoped the murk would lift in time to see land, should they miss the center of the channel. But he believed that to stop steaming or to run blind in foggy circles near islands encompassed by swirling, irregular currents could prove more deadly than running on direct course from the last observations. "It only required a little nerve." When they should have been about in the center of the pass—and much to everyone's relief—land appeared off either beam, and cross bearings to opposite headlands pinned them to the chart.

On 5 July they shot through the breach into the northern Pacific; off the port bow the desolate volcanic cone of Chagulak Island was spewing a huge column of black smoke. It would be the last land they would see for months. Waddell felt an unbounded sensation of freedom in that vast expanse of water where those who sail are at home. Looking back to where they had seen such hard and dangerous service, he no longer felt trammeled, would no longer hear the masthead lookout cry "Ice ahead." They had run out of gloomy vapor into bright, cheerful, sparkling ocean. "As soon as a hot sun thawed the frosty timbers and rigging of the craft she would be more than a match for anything she might [meet] under canvas." He made sail, hoisted the propeller, hauled fires, and blew water out of the boilers. The next morning a fresh breeze sprang up and she ran briskly on. "All hail it with delight," wrote Whittle as he sent aloft studding sail booms, rove the gear, and set these sails for the first time in weeks. He also began preparations to fight, if needed, by setting up new shot plugs and fuses for the guns, which Lining hoped would never be used.

The doctor observed their nine-month anniversary since leaving Liverpool and, contemplating the fate of those at home, had blues most of the day. The previous evening while reading James Fenimore Cooper's *Deerslayer*, he was carried away to the green country and forgot that he was on board ship, only to be startled to reality by the thud of a brace block. He also returned to navigation starting with Maury's *Physical Geography of the Sea* and then took up the sextant. Chew assumed that the Arctic visit completed their assignment:

"We are now *homeward bound!* That is, to Europe, for when shall I again see home?" He had read newspapers with dates up to 22 April, which deeply affected them all; their country had suffered great reverses and was in perilous condition if not overrun. "Under these circumstances our anxiety may be imagined."

All the capturing and burning had "played the duce" with discipline, noted Mason. It required time to restore normality along with cleaning up, making alterations, and repositioning boats and spare spars. He was deep in *Les Misérables* by Victor Hugo, which was long but so interesting that he didn't mind. The midshipman shaved his beard before the weather warmed and thereby, he thought, caught a bad cold but recovered as temperatures rose. On one calm, clear day, the crew went over the side to paint the hull. Then, with all sails set to royals and studding sails, they were pushed along by a gentle breeze at nine or ten knots. During his watch, Chew would peer over the side at the foam rushing swiftly by, or walk all the way forward and look back at the ship from the forecastle: "What a beautiful sight! Her tall, tapering masts and wide spread canvas reminding me of some large, graceful bird on the wing."

The captain's forty-first birthday on 13 July brought a storm and variable winds from southwest to southeast with heavy seas. Sail was reduced as she ran east under close reefed topsails and reefed foresail, wind on the starboard quarter. It was reported that the ship's cat had gone overboard, which was very bad seaman's luck and undoubtedly brought on the gale. The first lieutenant had not been fond of the feline—he previously had suggested that its loss would not displease him—so now the crew was labeling him a Jonah, a harbinger of bad luck. Suddenly up walked the cat. "No one was more surprised than I," wrote Whittle, "for I thought poor pussy gone. I gave orders to let the cat live. Ship is rolling fearfully but easily being in fine trim."

By invitation as custom required, Waddell celebrated his birthday dinner in the wardroom where the last surviving white tablecloth was spread. Chew thought the cloth gave the wardroom quite a homelike look. The meal consisted of roast shoat, fresh canned meat, vegetables, and all sorts of pies, puddings, and nuts, along with wine, port, and sherry. All hands joined in by splicing the main brace twice, once to drink the captain's health and once to fortify them against the weather. They had not encountered a storm like this for many weeks, so nothing in wardroom or cabins was properly secured and objects were tumbling about. A full slop tub upturned; it set the doctor's room afloat and had to be emptied in the middle of the night. Mason could not sleep as sofas, chairs, tables, trunks, and the like charged around the steerage like a "thousand of brick" making tremendous noise.

In Scales' cabin, the air port was closed but not fastened when a sea struck on that quarter and washed him out of bed. He came into the wardroom in a wet, clinging, night shirt, scratched his head, and declared, "I want to know when I shall get any more dry clothes!" Lining was called out of his bucking bunk at 6 a.m. to treat John Boy after the Hawaiian crushed his hand aloft in the upper gin block of the main topsail halyard. "I only wonder it had not taken it off, as it was, it hurt very severely." Chew awoke with a sore head from tossing about in his bunk, but said there was no sea sickness, "all of us having gotten bravely over that."

Good weather and good breeze returned and so it went, day after day. A few were punished for drinking; an Englishman reenlisted; the crew holystoned, washed, and scrubbed; sails were repaired. Lining treated an ulcer as big as his hand on the leg of a crewmember who was dismissed from duties as crew's cook. Having received additional stores from every capture, Whittle had to break out and restow the after hold for the seventh time. Amid worry and longing, everyone enjoyed warmer weather and welcomed the return of famil-iar contrast between day and night with bright stars in a velvet sky, never seen in the Arctic. The stove was removed from the wardroom. "I don't know how we should have got on without it," concluded Lining.

Whittle cherished Sundays even more, retiring to his cabin to be alone with his God and his letters. "Oh! how I wish that I was a Christian! And why am I not? Why can I not be?" He read the morning and evening services to cheer his poor heart, prayed humbly for guidance, and reflected gloomily on the fate of family, state, and country. "Oh! God teach me to trust in thee!!" But he felt better a few days later: "Today we have had strong breezes and occasional rain, and our noble Shenandoah has skipped merrily along." God was with them in this fine ship and good crew, in their mission, in the winds, and in his months-old missives of encouragement. "I feel more in earnest when I commune with my God and I feel more faith in my prayers being heard, listened to and answered than formerly."

Lining's blues continued, caused by he knew not what. "I don't know when I have felt so sad!" He wandered from wardroom to quarterdeck to take the sun, letting his thoughts wander back to other days and other scenes. The cat's presence nearby encouraged remembrances of past events. "A rainy, disagree-able day, so time hangs heavily on one's hands. Wind is fair, however & the 'Shenanigin' is running like a scared dog, long may she keep it up."

By mid-July, *Shenandoah* was eight hundred miles out in the Pacific, just south of the latitude of San Francisco near the northern edge of the northeast trade winds. Whittle mused that the citizens of that city would have heard nothing of them since the Melbourne visit six months previously and probably assumed the ship was wrecked. But reports of their activities in the Arctic should arrive soon and spread panic. In the meantime, they were booming along thousands of miles from where anyone would be looking for them. The first lieutenant hoped to encounter a vessel from California for news. He prayed that it would be good, contrary to the pessimism of some on board. They had had no word since learning of Lincoln's death. "I trust that none of our people had anything to do with it. If he had been killed in battle it would have been the fate of war; but not to be assassinated."

The crew was exercised at general quarters, firing blank cartridges from the starboard guns. They did remarkably well for the first attempt at broadside, thought Whittle, and for having not practiced. He worried that the 8-inch shell guns would strain the bulwark when fired together, but they recoiled only three or four feet. The captain, however, was not happy. Apparently, complained Chew, he was expecting them to perform in "trained man-of-war style." "No matter, the result will be a little more drill in future."

––––––––––

On 20 July *Milo* sailed through the Golden Gate with two hundred refugees. "Wholesale Destruction of American Whalers," trumpeted the *San Francisco Bulletin*, "Probable Destruction of Another Fleet of Sixty Whalers." "The most extensive and wholesale destruction of American shipping yet committed by any rebel pirate since the beginning of the war." The *Bulletin* opined the next morning that "this modern Viking," having proceeded despite information of Lee's surrender, was not waging honorable warfare, but was simply moved by "a diabolical desire to plunder and destroy." The commandant of the Mare Island Navy Yard reported, "Great apprehensions felt by mercantile community of San Francisco." Ship owners and underwriters requested authority to charter, arm, and man the fast Pacific Mail Company steamer *Colorado* to pursue *Shenandoah*.[1]

––––––––––

Breezes gradually freshened, coming on in squalls; the squalls producing fog. *Shenandoah* was flying along close to the wind, all sails set including staysails and royals, with the high sails filling most of the time. A heave of the log ran out the line at 12 and 13 knots—better sailing, noted Whittle, than they had ever done, "This is fine work." He was convinced that she would have done 15 or 16 knots with the same wind two points abaft the beam and yards braced in a little. Chew: "What fine winds we are having!" Lining: "Keep it up old girl!" On 24 July the noon-to-noon run was 249 nautical miles, a respectable 10.4 knots per hour.

They were rather high up to be catching the trades, thought Mason, but it was magnificent sailing. The midshipman longed for a prize with recent news, but, he groused, *Shenandoah* was well clear of trade routes to Hawaii and China and too far off the coast to meet mail steamers. Waddell seemed determined to get round the Horn quickly without seeking more captures, which would be just a matter of luck along this track. "The skipper of course must know best, but I think we might make the attempt." In his postwar report, Waddell claimed the intention to run along the coast with the north wind sweeping down lower California, looking for enemy cruisers and for packets on the Panama to San Francisco run. (He added in his later memoirs, "I had matured plans for entering the harbor of San Francisco and laying that city under contribution." There is no other evidence for such a plan.)

By this time, Waddell noted, "the ship had . . . lost that cold, cheerless aspect" which circumstances had imposed upon her in higher latitudes." Her decks once more were places of resort where sailors took shelter under the bulwarks from scorching tropical heat while thirty-seven head of live hogs sunned themselves. The captain had seen Jack scratch a hog to sleep in order to use him as a pillow. "A sailor bathes all over every morning, and that is cleanliness; but he is nevertheless a dirty fellow." The trades began dissipating into calms and baffling winds of the Doldrums. They snagged a four-foot shark and had him for dinner. By the end of the month, it was dead calm and disagreeably hot.[2]

The packet steamer *America* rushed from San Francisco to Acapulco, arriving on 29 July to notify Pacific Squadron commander Admiral G. F. Pearson of *Shenandoah*'s activities. With eight vessels, two of them sailing ships, Pearson was protecting U.S. citizens and property along the entire Pacific Coast of the Americas and in Hawaiian waters. Warships watched Acapulco, the Gulf of California, and Panama; sources of trouble included French efforts to conquer Mexico for Napoleon III. Pearson immediately dispatched the powerful side-wheel frigate *Saranac* (San Franciscans regarded her as the only available warship able to "cope with the *Shenandoah* in point of speed") and gunboat *Suwanee* on a months-long futile search to the north and west. From British Columbia to Samoa and Hawaii, both vessels would seek the rebel pirate, which was at this moment almost due west of them about a thousand miles and headed southeast. On 1 August *General Pike* reached San Francisco with refugees from seven more victims.[3]

On the evening of 2 August 1865, Whittle wrote, "The darkest day of my life. The past is gone for naught—the future is dark as the blackest night. Oh! God protect and comfort us I pray." They had encountered the English bark *Barracouta*, thirteen days from San Francisco bound for Liverpool and carrying newspapers only two weeks old that confirmed the worst: They had no country, no flag, no home. "We have lost all but our honor & self respect, and I hope our trust in God Almighty. . . . Were it not for my dear ones at home, I would rather die than live. Nearly all our work in the Arctic must have been done after this terrible visitation, but God knows we were ignorant. . . . My heart bleeds in anguish." He feared that his father, Captain Whittle, would be excluded from amnesty, imprisoned, or executed, and prayed that his army brother, Beverley, may be spared. His five sisters and two little brothers had no means or property and might starve. He could do nothing. "'I have been young, and now am old, but never have I seen the righteous man forsaken, or his children begging bread.' [Psalm 37:25] Let this be my motto until I can get safely to some port. Oh! God protect them for Christ's sake. I am almost mad, and will lay down my pen."

Scales entered official notice in the ship's log: "Having received . . . the sad intelligence of the overthrow of the Confederate Government, all attempts to destroy the shipping or property of the United States will cease from this date." Thus the captain ordered the first lieutenant "to strike below the battery and disarm the ship and crew." Wrote Chew, "The curtain has dropped, the bloody tragedy has finished. We are *Exiles!* A few particulars only have reached us with the overwhelming; the awful end. Our situation is very peculiar and very dangerous." Belligerents' rights were withdrawn, noted Mason; they were a ship with no government—"a novel position!" Vessels under the Confederate flag would be declared pirates, which any man-of-war could capture. "We were certainly a blue looking set. None of us able to fix our minds on reading or writing, were wandering about the ship with the most doleful countenances or sitting in knots about the deck talking over the dreadful news."

"Every man felt as though he had just learned of the death of a near and dear relative," recalled Hunt. Lining: "From today I must look forward *to begin life over again* starting where I cannot tell, how I cannot say, but I have learned for a certainty that I have *no country*. . . . Thus ends our dream! But I am too sad to think of it." The news cast a deep stillness over the ship's company, wrote Waddell. "My life had been checkered, and I was tutored to disappointment." But still, he had his duty, involving both personal honor and the honor of the flag entrusted to him, "which had been thus far triumphant."[4]

The propeller was hoisted and all plain sail set. Differences arose immediately over two questions. First, would Waddell be justified in destroying the ship or were they bound to give her up? Proponents of the first option said the war was over, the government and nation destroyed. *Shenandoah* was the last remnant of the old Confederacy, so why not blow her up and go ashore in a foreign land? On the other hand, maintained others, *Shenandoah* was the lawful prize of the enemy. Honor demanded that they proceed to an American port, deliver ship and their persons, and suffer the consequences. When Waddell half-heartedly broached that alternative, the doctor considered it a queer idea. However, there was a medium course: proceed to an English or French port and give up the vessel, which was public property, but not their persons, which belonged to no government. They were not bound to surrender themselves. This was agreed upon.

If they must give her up, the second question went, in what port would it be most advisable to do so? The captain and some officers initially favored Sidney from where they could take passage for England, thinking they would be less liable to capture en route and they could be confident of a warm reception upon arrival. The course was set accordingly. The next morning, however, Waddell changed course literally and figuratively, saying that it was nonsense to think of Australia, where they would be turned loose penniless. Paymaster Smith and Sailing Master Bulloch begged for Sidney, but it was no use. "He had made up his mind to go to Liverpool," wrote Lining, "he said he would be damned if he did not take her there." But why, asked the doctor in his journal, would Liverpool be any better than Sidney, in addition to the increased risk in transit? Mason was for Liverpool, believing the chance of capture minimal. The midshipman acknowledged Waddell's difficult and embarrassing position and did not envy him, but felt obliged to confess (to his journal) that their captain was "not the firmest, or most decided man alive." He vacillated, was never positive about anything, and was always afraid of doing too much or too little. "This morning when he spoke to several of us on the poop, his voice was thick & tears stood in his eyes. I was truly sorry for the poor man."

After the war, Waddell justified the long gauntlet of 17,000 miles to England: "Why should I not succeed in baffling observation or pursuit! There was everything to gain and only imaginary dangers." They had traversed over 40,000 miles without incident—searchers would be out in the Pacific not the Atlantic. The captain was determined to avoid any appearance of fear and to uphold the honor and duty of all concerned, and so, on this occasion, he made the decision without convening a conference of officers. Meanwhile, Lining pondered the fate of old and young ones at home: "I had the first hearty cry I have had for many a day. What will they do? How can they get on? Merciful God protect them, for in thee must be their only hope now!"

Going slowly and sorrowfully along with a light breeze, Whittle undertook what he considered his most painful piece of work. Purchases were rigged from the masthead, guns dismounted and lowered into the holds along with their carriages. Crewmen unrigged the purchases, swept down the decks, spliced the main brace, and were finished in less than three hours. As evening sun descended, all pistols were fired off and sent down along with the cutlasses to be locked up in the spirit room under Mason's charge. "Sic transit gloria mundi," he noted. "Our old ship is now as harmless as a woman without finger nails or teeth." Later, even the two signal guns—part of original *Sea King* equipment and for which they had only a single shot—were struck below. Gunports were sealed and the smokestack whitewashed to give the appearance of a peaceful trader.

With nothing warlike remaining on deck, it was beautifully clear for working the ship, noted Mason. "It's an ill wind that blows no body good." He longed for news of home—were Tom, Uncle R., and other dear friends and relatives alive, dead, wounded, or in prison? "The suspense is awful and I pray God that our passage may be a swift one." They would receive little mercy if captured. "If the worst comes to the worst however, I think I could hang as gracefully as any other man, though I must confess the idea is unpleasant & when I think of it, I feel a sort of choking sensation. And thus, after four long years of fighting, hardships &c. it has pleased the Almighty that we should be crushed." At that moment, the midshipman might have recalled his casual dinner conversation at the Melbourne Club with Dr. Barker concerning the advantages of placing the hangman's knot behind the neck.

Friday was a day of light airs and calms. Troubled crewmen presented a petition asking Waddell's intentions and respectfully requesting to be landed in the nearest English port. "However, if you think it best to go to Liverpool or any other port in England, we are, as heretofore, respectfully obedient to your commands." After dinner, all hands assembled aft for a speech by the captain, which Mason recorded. "My men, I have received your communication which is a very proper one," said Waddell. The South had indeed been subdued, but the position of the officers was far worse than that of any of the crew. "I shall take the ship into the *nearest* English port and all I have to ask of you, men, is to stand by me to the last. As for our cruise, it is a record which stands for itself & all you have to do is to be proud of it. I will share your fate, my brave men." Cries arose from all sides: "We are!" "We will be!" "We will stand by you Captain."

The speech had been delivered with much feeling, thought Mason. He observed several officers and men shedding tears while everyone seemed more or less affected, but he did not "exactly cry." The midshipman was gratified to see the crew behave so well under the circumstances and apologized to his journal for criticizing the captain. "I was too hard on the old gent." Chew and Lining seconded this account. Chew also praised the crew's conduct as noble and worthy of highest regard. Although they were of all nations and supposedly joined only for good pay—of which they now might receive little or nothing—no insubordination or disrespect manifested itself. "The crew to a man felt great sympathy for us, and if there is any change in their conducts, they are more respectful & polite."

However, painful uncertainty prevailed among the officers with respect to their destination. Some favored rounding the Horn, crossing the South Atlantic, and ending the cruise in Cape Town, South Africa, as passage to Europe would be easier from there than from Australia. In his memoirs, Master's Mate

Hunt accused Waddell of duplicity and greed, claiming to speak from personal knowledge that the captain's decision to go to Liverpool was an unnecessary risk "for the sake of securing a considerable sum of money which he knew to be lodged in the hands of one of our secret agents at Liverpool." (The availability of funds from James Bulloch in Liverpool to pay officers and crew what was due them would have been an element in Waddell's thinking, but there is no evidence of a conspiracy to acquire a "considerable sum." Subsequent events do not support this charge.) Lining reported that Hunt was sewing discord among the men by telling them that they would be paid only one shilling on the pound and by generating "hard talk" on the berth deck. Whittle then gave Hunt a talking-to and confined him to quarters.[5]

Chapter 18

"A Feeling Approaching Panic"

Shenandoah was no longer a warship. The captain still had supreme authority but presumably without naval discipline. She was sailed and maintained as usual and daily inspections were held. They beat against headwinds or steamed for days, struggling to make southing before crossing the equator on 17 August. The southeast trades were stormy, but good runs averaged 180 to 200 miles per day. Mason and Lining fussed that they could do better if the captain had the nerve to hold onto his canvas at night, which he did not do for fear of squalls. Scales suggested that the doctor administer a couple of drinks so Waddell would "carry sail until everything is blue." *Shenandoah* passed once more out of the torrid into the southern temperate zone, where winds became baffling and changeable with occasional moderate gales; then the cold returned along with heavy weather clothing and the little stove in the wardroom.

Waddell relieved Scales and Lee from duty for minor infractions of smoking on watch and oversleeping and then insulted them further by proposing to assign "clerk" Blacker as an officer of the watch. Confronted by a barrage of complaints, reported Lining, the captain seemed flummoxed and once more backed off. "So ended this row, in which like so many others the captain has come out to leeward. Weather getting right cold." The doctor's days consisted of eating, sleeping, loafing, and conversing with his messmates whose hands and fingers were sore from sewing shore bags and clothing. He treated Waddell for a painful stiff neck, had him sitting up all day, and at night administered to him a strong punch, "a hot toddy." The captain's swinging cot fell off its hook in the midwatch one night, which could not have helped either his neck or his disposition. Lining read a travel book by Daniel Webster, reviving an old desire to visit Spain, "which now alas! I see no prospect of gratifying!" He returned to studying navigation by making a chart of South America and a set of navigation dividers from walrus tusk.

On Lining's recommendation, the captain relieved Assistant Surgeon McNulty from duties for chronic drunkenness and stopped the source—the liquor allowance of all steerage officers: "A pretty state of affairs!" Hammocks were back in vogue in place of bunks for the seas around the Horn. Scales made a hammock and hung it in the wardroom with the approval of his messmates, but Waddell ordered it removed because it blocked his passing through to his cabin. The doctor was beyond complaining about the captain's invasion of the officers' private domain: "I am not particularly or individually interested & I hope soon to get out of this ship." Mason occupied himself with duties and reading, which included histories of the Reformation and France and Hume's *History of England* along with novels. But for him, twelve months at sea had destroyed all the romance of a sailor's life: the constant confinement and the "total deprivation of the society of females, which has so softening an influence on all men," along with miserable diet and other privations appreciated by only those who have experienced them. How much worse for the common sailor, he thought.

During stormy weather, complained Mason, one heard nothing but the old sail-handling cries: "Royal clewlines!" "Flying jib downhaul!" "Royal sheets!" "Flying jib halliards!" and the like. Chain sheets rattled against steel yards, men tramped and hauled, blocks screeched, the boatswain mate's hoarse voice shouted orders accompanied by an occasional yell from aloft. He was sick and tired of being knocked about when lying or sitting and of always walking on a continually changing inclined plane. He never wanted to hear a boatswain's whistle again. "It is about the only *music* we have, except perhaps some wretched accordion, horribly performed on by some amateur artist." Being officer in charge of the hold was not fun either. Empty beef barrels had to be put down on the ground tier and filled with seawater for ballast, a great deal of trouble. Mason considered resuming the study of navigation but had no intention of using the knowledge. "Certainly, if I can make an honest living anywhere else, I shall not [return to sea]." Nor did he wish to be put ashore at Cape Town where he could be delayed for months without funds for a steamer to England.

Paymaster Smith and Lieutenant Chew celebrated their twenty-fourth birthdays in the same week. "We are I expect the youngest set of officers who ever went to sea," concluded Whittle. But he now had little to say about the concerns of his fellow officers, and he withdrew from competition with his commanding officer. Career ambitions now meant little, so Whittle focused on duties while clinging to honor, self-respect, and love for family with all else gone. "I feel so melancholy that I can scarcely keep a cheerful face. . . . Oh! what a trial it is to think that I may never be in a position pecuniarily to ask [Pattie] to be mine." In one journal entry, a few scratched out words still can be read: "I have lost her. I can never love another."

––––––––––

The British secretary of state for the colonies issued a circular on 7 September directing that *Shenandoah* be detained in any British port she may enter, by force if necessary, if "sufficient force to command obedience" was at hand.

Colonial authorities were to deliver to her captain Commander Bulloch's previously forwarded letter, and to state that it was incumbent on him to deliver up vessel and armament to them. They were to prohibit any supplies of any description to the vessel, "so as to give her no facilities whatever for going to sea."[1]

––––––

Whittle took pleasure in sailing *Shenandoah*, not least because she was carrying them homeward. On 8 September she furrowed the ocean at between fourteen and sixteen knots for several hours without her royals. "This is fine work." The next day, she averaged eleven knots in a brisk southwesterly and would have done better had it not been for the opposing current. "That is the best she has ever made with us." Provisions were running down so they were eating mostly cured meat. "I would be ashamed to look at a salted pig or cow in the face." As stores were consumed, the ship lightened and rose in the water making stability a concern, but having the guns below helped. "All will be well, if God so wills it. Trust in him."

Finally approaching the Horn and once again in the stormy roaring forties between 40° and 50° south latitude, they battened down in anticipation of harsh westerly winds, preparing to turn eastward under the icy tailbone of America. Studdingsail booms and royal yards were sent down, the flying jib unbent. Some complained that these precautions would impede progress and lose time, wrote Mason. "This is the all absorbing theme of conversation, morning, noon, & night."

On 12 September, at 54° south, the first ship since *Barracouta* was sighted ten miles off the starboard quarter, heading eastward with them but sailing higher up into the wind. She appeared to be a six-topsail-yarder; some thought she flew fore and main skysails above royals and studding sails. These homeless Confederates still had their pride, so in a fresh breeze they sent back up and set royals and staysails. Through the day and the night, however, *Shenandoah* was easily overtaken and passed. "She walked right away from us most shamefully," wrote Whittle. Lining declared, "Never did I expect to be beaten in such a shameful manner by any ship short of a first class extreme clipper!" Waddell attributed this poor performance to accumulation of weed on the bottom, "an unpleasant circumstance, for it might require all her fleetness to escape a Federal cruiser." Other vessels passed in the opposite direction, one identifying herself as the English ship *West Australian*, Cardiff to Valparaiso. Signals were not returned. The wind increased by night, noted Lining, but no sails were taken in, and, in fact, they were carrying more than ever.

Whittle's entry of 15 September noted, "Today we passed Cape Horn, and we got a tartar." A fresh gale slammed in from north-northwest in beautifully clear weather with heavy seas and quite cold. Given the good conditions so far,

Mason had hoped to double the Horn without reducing sail, but no such luck. He was furling and reefing the entire midwatch; the fore royal halyard parted, bringing the yard crashing down in the topmast rigging, but they were able to secure it. The yard could have gone on down through the deck and thrown two or three sailors overboard. No bones were broken but two men had the flesh torn from their hands by running ropes. As the ship rolled in the night Lieutenant Lee's dog, closed in the wardroom, started howling, much to the disgust of sleepers. Nothing else amusing going on, noted Lining, except that Grimball and Bulloch were doused by a big sea coming over the rail as they scrambled up the rigging.

Gunmetal seas tossed *Shenandoah* around through bitter cold rain and intermittent squalls from glowering cloud cover, drenching everyone on deck. "Everything uncomfortable, no pleasure at meals or anywhere else," wrote Mason. They intended to sail northward for the Falkland Islands; but under minimal sail and close hauled against northerly winds, they were driven eastward instead. Lining spent most of the day in bed with a cold and cough, the only place he could keep warm and comfortable. Whittle worried about fetching up on the Georgian Islands and Shag Rocks southeast of the Falklands. "O! how I wish that our dear ones could know that we are still in the 'water of the living.' I have no doubt that a great many think us lost."

Their old enemy, ice, appeared—small pieces at first and then large bergs, some quite close. The big ones carried along their own fog banks and bitter cold air. Mason was glad for the opportunity to see them. He estimated one at less than two miles off with a church-spire pinnacle soaring to three hundred feet and breaking seas throwing spray fifty feet in the air. "The sun shining on this white sparkling surface had a very pretty effect." Mason was less enthused about standing ice lookout forward on the forecastle. "I verily believe that if [Waddell and Whittle] live to get through this cruise, they will be shy of ice-cream even, forever afterwards." The midshipman reported on deck without oilskins and caught the first sea coming over the rail—it was too late then so he stuck it out. Wind increased to half a gale as wave after frigid wave swept the forecastle with the lee rail underwater most of the time. Mason was drenched to the skin, half-blinded by wind and salt water, and "mad & cross as a bear with a sore head." Icebergs glided by, which, according to Lining, were entirely too thick to make navigation safe or comfortable: "It would be dreadful to run into one of these things out here after escaping so well in the Arctic."

As head seas went down and wind moderated, more canvas was set. They were comparatively comfortable but still conflicted as to destination. Those wishing to go to Cape Town watched easterly change in longitude; those for England watched northerly change in latitude. Mason again criticized the captain for inconsistency and vacillation. Chew's twenty-fourth birthday passed as they hauled northward through intermittent gales, heading up the Atlantic under every possible stitch and turning their backs on ice and cold. But returning fair weather did not moderate the brewing storm within.

On 28 September the captain received a petition signed by Lieutenant Chew, Sailing Master Bulloch, Chief Engineer O'Brien, Paymaster Smith, Surgeon Lining, and Midshipman Browne expressing "anxiety and regret" concerning passage to a country so distant as England. The "present unparalleled state of affairs" had rendered the vessel defenseless, at the mercy of any passing cruiser. "We regard with a proper horror any prospect of capture or imprisonment," with no access to amenities usually granted to prisoners of war. It was a well-known fact that U.S. authorities "frequently, almost generally, treated our prisoners with great rigor and severity. How much more will such be the case now that the war has concluded in the manner that it has!"[2]

The risks of proceeding to Cape Town would be comparatively small; the letter continued in considerable and emotional detail, suggesting that all on board should be given a choice with the majority deciding and intimating that the majority would prefer Cape Town. The signers wished it understood that they acted from a sense of duty. "We distinctly disclaim any intention or desire to trammel your judgment or interfere with your functions. We have the honor to be, very respectfully, your obedient servants." Mason characterized it as a "lengthy, profuse and remarkable" communication, which had been drawn up by Smith, "a shrewd, thinking man" who had studied law. Because he was asked, Lining signed the letter, but did so reluctantly; he believed the captain's mind was made up for Liverpool.[3]

Waddell received a similar petition prepared by John Blacker and signed by all junior officers in the steerage except Master's Mate Hunt, Midshipman Mason, and Midshipman Browne. "We cannot reasonably expect any good treatment if we fall into the hands of [the] U.S. Government." It complained that the ship was unstable and would not be safe in North Atlantic gales, "a most dangerous condition." If the captain bypassed Cape Town, signatories requested to be landed somewhere on the African coast, "which we would infinitely prefer to the chances of capture or shipwreck." The letter laid aside all ranks and titles, noted Mason, and, in his opinion, was disrespectful, dictatorial, and insubordinate. A ship was not a democracy; petitions were close to mutiny. "This was the worst, the most pusillanimous part of the whole affair." Both missives expounded on the probabilities of capture with "wholesome terror and painted in the liveliest colors."[4]

The captain summoned a council of his five lieutenants, laid the two letters before them, and left the cabin. It was a stormy session. Whittle preferred Cape Town but would go wherever the captain and others decided; Chew reiterated his desire for Cape Town while Grimball, Lee, and Scales voted for Liverpool, thus deciding the issue on a majority. Lining considered this the smartest move Waddell ever made. The topic had been openly, loudly, and angrily discussed; the captain knew beforehand all opinions, and he excluded from the meeting those—the doctor and Bulloch among them—who had participated in previous consultations. So Waddell knew it would be settled as he wished while throwing responsibility on the council and saying coolly, "Gentlemen I will be guided by you." Lining regretted that he had revealed his position in the first letter. "Loud were the cries of the Cape Town men about this decision," wrote Mason, who thought it should have been resolved with more discretion, but the affair was all over the ship before the documents reached the captain's hands.

More than seventy petty officers and crewmen prepared their own petition expressing "complete denial" of the first letter and its object, and of petitioning him "on such a subject whatsoever." They wished to show "complete reliance and trust in whatever it should please you to do under any circumstances." Mason thought they had good reasons for not wishing to go to Cape Town: the uncertainty of being paid off, the difficulty of getting employment, and the virtual impossibility of getting away from there. This communication was, Mason concluded, perfectly subordinate and respectful. He believed that other crewmembers were of the same opinion, but sharing a revulsion for petitions, did not sign it. The letter was addressed in due form to Lieutenant Commanding James I. Waddell, CSS *Shenandoah*.[5]

At breakfast the next morning, wrote Mason, everyone looked as black as midnight. "I scarcely dared speak to any of the Cape Town crowd." Even Breedlove Smith, always so cool, could not conceal his disappointment and wounded pride. Mason, on the other hand, felt immense satisfaction. He, along with Lee, Grimball, Scales, and Assistant Surgeon McNulty, prepared yet another missive as officers of the Confederate States navy, addressed properly to the captain through the first lieutenant, expressing their "unqualified approbation of the course you have determined upon. Be the fortune of war and shipwreck in our passage (which appears to excite so much uneasiness in some) what they may, we consider either England or France the only proper destination for the *Shenandoah*."[6]

Whittle noted "a feeling approaching panic" among Cape Town proponents, which he considered disgraceful: "Some look as though they had already been hung." In the name of honor, birth, and property, he continued, they should support the captain. Could they not stand their fate, unjust as it might be, like men? "No! Let us throw aside this childishness" and trust in God. They had done their work nobly and honorably; the struggle had ended by divine will. Papers and petitions were not his forte, and as executive officer, Whittle would have nothing to do with them. The captain had his support in all things except one—any attempt to go to a Yankee port. "I am very sorry to see so much temper shown on both sides."

That night they crossed their outbound track of exactly ten months previous after traveling 45,000 statute miles. Waddell sent a bottle of champagne into the wardroom at dinnertime with a note of congratulation for circumnavigating the globe. Sailing Master Bulloch, Engineer O'Brien, and Paymaster Smith walked out, refusing to share the wine in protest of the Liverpool decision. To Mason, this was exceedingly bad taste. The captain had been actuated by the best motives, having saved this bottle for the occasion, "little dreaming what unpleasant circumstances would attend the event." Lining, still suffering from a headache and troublesome cough, believed the captain's gesture was kindly and politely meant.

On through October with bright sun, smooth sea, and fair tropic winds, the unhappy ship sailed back across the equator. Light winds of the Doldrums slowed them down, but the engine could be used only sparingly; what heavy coal remained below was needed as ballast.

The frosty atmosphere in the wardroom thawed, but did not regain its original camaraderie. Whittle continued to fret over the fate of his father: "Have they bathed his silvery locks with blood[?]" Had his army brother been slain? Were his younger brothers and sister suffering from want of food? "These thoughts harrow my brain. . . . God alone can tell. He alone can afflict, and He alone can comfort when afflicted!" Lining had a long talk with the gloomy first lieutenant, considering him the most to be pitied on account of his family.

———

On 6 October Foreign Secretary John Russell obtained information that *Shenandoah* had continued her "captures and depredations on the high seas" after having been appraised that the flag had ceased to be recognized. He instructed the Admiralty that Her Majesty's ships of war were to forcibly detain said vessel anywhere encountered and deliver it to the nearest U.S. authority ashore or afloat; the crew, however, should be allowed to go free. The source of the information is not specified, but it has the ring of U.S. minister Adams' work.[7]

———

"The passion now is for puzzles," wrote Mason, "and you would be surprised to see how everyone is amused by the most simple thing, so little have we to occupy our minds." On the anniversary of their departure, 9 October, Lining looked back on the year as a dream. What changes will be found? Who was dead? Who married? Who will remember him? With no means of support, what will be his prospects? He had nothing to look forward to except hard work and a cold shoulder from former friends. "But I have youth & strength, & if my health is only spared me I will get along yet, even if I have to work my hands bare for it."

Condensing of freshwater was curtailed to save coal—the daily allowance cut to two-thirds, about ninety-nine gallons per day for 134 men. The crew had no water for washing and no coffee in the morning watch; but grog three times a day was a good substitute. Strangely no rain had fallen since the ship entered the tropics. All sorts of canvas pieces were suspended in the rigging to catch any drop that might descend.

Assistant Surgeon McNulty again got boisterously drunk, insulted fellow Irish Catholic John Blacker by calling him an "English-Irish Orangeman," and pulled a pistol on Whittle before being restrained. (Mason thought the disagreement involved the selling of oranges until the Irish problem was explained to him.) McNulty blamed Blacker and Whittle for the confrontation. The captain seemed to give credence to McNulty's excuses, which put Whittle in a towering passion. He called the Irishman a liar and was challenged in return for "satisfaction as is looked for between gentlemen." Despite his opposition to dueling, honor demanded from him a response. The first lieutenant concluded, however—with encouragement from the doctor—that it would set a bad example. He himself had punished men for fighting, and there was danger of hitting someone else in a crowded and rolling ship. The parties agreed to settle as soon as they reached port. "So ends for the present this disagreeable business," concluded Lining. "I, for one, hope it may never go any further."

Occasional vessels were sighted and some passed close aboard, but there were no attempts to communicate and no respectful raising and dipping of the flag. One sail was reported on a converging track, which from its rig and behavior could have been a warship. After dark, Waddell extinguished all lights, wore ship, got up steam, took in sail, and steamed dead to windward for sixteen miles before returning to course, intending that the stranger should see only an empty horizon at dawn. "Everything looks as nice as a new pin," wrote Mason, as all hands were employed painting inside and out, "but afterwards we do not feel the same interest in things as we did before." Waddell once more harassed his officers with petty regulations, forbidding them to sit on watch, which Lining thought was ridiculous. The doctor discovered a multitude of bedbugs and applied alcohol all over his bunk to discourage them.

The northeast trades wafted them along in delightful weather through *Shenandoah's* birthday, 18 October. Light hearts and high hopes were long gone, thought Lining. "Our ship is fast becoming a perfect hell afloat, & only wants a few more quarrels in the ward room to become entirely so." Arguments in the steerage were audible in the wardroom; one spree turned into a general drunk ending in a brawl. "There are some awful hurting eyes this morning, [and] I dare say a good many swelled heads." The crew, however, seemed relaxed. Lee assembled the men by the main hatch one evening, provided some whisky, and set them dancing until after nine o'clock. Among the crew were two or three accomplished dancers, one of whom had performed on stage in San Francisco. On another night, three Hawaiians entertained the officers with sweet singing. Mason listened as he wrote in his journal with the wardroom door open, but the Hawaiian dancing was, according to Lining, execrable.

A few cases of scurvy developed, a condition Whittle considered disgusting and often fatal; the doctor hoped it would not spread. Seaman William Bill, a native of Maui, had long suffered from venereal disease, was covered with ulcers about the throat and chest, and had all the symptoms of "sub-acute inflammation of the brain & chest." He died so easily and suddenly that those with him thought he was asleep. Bill was sewn up in canvas containing two 8-inch shot and laid on the lee side of the poop with a watch over him through the night. The following morning at 9:15, all hands were called aft. Waddell read the service and the seaman was committed to the deep. "We half masted our poor down trodden flag," wrote Whittle. "At all times a burial is sad, but particularly at sea. And when I saw our poor flag weeping I could but be plunged into the depths of thought connected with it which made me still more melancholy." They were a little north of the latitude of his home in Norfolk, Virginia, and about two thousand miles eastward. "How much would I not give to be there now!" Mason did not feel particularly affected by his first sea burial: "I don't think a tear was shed for the poor fellow."

Fresh breezes with intermittent squalls and heavy seas pushed them rapidly northward of the Azores. Marine Sergeant Canning's old chest wound from Shiloh opened up; he had been declining for several weeks. The doctor diagnosed the problem as phthisis—a wasting away of part of the body. Canning quietly expired on the evening of 31 October. In the morning, the solemn call of "All Hands to bury the dead" brought the crew aft again where McNulty read the Catholic burial service and Canning was dropped over the side to join William Bill—the only deaths, friend or foe, during the cruise.

By 2 November they were about four hundred miles and perhaps four days from the southeastern tip of Ireland. Waddell ordered steam up and propeller lowered. Whittle did not look forward to their arrival with as much hope and good cheer as the others: "I feel that we are men with something awful hanging over us." They would be safe from capture inside English territorial waters, but when dealing with governments, he had little faith that honor would prevail over interest; the English might acquiesce to Yankee threats and hand over the former rebels. He ordered a thorough holystoning of the spar deck and thought it looked good.

Waddell commenced paying officers and crew with English gold and American coin captured prior to surrender of Southern armies. They were owed some $30,000 but only $4,000 was available minus pilotage fees, leaving about fourteen cents on the dollar. There was little grumbling among the crew, however. The captain complimented them on their good conduct during the cruise and added, "You have gained a name by serving in this vessel that will never be forgotten. Your acts will be talked of all over Europe." He promised them he would personally attempt to procure from grateful Southerners residing in Liverpool the remainder due them. Chew reported his share as $90. Whittle received $45.90 of $360 due, probably the last money he would see for a long time. All he wanted was enough to live on and support his family. "Where there is a will there is a way"; he would not starve. Lining was paid $77.26 of $547.19. The doctor heard rumors that crewmembers were getting drunk and intended to come aft to demand all that was due them. "But all this is bosh! The men are too near England if nothing else to attempt such a thing. Besides they know the officers too well to attempt it."[8]

Chew was counting the hours to the dropping of the anchor and blessed the engine for moving them onward despite light and fickle breezes. "The thoughts of getting ashore fill me with strange emotions; I can hardly realize it." He should have been eagerly anticipating letters from home but did not expect any. Upon departure over a year earlier, and not knowing where the ship would be, he had requested family and friends not to write. He also had expected the cruise to terminate in a port of the Confederate states. "How greatly I have been mistaken; we are about to enter Liverpool with everything lost save honor." Dr. Lining lay awake most of the night, his mind crowded with thoughts of arrival, an affliction now referred to as "channel fever."

On the morning of 5 November, they entered St. George's Channel with Ireland to port and Wales to starboard. The 116-foot white tower of Tuskar Lighthouse appeared through the mist on a bare rock seven miles off the Irish coast. "I cannot describe with what pleasure we again looked upon land, after having been so long out of sight of it," wrote Chew. The last bits of Mother Earth they had seen were the snowcapped peaks of the Aleutian Islands, 122 days of nothing but "sea & sky, ice, gales, and calms." The Emerald Isle floated by the whole day and many vessels passed, the majority outward bound. Lining surveyed lady passengers on one ship, "the first petticoats I have seen for many a day." As dusk gathered, attentive watch was kept for navigation lights along the channel; rockets were fired and blue lights lighted to signal for a pilot. Chew admitted to his journal that he had had enough of hardship, anxiety, discomfort, and separation from home and friends. "Man has adapted many strange and unnatural habits, and this going to sea is one of them; henceforth, ships, sea gales, squalls, calms, long, weary four hour watches, royal clewlines &c farewell!!! And you 'salt horse and hardtack,' may I never be found to eat you again!" He was resolved to earn his bread on land however laborious it may be, and only if reduced to *"stealing or starving"* would he consider returning to sea.

The pilot boat approached and hailed the ship around midnight. To prevent the boat from reporting them in town and raising an alarm, Bulloch responded that they were the merchant vessel *Araminta*. Whittle thought this disgraceful, but Lining considered the precaution quite right. Once on board and appraised of the vessel's true identity, the astonished pilot had little to relate except that the war was over so long that it was no longer news and that he had read a few days earlier of *Shenandoah* in the Arctic. Yet the little information the pilot possessed was a relief to all, for having imagined all sorts of calamities including the execution of Jefferson Davis and other leaders, they had feared the South was suffering much more than apparently was the case.

The pilot explained that tide was past flood so they might not make it over the Mersey River bar until morning. But the ship didn't belong to anyone, so Waddell didn't care; he ordered steam at full speed ahead. Sure enough about 4 a.m., she slid up on the sand and stuck fast. Three hours and three attempts later, with the turn of the tide and the brightening of dawn, they freed her without damage and steamed unobserved upriver through morning haze with the Confederate flag flying at the peak. The anchor dropped at nine o'clock near the guard ship HMS *Donegal*. Customhouse officers boarded and granted entry.

Chapter 19

"Having Done My Duty"

A lieutenant from *Donegal* visited, providing what Waddell recorded as "official intelligence" of termination of the war. "He was very polite toward me, and left me to believe he felt a sympathy for us in our situation." The last Confederate banner was hauled down without ceremony about 10 a.m., 6 November 1865. The captain then dispatched a communication, which had been in careful preparation for several days, to Her Britannic Majesty's minister for foreign affairs: "I have the honor to announce to your lordship my arrival in the waters of the Mersey with this vessel, lately a ship of war, under my command, belonging to the Confederate States of America. The singular position in which I find myself placed and the absence of all precedents on the subject will, I trust, induce your lordship to pardon a hasty reference to a few facts." He had cruised as ordered against the enemy's commerce, eventually in locations so far removed that timely news of the war could not be received. "In consequence of this awkward circumstance I was engaged in the Arctic Ocean in acts of war as late as the 28th day of June, in ignorance of the serious reverses sustained by our arms in the field and the obliteration of the Government under whose authority I have been acting."[1]

He first learned these facts from *Barracouta* on 2 August off the California coast—"Your lordship can imagine my surprise at the receipt of such intelligence"—and he would have given them little consideration then, except the news came from an Englishman. However, to surrender the vessel in an American port simply because the master of *Barracouta* had said the war was ended would not have been intelligent, so he desisted from further acts of war and shaped course for a European port where confirmation could be obtained. He had diligently examined all law writers at his command, searching for a precedent and for guidance in the management and disposal of the vessel. "I could find none. History is, I believe, without a parallel." Waddell did not consider that he had any right to destroy the ship or any further right to command her, and because Confederate States' property had reverted by fortune of war to the government of the United States, this vessel should also. "I therefore sought this port as a suitable one wherein to 'learn the news,' and, if I am without a Government, to surrender the ship with her battery, small arms, machinery, stores, tackle, and apparel, complete, to her Majesty's Government for such disposition as in its wisdom should be deemed proper."[2]

Captain Paynter of *Donegal* informed the Admiralty by telegraph and requested instructions, noting that some *Shenandoah* crewmembers had scurvy and should be landed as soon as possible. The customs officer similarly telegraphed the treasury department; word then bounced over to the Home Office, in whose jurisdiction the vessel now lay, and to the Foreign Office. The Admiralty ordered Paynter to prevent *Shenandoah* from coaling or leaving the port. Having interviewed Waddell, Paynter did not anticipate any such move but would take no chances. The coast guard was notified and artillery batteries in the North Fort at the river entrance were put on alert. Custom authorities returned later in the day to take possession of the ship. Paynter instructed that no one, officers or crew, was to leave until further instructions were received from London. He ordered Lieutenant Cheek commanding the steam gunboat *Goshawk* to lash his vessel alongside *Shenandoah* with fires banked.[3]

Cheek was to maintain sentries on board *Shenandoah*, assist custom officers, and give timely notice of any infringement of the laws of the port. No property that might belong to the American government would be hoisted out and no communications were allowed between the crews of the two vessels. The crew and marines of *Goshawk* were to be kept ready for immediate service. "Should any attempt be made during the night to weigh, or light fires, you are to send up a rocket and burn a blue-light; and the *Donegal* will fire a gun as a precautionary signal to the North Fort."[4]

Waddell informed Lieutenant Cheek and the customs inspector general that he considered himself, the officers, and crew relieved of all further charge and responsibility, and that his authority over the crew was ended. All hands were relieved from duty and allowed to do as they pleased. "The day hung heavily on our hands," wrote Chew, "everything ready to go on shore and not to make a move." He walked the poop and gazed at the shore, but obscured by fog and industrial smoke, it presented "such a cold & uninviting appearance!" As night came on and fog lifted, "chimneys ceased to send forth their dark streams of smoke and thousands of lights peeped out, giving animation to the scene. A promenade on deck was then more pleasant."

With fresh provisions from shore, the officers retired to the wardroom where they ate, sang, laughed, and rejoiced in full bellies. The custom officers were escorted into the steerage and made so roaring drunk that one slept in the scuppers all night. About 8 p.m., a sympathetic Royal Navy captain came off in a steamboat carrying fresh beef, mutton, vegetables, eggs, and cheese for all hands and apples for the sick. For the officers, he brought two casks of beer, one cask each of porter and whisky, along with tea, white sugar, pipes, tobacco, and other luxuries. "His present was the most acceptable that he could possibly have brought," wrote Lining. "[We] spent the rest of the evening most jollily." Chew noted, "[We] banished all thoughts of our condition from our minds. I thought, let us eat, drink and be merry for tomorrow we shall be given up to the U.S.?"

Good spirits prevailed the next morning. Fresh eggs, milk, and other provisions appeared as they lounged through the day watching steamboatloads of people cruising by to gawk "as if we were wild beasts." But time began to pass wearily; boredom and restlessness took over. The crew requested that Lieutenant Cheek allow them to land after nine months at sea, demanding his authority for detaining American subjects. He told them it was not within his power to grant and, with difficulty, persuaded them to remain quiet for a day or two. Lining groused about *Goshawk* alongside: "The ridiculous idea, as if we had not just come off such a sea voyage as to wish to go to sea again." Another boatload of fresh provisions arrived in the evening, but custom officials would not allow them on board. A few officers took "French leave" going ashore overnight without permission while those remaining had their milk punch in the wardroom and invited Cheek and Waddell to join them for refreshment—smoking, drinking, singing songs, and spinning yarns or "cuffers." "We had quite a merry evening of it," concluded Lining. The old customs officer was drunk again.

But *Shenandoah*'s arrival in the Mersey rekindled passions that the British hoped were dying out and generated a slew of correspondence around the government—up to and including cabinet ministers—concerning how to proceed. Primary questions concerned ownership and disposal of the vessel and status of officers and crew. With fervent hopes for a quick and quiet resolution, the foreign minister turned to the law officers of the Crown. Government and press were highly chagrined at this reminder of the recent unpleasantness, complicating already strained relations over rebel cruisers.[5]

U.S. minister Adams respectfully requested that Her Majesty's government take possession of said vessel with a view to delivering it into the hands of his government, "in order that it may be properly secured against any renewal of the audacious and lawless proceedings which have hitherto distinguished its career." Adams maintained that *Shenandoah* had continued her ravages after she ceased to be a belligerent and that British citizens were on board. While not prepared to suggest any particular course of action, he hoped the government would mark his countrymen's "high sense of the flagrant nature of their offenses."[6]

Waddell surrendered a bag of gold and silver valued at $820.38 to the paymaster of *Donegal* for safekeeping and eventual transfer to American authorities. The bag contained coins from vessels captured after Lee's surrender—mostly from Mexico and South America, with some other foreign coins and a few

American and English pieces. Waddell took pains to assert scrupulous and honorable management of funds, and the record offers no evidence to the contrary.

By the third morning, Wednesday, 8 November, there still was no news and no more fresh provisions either. "The thing is being pushed too far now," complained Lining, "it is being rubbed in, and everybody has a 'big disquiet' on & loud talking is going." Bulloch returned from shore early that morning, but Lee did not get back to the ship until 10 a.m. and looked pretty seedy with his hat lost and his knuckles skinned. Where he had been, no one knew. Hunt apparently did not return at all. The crewmen, according to Lieutenant Cheek, were getting riotous. Captain Paynter could only appeal for patience; instructions were expected soon. Chew considered this day ten times worse than the last. "I began to think seriously that we would have to stand a trial in an English court."

Former Confederates visited to cheer them up but did not mollify anyone. As evening approached, most officers were of a mind to leave with or without permission or possessions. Several crewmen departed in civilian dress, swearing they did not belong to the ship. Dr. Lining was determined to remain and treat the scurvy cases no matter the consequences, but began to grow very uneasy. Around dusk, guards were doubled; the dingy was hoisted onto the deck of the gunboat, and orders issued that no boats would come alongside *Shenandoah*. The only exit was across the deck of *Goshawk* with armed sentries posted.

A three-judge panel of law officers (including the eminent Sir Robert Phillimore, whose works Waddell and Semmes had so closely studied) advised the foreign minister that ship and appurtenances should be surrendered to the United States. However, on basis of facts as stated by Waddell and without contravening evidence, there were no grounds for prosecution on charges of piracy. If evidence could be obtained that crewmembers were natural-born British subjects, then proceedings against them should be initiated for breach of the Foreign Enlistment Act. In the absence of warrants for criminal arrest under British law, there were no grounds for preventing *Shenandoah* personnel from "going on shore without restraint and disposing of themselves as they thought fit."[7]

Shenandoah officers sat at supper in the wardroom when a shout was heard on deck as a steam launch bumped alongside with Captain Paynter on board. A number of sailors swarmed on board the launch by the hawsers and attempted to conceal themselves, but were persuaded to return to the ship. Accompanied by his paymaster, Mr. Warwick, Paynter entered Waddell's cabin and asked the former captain on his honor whether he was aware of British subjects among the crew. Waddell assured Paynter that he was not and that he had no evidence, certificates of birth, or nationality tickets, to prove nationality. They were "a desperate and motley set of men," he said, who had been picked up on the high seas and who ran the risk for high wages and prize money. Paynter proceeded to the wardroom and inquired if any of the officers were British subjects. They were not, nor did they think any of the crew were.[8]

Paynter requested that the crew be mustered. (One sailor later testified that the captain sent marines among them saying that they all were to be Southerners when their name was called. Waddell denied it.) Each man passed before Paynter. Most stated—many in English, Scottish, or Irish accents—that they came from one or other of the Southern states. Some were Sandwich Islanders, a few Portuguese, with a smattering of other nationalities. None acknowledged being British, and, judging from their appearance and dress, paymaster Warrick did not think they were. Furthermore, they appeared to him to be in a very excited state at having been held on board without reason or authority. "I have no doubt that any further detention would have resulted in a serious riot." Paynter then read out orders from London that all were to be released who were not British citizens. "With what joy it was received!! The men cheered heartily," wrote Chew.[9]

Paynter was required to justify these proceedings following pointed allegations of prevarication from Minister Adams. The British captain vented his spleen: it was nearly impossible, he explained, to ascertain with certainty the nationality or birthplace of such seamen. The enormous shipping trade with America and the facility with which American naturalization papers could be obtained obscured the issue, while the dress, style, and habits of these mongrel crews—including Yankee drawls and swaggering gaits—were complete disguises. He was a British officer accustomed to the uniform and clean appearance of British men-of-war's men. "I trust I may be pardoned . . . if I could not pronounce on my own responsibility whether some of the dirty, drawling, ill-looking, grey-coated, big-bearded men, who passed before me as the crew of *Shenandoah*, were British subjects or American citizens." Furthermore, it might be presumed that any British subjects already had made their escape and, he believed, would have had every assistance from those on board in doing so.[10]

Thomas Dudley, U.S. consul in Liverpool, compiled a list of *Shenandoah* personnel with places of origin. Of 137 persons named, 55 percent (75) of them were English (46), Irish (14), Scotch (10), Canadian (3), or Welsh (2). It seems that quite a few subjects of the Crown walked off, including most senior warrant officers. It also would have been highly inconvenient for the British government to witness public prosecutions of its citizens in the heat of ongoing controversy. Minister Adams, supported by a scathing (and somewhat inaccurate) letter from Secretary of State Seward, rehashed the issues of British complicity in piracy. Foreign Minister the Earl of Clarendon voluminously countered these allegations as having no basis or evidence. No American minds were changed, however, as they prepared litigation that would lead to the *Alabama* Claims.[11]

By about nine o'clock on the evening of 8 November, customs officials had examined all baggage; everything had been loaded onto the ferry *Bee*, and they steamed away from *Shenandoah*. Francis Chew recorded, "I grew sadder & sadder as the outlines of the old ship became fainter & fainter in the increasing distance. Farewell dear old ship, farewell! I have seen you for the last time. I shall never again tread your deck! You now go to the U.S., but with no dishonor to yourself; you roamed the seas in spite of cruisers, some of which are now searching for you in the North Pacific and you [are] quietly anchored off Liverpool, twenty thousand miles away."

"We *bid a final adieu* to the *old Shenandoah* which had carried us safely over so many hundred miles of water," wrote Charles Lining in his last journal entry. "It is all over & I thank God for it. We were the last thing that flew the Confederate flag & that is something to be proud of." He and Whittle took a cab and, after trying three hotels, landed at the Clifton, then washed and dressed and went to dinner and a play. They met there a Confederate major Hughes, learned a great deal of news and had a pleasant evening. William Whittle recalled, "Thus ended our memorable cruise—grand in its conception. Grand in its execution, and unprecedentedly, awfully grand in its sad finale. To the four winds the gallant crew scattered, most of them never to meet again until called to the Bar of that Highest of all Tribunals."[12]

Waddell set up temporary lodging at the George's Hotel and contacted Commander Bulloch to make arrangements that the crew should receive their full pay, which apparently was accomplished. Within two weeks Waddell would suffer several lung hemorrhages and for several months, cough up large amounts of blood, near death under Bulloch's care. Waddell and his wife had been excluded from the amnesty. She had been imprisoned by order of Secretary of War Stanton while *Shenandoah* was still in the South Atlantic, and even after the vessel's return to Liverpool the secretary refused for a time to release her so she could join him in England. "Now is this not tyranny, cruel and barbarous," commented Whittle.[13]

In his final report, Waddell thanked Captain Paynter for his kindness and then summarized: *Shenandoah* actively cruised for eight months and made thirty-eight captures—an average of over four per month—releasing six on bond and destroying thirty-two. She was the only vessel to carry the flag around the world, visiting every ocean except the Antarctic and flying it six months after the overthrow of the South. The last gun in defense of the South was fired from her deck on 28 June in the Arctic Ocean (more accurately the

Bering Strait). She was abandoned to the British on 6 November 1865 after running a distance of 58,000 statute miles and meeting with no serious injury in thirteen months at sea. She never lost a chase and was second only to the celebrated *Alabama*. (In terms of tonnage captured, *Florida* is considered second and *Shenandoah* third.) "I claim for her officers and men a triumph over their enemies and over every obstacle, and for myself I claim having done my duty."

Epilogue

The CSS *Shenandoah* was turned over to the American consul in Liverpool and sold in March 1866 to the Sultan of Zanzibar as a yacht. She was damaged in a hurricane and sank off the east coast of Africa in September 1872.

Fearful of returning home, many of the officers attempted to make a life in South America or Mexico, but as animosity softened and amnesty policies loosened over the next decade, they returned to the United States. These former rebels were bitter about having been banished from homes and loved ones, and were acutely sensitive concerning their roles in the war. But they accepted the outcome with no ideological qualms and no desire to escape political and social reconstruction. They were eager to and did resume lives as responsible citizens.[1]

James Waddell returned to Annapolis with his wife, Ann, in July 1867. In 1875 the Pacific Mail Line engaged him to command *City of San Francisco*, its newest liner, on her maiden voyage from San Francisco to Sydney via Honolulu. But San Francisco papers carried angry editorials decrying the presence of a Confederate marauder in the city; mobs of whalemen threatened violence over losses suffered a decade earlier, and Hawaiian authorities swore to arrest Waddell on charges of piracy for destroying the *Harvest* in Pohnpei. *City of San Francisco* sailed with a substitute captain. Waddell assumed command on a later voyage but never visited Hawaii or revisited Australia. In the 1880s he commanded Maryland's "Oyster Navy," fighting illegal oyster dredging. As an old man, he was a fixture around the grounds of the Naval Academy. When Waddell died on 15 March 1886 at age sixty-one, the Maryland General Assembly adjourned and both houses attended his funeral next door at St. Anne's Church.

William Whittle came home to Norfolk, Virginia, in 1867; married Elisabeth Calvert Page (daughter of a Confederate general and first cousin to Robert E. Lee); and raised two boys and four girls. For twenty years Whittle commanded coastal steamers and superintended a fleet of them. In 1901 he helped organize the Virginia Bank and Trust Company, rising to vice president and director, all the while active in Confederate veterans' affairs. Whittle died in 1920 at the age of eighty-two.

Charles Lining was appointed as a government surgeon in Argentina and did not return to the United States until 1874 to reside in Tennessee. John Grimball settled into his family's recovered plantation in January 1867, passed the South Carolina bar, and practiced law in New York for sixteen years. In 1884 Grimball returned to Charleston and married Mary Georgianna Barnwell who bore four sons. He owned homes in Charleston and Waynesville, North Carolina, and owned and for a time operated a rice plantation on the Pon Pon River. Sidney Lee settled on a farm in Stafford County, Virginia. Francis Chew returned to Missouri to raise a family, passing in 1893 at age fifty-two.

Dabney Scales was back in Mississippi by November 1866 without waiting for a pardon. He taught French at the University of Mississippi while studying law, and then practiced in Memphis, where he married and had three children. He refused to take an oath of allegiance because it would imply guilt regarding his service. Scales was elected to the Tennessee legislature and served in the state senate. In 1884 he became commander of the Memphis Camp of the United Confederate Veterans. At age fifty-six he was commissioned into the U.S. Navy as a lieutenant during the Spanish American War. Scales offered his services in World War I only to be refused because he failed to take the oath, but he persisted and in 1917 was commissioned a captain in the National Guard at the age of seventy-six. Scales died on 26 May 1920.

John Mason studied law at the University of Virginia and settled in Baltimore. Irving Bulloch remained with family who had resided in Liverpool since the early days of the war. He and his half brother, James, became successful cotton brokers. Their mother and sister (mother of Theodore Roosevelt) lived in New York throughout the war and suffered no hardship. Irving returned briefly and illegally under an assumed name to visit the family in 1868. His brother James did not visit until May 1870 after unconditional amnesties had finally been issued by President Johnson. (Stories of his uncles' wartime adventures were among Teddy's favorites, undoubtedly inspiring a future interest in naval affairs.)[2]

In July 1866 San Francisco's *Daily Alta Californian* reported a story attributed to former crewmembers of the New York City bark *Mustang*, which had been anchored near *Shenandoah* in Melbourne. Captain W. Q. Sears and five others allegedly assembled a "torpedo" with 250 pounds of gunpowder, rigged it with a cocked revolver, and under cover of darkness rowed quietly up to *Shenandoah* to place the bomb alongside the hull. However, the line to the pistol trigger broke, aborting the attempt, according to the article. That such a scheme was contemplated is entirely believable, but that it occurred without notice by the Confederates is doubtful considering their high state of alert at the time. Had it succeeded, the irony would have been manifest as a rare instance in which one of the Confederacy's most innovative and successful weapons was turned against it.[3]

In June 1872 an international tribunal arbitrating the *Alabama* claims found in favor of Great Britain in the cases of all confederate cruisers except *Alabama*, *Florida*, and *Shenandoah*. The United States was awarded $15.5 million in gold coin. Great Britain accepted responsibility for breach of neutrality in supplying and repairing *Shenandoah* at Melbourne and paid claims for vessels destroyed after she departed; however, because *Sea King* had sailed from England as a registered merchant vessel, the British government accepted no blame for captures prior to Melbourne.[4]

Shenandoah's mission, commerce raiding or *guerre de course*, first emerged as a naval strategy in the sixteenth century coincident with the development of oceangoing square-rigged ships and the Age of Discovery. Queen Elizabeth I set loose her "gentlemen adventurers" to break Spanish monopolies of sea power and trade, but on their own coin. In subsequent European wars, swarms of privately financed armed merchant vessels—"privateers" or "licensed pirates"—accounted for the vast majority of commercial losses, affecting the wealth of all trading nations while expanding the scope and impact of maritime conflict. Americans inherited the strategy and applied it vigorously throughout their history. But the strategic impact of this approach in any contest is difficult to evaluate—it causes incremental transfers of wealth and material and could affect home-front morale, but does not produce victory or defeat in battle or gains or losses of territory.

Naval strategist Captain A. T. Mahan, speaking of French policy during that nation's wars with Great Britain, wrote in 1890, "The harassment and distress caused to a country by serious interference with its commerce will be conceded by all." He considered *guerre de course* a most important secondary operation of naval war, but "regarded as a primary and fundamental measure, sufficient in itself to crush an enemy, it is probably a delusion"—most misleading when the target nation possesses the two requisites of a strong sea power: "a wide-spread healthy commerce and a powerful navy." Great Britain had these two advantages against France (and America) for most of the preceding two centuries, and so did the Union vis-à-vis the South. In addition, Confederates were compelled by circumstances and evolving international law to abandon low-cost privateering in favor of state-financed, commissioned cruisers. But the Confederates prescribed to the delusion of commerce warfare; it was an American tradition, and really they had little choice.[5]

On the other hand, wrote one historian, "If there was one single factor that could have assured Southern independence," it was that Great Britain might have permitted the Confederate States to build warships in British yards and get them to sea where they could prey on Northern commerce, break the blockade, and "give the Southern army access to almost unlimited war material." Another historian concluded, "The cruisers were not able to win the war, but relative to their cost they did far more damage . . . than any other class of military investment made by the Confederacy." *Alabama* and her sisters crippled the powerful northeast shipping and whaling industries while greatly boosting the spirits of Southerners who revered the ships and lionized the men. The cruisers proved that the Confederacy could carry the fight to the Union anywhere in the world. Their exploits exacerbated international tensions and encouraged England and France to consider intervention, recognition, and support for the new nation—the primary objective of Confederate foreign policy. President Lincoln considered any kind of international interference a dire threat to victory and union, and he was determined to prevent it.[6]

Confederate navy secretary Mallory also hoped that the cruisers would draw federal blockaders away from the coasts to chase them down. His Union counterpart, Gideon Welles, generally resisted this temptation, diverting only a few ships despite howls of protest from those who stood to lose so much. Welles probably would have agreed with this historical assessment: "From the Dutch Wars of the seventeenth century through to the close of World War II, search-and-destroy missions at sea against privateers or naval raiders were an exhausting exercise in futility, just as they tend to be in counterguerrilla operations on land." Whatever the costs to particular interests, the cruisers put not a dent in the industrial war machine of the United States or in the burgeoning trade that supported it. Commerce just shifted to neutral bottoms; whaling was declining from other causes anyway while the blockade progressively throttled the South.[7]

But Confederate commerce raiding was also carefully planned psychological warfare, a bit of W. T. Sherman. What if *Shenandoah* had cruised a year earlier, achieving the same results? How would news of another *Alabama* loose in the Pacific during the military stalemate of summer 1864 have contributed to Northern malaise and to George McClellan's prospects for the presidency? The Confederacy might have been as close to independence that summer as at any time during the war. It was not an irrational strategy. By the spring of 1865, however, there could be no such hope.

The success of rebel raiders also encouraged brief enthusiasm for large, fast, commerce-destroying cruisers. In 1863 the Union secretly designed a new class specifically to go against the British should they intervene for the South and start a third war with former colonies. By 1868 the USS *Wampanoag* was the fastest warship in the world, able to steam across rough water at seventeen knots. The sleek hull—355 feet long, 45 feet wide—was designed around a huge and complex steam propulsion system crowned by four stacks; she carried little armament as befitted the mission. *Wampanoag* had been a logical extension of the strategy behind *Alabama* and *Shenandoah* now that privateering was dead, but the threat of British meddling no longer existed and the design was not efficient. *Wampanoag* was decommissioned as too expensive to operate and maintain.[8]

The legacy of *Shenandoah* and her sisters continued into the twentieth century, but commissioned surface raiders became too expensive and more easily rounded up and destroyed. As the naval underdog, however, Germany pursued the mission with considerable success by using nondescript armed merchant vessels and submarines, although Count von Luckner's World War I raider, *Seeadler*, was a sailing ship with no small resemblance to Confederate predecessors.

On 28 August 1964 the USS *Waddell* (DDG 24), named for James Waddell, was commissioned as a *Charles F. Adams*–class guided-missile destroyer. *Waddell* made several deployments to Vietnam performing naval gunfire, plane guard, and search-and-rescue duties, along with interdiction of enemy waterborne logistics traffic, that is, commerce destruction. She was decommissioned on 1 October 1992, sold to Greece and renamed *Nearchos*. The USS *Waddell* received eleven engagement stars and two Navy Unit Commendations.

In August 2000 maritime archeologists from the University of Hawaii at Manoa and East Carolina University investigated the remains of vessels in Lohd Pah Harbor. They identified material from three wrecks: portions of keels, floor timbers, planking, frames, and other hull structures with associated iron and copper hardware and tryworks bricks. Historical records and clues passed down through oral history indicate one of the two vessels is the *Harvest*. *Harvest*'s captain Eldridge had remained on the island; his grandson, Sakies Eldridge, age 75, was one of those interviewed. The team submitted a preservation plan recommending that the harbor, a quiet place and virtually unchanged, be declared an American Battlefield site.[9]

In conclusion, the CSS *Shenandoah* was the epitome of an ancient maritime heritage combined with the most advanced technology of the time. She represented a new concept in an old strategy of naval warfare and was a good example of what a weaker naval power can accomplish in what we today call asymmetric warfare. The cruise also illustrates the difficulties emerging states or revolutionary movements encounter when claiming what they perceive as their rights and when trying to achieve accommodation in the international arena. The men of *Shenandoah* heeded the call of their leaders, putting their lives, fortunes, and honor on the line. They sought to serve in the best traditions of the U.S. Navy, which they took as their model and from which several of them came. Judging by their accomplishments, they succeeded. The ship and men deserve to be remembered.

Notes

Chapter 1. "Otro *Alabama*"

1. James I. Waddell, "Extracts from notes on the C.S.S. *Shenandoah* by her commander, James Iredell Waddell, C.S. Navy," in *The Official Records of the Union and Confederate Navies in the War of the Rebellion* (Washington, DC: U.S. Government Printing Office, 1896) (hereafter cited as *ORN*), 1, 3:792–836. Unless otherwise noted, quotes from James Waddell are from this source on or about the date in context.
2. John T. Mason, Journal, Eleanor S. Brokenbrough Library, Museum of the Confederacy, Richmond, VA. Unless otherwise noted, quotes from Mason are from this journal on or about the date in context.
3. Charles E. Lining, Journal, Eleanor S. Brokenbrough Library, Museum of the Confederacy, Richmond, VA. Unless otherwise noted, quotes from Lining are from this journal on or about the date in context.
4. William C. Whittle Jr., "The Cruise of the *Shenandoah*," *Southern Historical Society Papers* 35 (1907): 244.
5. "Deposition of John Hercus," *Case of Great Britain as Laid before the Tribunal of Arbitration: Convened at Geneva Under the Provisions of the Treaty Between the United States of America and Her Majesty the Queen of Great Britain, Concluded at Washington, May 8, 1871. Together with Volumes V, VI, and VII of Appendix to the British Case. Transmitted to congress by the President of U.S.*, 3 vols. (Washington, DC: Government Printing Office, 1872) (hereafter cited as *Case of Great Britain*), 1:751–52.
6. James D. Horan, ed., *C.S.S. Shenandoah: The Memoirs of Lieutenant Commanding James I. Waddell* (New York: Crown Publishers, 1960), 66.
7. Grimball to Father, 23 December 1864, John Berkley Grimball Papers, David M. Rubenstein Rare Book & Manuscript Library, Duke University. Unless otherwise noted, quotes from John Grimball are from this source.
8. Raphael Semmes, *Memoirs of Service Afloat during the War between the States* (Baltimore: Kelly, Piet and Company, 1869), 409–12.
9. Ibid.
10. Bulloch to Mallory, *ORN*, 1, 3:758; Bulloch to Waddell, *ORN*, 1, 3:752.
11. "Deposition of John Wilson," *Case of Great Britain*, 1:753.
12. "Deposition of John Ellison," *Case of Great Britain*, 1:742.
13. Whittle, "Cruise of the *Shenandoah*," *Southern Historical Society Papers*, 245.
14. James D. Bulloch, *The Secret Service of the Confederate States in Europe; or, How the Confederate Cruisers Were Equipped*, 2 vols. (reprint, New York: Thomas Yoseloff, 1959), 2:146.
15. Ibid.
16. Whittle, "Cruise of the *Shenandoah*," *Southern Historical Society Papers*, 243.

Chapter 2. "Do . . . the Greatest Injury"

1. Alexander Stephen and Co., *A Shipbuilding History, 1750–1932: A Record of the Business founded, about 1750, by Alexander Stephen* . . . (London: Printed for Alexander Stephen and Co., 1932), 46; Bulloch, *Secret Service*, 2:125.
2. Adams to Earl Russell, *Case of Great Britain*, 1:847; Raimondo Luraghi, *A History of the Confederate Navy* (Annapolis, MD: Naval Institute Press, 1996), 9–12.
3. Semmes, *Memoirs of Service Afloat*, 92.
4. Spencer C. Tucker, *Blue & Gray Navies: The Civil War Afloat* (Annapolis, MD: Naval Institute Press, 2006), 72–76; also William Morrison Robinson Jr., *The Confederate Privateers* (Columbia: University of South Carolina Press, 1928).
5. Mallory to Bulloch, *ORN*, 2, 2:687.
6. Bulloch, *Secret Service*, 1:55; Mallory to Bulloch, *ORN*, 2, 2:687.
7. Bulloch, *Secret Service*, 2:125.
8. John H. Schroeder, *Shaping a Maritime Empire: The Commercial and Diplomatic Role of the American Navy, 1829–1861* (Westport, CT: Greenwood Press, 1985), 159–63.
9. Bulloch to Mallory, *ORN*, 2, 2:589.
10. Chester G. Hearn, *Gray Raiders of the Sea: How Eight Confederate Warships Destroyed the Union's High Seas Commerce* (Camden, ME: International Marine Publishing, 1992), xv; George W. Dalzell, *The Flight from the Flag: The Continuing Effect of the Civil War upon the American Carrying Trade* (Chapel Hill: University of North Carolina Press, 1940), 237–48.
11. Mallory to Bulloch, *ORN*, 2, 2:613; Mallory to Bulloch, *ORN*, 2, 2:701.
12. Dalzell, *Flight from The Flag*, 198–204.
13. David R. MacGregor, *Fast Sailing Ships: Their Design and Construction, 1775–1875*, 2nd ed. (Annapolis, MD: Naval Institute Press, 1988), 224.
14. Mallory to Bulloch, *ORN*, 2, 2:708; Brook memo, *ORN*, 2, 2:708–9.
15. Bulloch to Mallory, *ORN*, 2, 2:723–24.
16. Bulloch, *Secret Service*, 2:127.
17. Bulloch to Whittle, *ORN*, 2, 2:731–32.
18. Bulloch to Waddell, *ORN*, 1, 3:749–55.
19. Ibid., 749–55.
20. Ibid.
21. Barron to Waddell, *ORN*, 1, 3:755–56.
22. Bulloch to Mallory, *ORN*, 2, 2:736–37; Report of Commodore Craven, *ORN*, 1, 3:341–43.
23. Bulloch to Mallory, *ORN*, 1, 3:758; Mallory to Bulloch, *ORN*, 2, 2:767.

Chapter 3. "None but Fiends Could"

1. William C. Whittle, Journal, Eleanor S. Brokenbrough Library, Museum of the Confederacy, Richmond, VA. Unless otherwise noted, quotes from Whittle are from this journal on or about the date in context. Also William C. Whittle Jr., *The Voyage of the CSS* Shenandoah: *A Memorable Cruise* (Tuscaloosa: University of Alabama Press, 2005), a published version of the journal.
2. Angus Curry, *The Officers of the CSS* Shenandoah (Gainesville: University Press of Florida, 2006), 34–35.

3. Francis Thornton Chew, "Reminiscences and Journal of Francis Thornton Chew, Lieutenant, C.S.N.," Chew Papers #148, Southern Historical Collection, University of North Carolina Library. Unless otherwise noted, quotes from Chew are from this source on or about the date in context.

4. Horan, ed., *C.S.S. Shenandoah*, 58–59.

5. Hearn, *Gray Raiders of the Sea*, 45–49.

6. Curry, *Officers of the CSS* Shenandoah, 26.

7. Ibid., 19–22. The following information concerning the officers' previous war experiences are primarily from this source.

8. Semmes, *Memoirs of Service Afloat*, 167, 223, 481.

9. Ibid., 482–83.

10. Ibid., 489–90.

11. Cornelius E. Hunt, *The* Shenandoah; *Or, The Last Confederate Cruiser* (New York: G. W. Carelton, 1867), 32–33.

12. Curry, *Officers of the CSS* Shenandoah, 85–86.

Chapter 4. "Now Came the Trouble"

1. Testimony of William Bruce, *Case of Great Britain*, 1:863.

2. Hunt, Shenandoah, 35.

3. Melbourne *Age*, 15 February 1865; Dennis J. Ringle, *Life in Mr. Lincoln's Navy* (Annapolis, MD: Naval Institute Press, 1998), 3–4; James E. Valle, *Rocks & Shoals: Naval Discipline in the Age of Fighting Sail* (Annapolis, MD: Naval Institute Press, 1980), 83–84; Curry, *Officers of the CSS* Shenandoah, 98.

4. Hunt, Shenandoah, 39–40.

5. Testimony of John Williams, "Papers Relating to Foreign Affairs, Great Britain" in *Executive Documents Printed by Order of the House of Representatives during the First Session of the Thirty-Ninth Congress, 1865–66.* Vol. 1, No.1, Part 1 (Washington, DC: U.S. Government Printing Office, 1866) (hereafter cited as "Papers Relating to Foreign Affairs"), 478–79.

6. Consul Grattan to Earl Russell, *Case of Great Britain*, 1:741–42.

7. Benjamin Moran, *The Journal of Benjamin Moran, 1857–1865*, 2 vols. (Chicago: University of Chicago Press, 1948–49), 2:1348; Dudley to Craven, *ORN*, 1, 3:372–73.

Chapter 5. "Oh, It's a Grand Sight"

1. Lynn Schooler, *The Last Shot: The Incredible Story of the CSS* Shenandoah *and the True Conclusion of the American Civil War* (New York: Harper Collins, 2005), 77 footnote.

2. Hunt, Shenandoah, 50–52.

3. Ibid.

4. Ibid.

5. Mr. Adams to Earl Russell, *Case of Great Britain*, 1:749–51.

6. William N. Still Jr., ed., *The Confederate Navy: The Ships, Men and Organization, 1861–65* (Annapolis, MD: Naval Institute Press, 1997), 126.

7. Clark to Welles, *ORN*, 1, 3:400.

8. Horan, *C.S.S. Shenandoah*, 116.

9. Rodgers to Welles, *ORN*, 1, 3:403–4.

Chapter 6. "Running Her Easting Down"

1. Hunt, Shenandoah, 65–66.
2. MacGregor, *Fast Sailing Ships*, 224; William F. Baker, *Running Her Easting Down: A Documentary of the Development and History of the British Tea Clippers Culminating with the Building of the* Cutty Sark (Caldwell, ID: Caxton Printers, 1974), 31.
3. Gary McKay, *The Sea King: The Life of James Iredell Waddell* (Edinburgh: Birlinn Limited, 2009), 129–30; Ann Jensen, "Rebel Captain from Annapolis, The Last Confederate Raider," *Annapolitan*, March 1990, 46.
4. Hunt, Shenandoah, 67–69, 70.
5. Measurements approximated from the CSS *Shenandoah/Sea King* Builder's Plans, National Maritime Museum, Greenwich, England.
6. John Harland, *Seamanship in the Age of Sail: An Account of the Shiphandling of the Sailing Man-of-War, 1600–1860, Based on Contemporary Sources* (Annapolis, MD: Naval Institute Press, 1984), 124–25.
7. Hunt, Shenandoah, 72.
8. Clark to Welles, *ORN*, 1, 3:400; Seward to Welles, *ORN*, 1, 3:426–28.
9. Clark to Welles, *ORN*, 1, 3:424–25.
10. Rodgers to Welles, *ORN*, 1, 3:403–4.

Chapter 7. The Queen of the *Delphine*

1. Hunt, Shenandoah, 74.
2. Ibid., 75, 78.
3. Ibid., 78.
4. Waddell, "Extracts," 807–8.
5. Hunt, Shenandoah, 79.
6. Ibid., 87–89.
7. Ibid., 84–86.
8. Ibid., 91.
9. Rodgers to Welles, *ORN*, 1865, 1, 3:405–6.
10. Welles to Shirley, *ORN*, 1, 3:407.
11. H. H. Swift & Co. to Welles, *ORN*, 1, 3:412; Welles to H. H. Swift & Co., *ORN*, 1, 3:413; Dahlgren to Williamson, *ORN*, 1, 16:164.

Chapter 8. End of the International Road

1. Waddell to Darling, *ORN*, 1, 3:761.
2. King to Wiseman, *Case of Great Britain*, 1:764.
3. Donald A. Petrie, *The Prize Game: Lawful Looting on the High Seas in the Days of Fighting Sail* (Annapolis, MD: Naval Institute Press, 1999),162; Russell to Newcastle, *Case of Great Britain*, 1:778–79.
4. Norman Bartlett, *1776–1976, Australia and America through 200 Years* (Sidney: Fine Arts Press, 1967), 147; Extracts from minutes, *Case of Great Britain*, 1:776–77; Francis to Waddell, *ORN*, 1, 3:761–62.
5. Melbourne *Age*, 26 January 1865; Melbourne *Argus*, 26 January 1865.
6. Melbourne *Age*, 27 January 1865.
7. Cyril Pearl, *Rebel Down Under: When the* 'Shenandoah' *Shook Melbourne, 1865* (Melbourne: William Heinemann, 1970), 43.

8. Lillias L. Nichols, "Papers Relating to Foreign Affairs," 463.
9. Blanchard to Seward, "Papers Relating to Foreign Affairs," 458; Blanchard to Adams, 26 January 1865, "Papers Relating to Foreign Affairs," 463.
10. Semmes, *Memoirs of Service Afloat*, 708–9.
11. Waddell to Barron, *ORN*, 1, 3:759–60.
12. Ibid.
13. Blanchard to Darling, "Papers Relating to Foreign Affairs," 464.
14. Raphael Semmes, *The Cruise of the* Alabama *and the* Sumter: *From the Private Journals and Other Papers of Commander R. Semmes, C.S.N., and Other Officers* (New York: Carleton, 1864), 74–75; Blanchard to Seward, "Papers Relating to Foreign Affairs," 459.
15. Blanchard to Darling, "Papers Relating to Foreign Affairs," 464–65.

Chapter 9. The War Down Under

1. James Grant and Geoffrey Serle, eds., *The Melbourne Scene, 1803–1956* (Melbourne: Melbourne University Press, 1957), 3–5, 11, 14, 77, 84, 130.
2. Ibid, 117; Bartlett, *Australia And America*, 146.
3. Sheldon Vanauken, *The Glittering Illusion: English Sympathy for the Southern Confederacy* (Washington, DC: Regnery Gateway, 1989), 41; Curry, *Officers of the CSS* Shenandoah, 134.
4. Ballarat *Evening Post*, 31 January 1865; Hunt, Shenandoah, 102.
5. Curry, *Officers of the CSS* Shenandoah, 135–36.
6. Melbourne *Herald*, 4 February 1865.
7. Pearl, *Rebel Down Under*, 45–46.
8. Melbourne *Age*, 27 January 1865.
9. Ibid.
10. Ibid., 30 January 1865.
11. Ibid., 27 January 1865.
12. Ibid.
13. Pearl, *Rebel Down Under*, 41–42; Melbourne *Herald*, 4 February 1865.
14. Semmes, *Memoirs of Service Afloat*, 619.
15. Melbourne *Herald*, 4 February 1865.
16. Blanchard to Darling, "Papers Relating to Foreign Affairs," 467.
17. Waddell to Francis, *ORN*, 1, 3:764–65.
18. Minutes of the Council, *Case of Great Britain*, 1:782.
19. Melbourne *Age*, 1 February 1865.
20. Melbourne *Argus*, 2 February 1865.
21. Ibid.
22. Blanchard to Seward, "Papers Relating to Foreign Affairs," 459.
23. Lillias L. Nichols, "Papers Relating to Foreign Affairs," 476–77.

Chapter 10. Charley the Cook

1. Walke to Welles, *ORN*, 1, 3:420–21.
2. Melbourne *Age*, 11 February 1865.
3. Ibid., 6 and 11 February 1865.
4. Ibid., 13 February 1865.

5. Ibid., 6 February 1865.
6. Ibid., 11 February 1865.
7. Melbourne *Argus*, 20 February 1865.
8. John Williams, "Papers Relating to Foreign Affairs," 478.
9. Chomley to Blanchard, "Papers Relating to Foreign Affairs," 478.
10. Police report, Sandridge, *Case of Great Britain*, 1:788–89; Melbourne *Argus*, 20 February 1865.
11. Curry, *Officers of the CSS* Shenandoah, 137, 356, n74.
12. Walter J. Maddon, "Papers Relating to Foreign Affairs," 479.
13. Hermann Wicker and F. C. Behucke, "Papers Relating to Foreign Affairs," 482–83.
14. Lyttleton to Chief Commissioner, *Case of Great Britain*, 1:789–90.
15. Minutes of Council, *Case of Great Britain*, 1:789; Pearl, *Rebel Down Under*, 94–95.
16. Francis to Waddell, *ORN*, 1, 3:769–70.
17. Melbourne *Age*, 15 February 1865.
18. Melbourne *Argus*, 15 February 1865.
19. Melbourne *Herald*, 15 February 1865.
20. Waddell to Francis, *ORN*, 1, 3:770–71.
21. Lyttleton, *Case of Great Britain*, 1:805; Littleton to the Commissioner, *Case of Great Britain*, 1:792.
22. Blanchard to Darling, "Papers Relating to Foreign Affairs," 484–85; Frank J. Merli, *Great Britain and the Confederate Navy, 1861–1865* (Bloomington: Indiana University Press, 2004), 160–77.
23. Blanchard to Darling, "Papers Relating to Foreign Affairs," 484–85.

Chapter 11. "On the Bright Blue Sea"

1. Waddell to Francis, *ORN*, 1, 3:771; Melbourne *Argus*, 16 February 1865.
2. Mr. Higgenbotham, *Case of Great Britain*, 1:813–14.
3. Minutes of council, *Case of Great Britain*, 1:791; Theo, "Case of the Australian government versus the C.S.S. *Shenandoah*," *ORN*, 1, 3:773–74.
4. Melbourne *Herald,* 16 February 1865; *Illustrated London News*, 15 April 1865.
5. Francis to Waddell, *ORN*, 1, 3:772–73.
6. Waddell to Francis, *ORN*, 1, 3:774.
7. Horan, ed., *C.S.S.* Shenandoah, 137.
8. Semmes, *Memoirs of Service Afloat*, 671.
9. Waddell to Barron, *ORN*, 1, 3:759; Michael Cashmore, *Case of Great Britain*, 1:881.
10. Bartlett, *Australia and America*, 128.
11. Pearl, *Rebel Down Under*, 104–11.
12. Ibid.
13. Melbourne *Age*, 16 February 1865.
14. *Case of Great Britain*, 1:811.
15. Ibid., 1:811–13.
16. Welles to Townsend, *ORN*, 1, 3:429–30.
17. Blanchard to Darling, "Papers Relating to Foreign Affairs," 487.
18. Ibid., 462.
19. Rodgers to Welles, *ORN*, 1, 3:430–31.
20. Welles to Bankhead, *ORN*, 1, 3:472.
21. Semmes, *Memoirs of Service Afloat*, 424.

22. Hunt, Shenandoah, 100.
23. Melbourne *Argus*, 20 February 1865.

Chapter 12. "The Abomination of Isolation"

1. Hunt, Shenandoah, 113–14.
2. Hull to Bateson, *Case of Great Britain*, 1:994.
3. Boggs to Welles, *ORN*, 1, 3:433.
4. Hunt, Shenandoah, 116–18.
5. John R. Bockstoce, *Whales, Ice and Men: The History of Whaling in the Western Arctic* (Seattle: University of Washington Press, 1986), 110; Newspaper clipping, *ORN*, 1, 3:581.

Chapter 13. "Upon a Stone Altar"

1. David Hanlon, *Upon a Stone Altar: A History of the Island of Pohnpei to 1890* (Honolulu: University of Hawaii Press, 1988), xiii; F. W. Christian, *The Caroline Islands: Travel in the Sea of the Little Lands* (London: Methuen & Co., 1899), 59–62. Pohnpei is the largest island in the eastern Caroline Islands, capital of the Federated States of Micronesia.
2. Hanlon, *Upon a Stone Altar*, xvii, 4.
3. Ibid., 6–7, 25.
4. Ibid., 26–58, 73–74, 85.
5. "Pohnpei (Southeast), Topographic Map of the Island of" (Washington, DC: U.S. Geological Survey, 2001).
6. Hunt, Shenandoah, 123.
7. Hanlon, *Upon a Stone Altar*, 59–62.
8. Rodgers to Welles, *ORN*, 1,3:486–487, 559.
9. Alexander Starbuck, *History of the American Whale Fishery* (reprint, New Jersey: Castle Books, 1989), 550–51, 564–65.
10. *Letters and Documents Relating to the Claim of the Owners, Officers, and Crew of the Ship* Harvest *Captured by the* Shenandoah (Washington, DC: Committee on Foreign Relations, United States Senate, August 1, 1894), 23–24.
11. Ibid.
12. Hanlon, *Upon a Stone Altar*, 39, 59, 69–71.
13. Ibid., 47, 59.

Chapter 14. The World on Fire

1. *Civil War Naval Chronology, 1861–1865* (Washington, DC: U.S. Government Printing Office, 1971), 5:75.
2. Hunt, Shenandoah, 129.
3. *Civil War Naval Chronology*, 5:76.
4. Edward A. Pollard, *The Lost Cause: A New Southern History of the War of the Confederates* (New York: E. B. Treat and Co., 1867), 696.
5. *Civil War Naval Chronology*, 5:78; Geoffrey Perret, *Lincoln's War: The Untold Story of American's Greatest President as Commander in Chief* (New York: Random House, 2004), 402.

6. Hunt, Shenandoah, 129.
7. Hanlon, *Upon a Stone Altar*, 79–81.
8. Christian, *The Caroline Islands*, 61.
9. Hanlon, *Upon a Stone Altar*, 80.
10. Ibid., 13–22; Christian, *The Caroline Islands*, 78–79, 108–9.
11. Price to Wells, *ORN*, 1, 3:509; Russell to Welles, *ORN*, 1, 3:511.

Chapter 15. Invading the North

1. Colvocoresses to Welles, *ORN*, 1, 3:533–34; Colvocoresses to Welles, *ORN*, 1, 3:545.
2. Hunt, Shenandoah, 158.

Chapter 16. High Tide of the Confederacy

1. Bockstoce, *Whales, Ice, and Men*, 113.
2. Hammond to Mason, *Case of Great Britain*, 1:919.
3. Bulloch, *Secret Service*, 2:157–59.
4. *San Francisco Bulletin*, 7 July 1865.
5. Hunt, Shenandoah, 181; *San Francisco Bulletin*, 7 July 1865.
6. Bockstoce, *Whales, Ice, and Men*, 116.
7. Jefferson Davis, *Rise and Fall of the Confederate Nation*, 2 vols. (reprint, New York: Thomas Yoseloff, 1958), 2:700.
8. Bockstoce, *Whales, Ice, and Men*, 116–17.
9. In his writings, Waddell would confuse Clark with Ebenezer Nye of *Abigail* (Waddell, "Extracts,") 823.
10. Bockstoce, *Whales, Ice, and Men*, 120–21.
11. Ibid., 122.

Chapter 17. "The Darkest Day"

1. McDougal to Welles, *ORN*, 3, 1:571.
2. Horan, *C.S.S. Shenandoah*, 175.
3. Pearson to Welles, *ORN*, 1, 3:577; *San Francisco Bulletin*, 20 July 1865; McDougal to Welles, *ORN*, 1, 3:589.
4. Hunt, Shenandoah, 218.
5. Ibid., 223.

Chapter 18. "A Feeling Approaching Panic"

1. Circular to the Colonies, *Case of Great Britain*, 1:923.
2. Petition, *ORN*, 1, 3:779–80.
3. Ibid.
4. *ORN*, 1, 3:781–82.
5. Ibid., 782–83.
6. Ibid., 782.
7. Earl Russell to the Lords Commissioners of the Admiralty, *Case of Great Britain*, 1:923.
8. William A. Temple, *Case of Great Britain*, 1:973.

Chapter 19. "Having Done My Duty"

1. Waddell to Russell, *ORN*, 1, 3:783–84.
2. Ibid.
3. Letters, *Case of Great Britain*, 1:928–34.
4. Order to Lieutenant A. D. Cheek, *Case of Great Britain*, 1:946.
5. Letters, *Case of Great Britain*, 1:928–34.
6. Adams to Clarendon, *Case of Great Britain*, 1:937–38.
7. Law-officers to Clarendon, *Case of Great Britain*, 1:938–40.
8. Paynter to the Admiralty, *Case of Great Britain*, 1:953–54.
9. Temple, *Case of Great Britain*, 1:974; Warwick to Paynter, *Case of Great Britain*, 1:989–90.
10. Paynter to the Admiralty, *Case of Great Britain*, 1:953–54; Paynter to the Admiralty, *Case of Great Britain*, 1:988.
11. "List of the officers and men of the *Shenandoah*," *Case of Great Britain*, 1:974–77; letters, *Case of Great Britain*, 1:963–98.
12. Whittle, "Cruise of the *Shenandoah*," *Southern Historical Society Papers*, 258.
13. Curry, *Officers of the CSS* Shenandoah, 272.

Epilogue

1. See Curry, *Officers of the CSS* Shenandoah, Chapter 10, 265–93 for officers' postwar lives.
2. Stephen Chapin Kinnaman, *Captain Bulloch: The Life of James Dunwoody Bulloch, Naval Agent of the Confederacy* (Indianapolis, IN: Dog Ear Publishing, 2013), 413, 419.
3. Tom Chaffin, *Sea of Gray: The Around-the-World Odyssey of the Confederate Raider* Shenandoah (New York: Hill and Wang, 2006), 157–58.
4. Curry, *Officers of the CSS* Shenandoah, 289–91.
5. Captain A. T. Mahan, *The Influence of Sea Power upon History, 1660–1783* (Boston: Little, Brown and Company, 1890), 539.
6. Merli, *Great Britain and the Confederate Navy*, 3; Frank Lawrence Owsley Jr., *The C.S.S.* Florida: *Her Building and Operations* (Tuscaloosa: University of Alabama Press, 1965), 10.
7. Colin S. Gray, *The Leverage of Sea Power: The Strategic Advantage of Navies in War* (New York: Free Press, 1992), 13.
8. Robert Gardiner, ed., *Steam, Steel & Shellfire: The Steam Warship 1815–1905* (London: Conway Maritime Press Ltd., 1992), 88–89.
9. Suzanne S. Finney and Michael W. Graves, "Site Identification and Documentation of a Civil War Shipwreck Thought to Be Sunk by the C.S.S. *Shenandoah* in April 1865" (Washington, DC: Prepared for the American Battlefield Protection Program, National Park Service, 2000).

Selected Bibliography

Alexander Stephen and Co. *A Shipbuilding History, 1750–1932: A Record of the Business Founded, about 1750, by Alexander Stephen at Burghead, and subsequently carried on at Aberdeen, Arbroath, Dundee and Glasgow.* London: Printed for Alexander Stephen and Co., 1932.

Baker, William F. *Running Her Easting Down: A Documentary of the Development and History of the British Tea Clippers Culminating with the Building of the* Cutty Sark. Caldwell, ID: Caxton Printers, 1974.

Bartlett, Norman. *1776–1976, Australia and America through 200 Years.* Sidney: Fine Arts Press, 1967.

Bennett, Michael J. *Union Jacks: Yankee Sailors in the Civil War.* Chapel Hill: University of North Carolina Press, 2004.

Bockstoce, John R. *Whales, Ice and Men: The History of Whaling in the Western Arctic.* Seattle: University of Washington Press, 1986.

Brady, William N. *Kedge-Anchor; or, Young Sailor's Assistant.* New York: Published by the author, 1864.

Brooke, George M., Jr. *John M. Brooke, Naval Scientist and Educator.* Charlottesville: University of Virginia Press, 1980.

Bulloch, James D. *The Secret Service of the Confederate States in Europe; or, How the Confederate Cruisers Were Equipped.* 2 vols. Reprint, introduction by Philip Van Doren Stern. New York: Thomas Yoseloff, 1959.

Campbell, George F. *China Tea Clippers.* Camden, ME: International Marine Publishing, 1974.

Canney, Donald L. *Lincoln's Navy: The Ships, Men, and Organization, 1861–65.* Annapolis, MD: Naval Institute Press, 1998.

———. *The Old Steam Navy, Volume One: Frigates, Sloops, and Gunboats, 1815–1885.* Annapolis, MD: Naval Institute Press, 1990.

Carvel, John L. *Stephen of Linthouse: A Record of Two Hundred Years of Shipbuilding, 1750–1950.* Glasgow: Alexander Stephen and Sons, 1950.

Case of Great Britain as Laid before the Tribunal of Arbitration: Convened at Geneva Under the Provisions of the Treaty Between the United States of America and Her Majesty the Queen of Great Britain, Concluded at Washington, May 8, 1871. Together with Volumes V, VI, and VII of Appendix to the British Case. Transmitted to congress by the President of U.S., 3 vols. Washington, DC: U.S. Government Printing Office, 1872.

Chaffin, Tom. *Sea of Gray: The Around-the-World Odyssey of the Confederate Raider* Shenandoah. New York: Hill and Wang, 2006.

Cheneviere, Alain. *Pacific, The Boundless Ocean.* New York: Konecky and Konecky, 1995.

Chew, Francis Thornton. "Reminiscences and Journal of Francis Thornton Chew, Lieutenant, C.S.N." Chew Papers #148, Southern Historical Collection. University of North Carolina Library.

Christian, F. W. *The Caroline Islands: Travel in the Sea of the Little Lands.* London: Methuen & Co., 1899.

Civil War Naval Chronology, 1861–1865. Washington, DC: U.S. Government Printing Office, 1971.

Coski, John M. *The Men, Ships, and Operations of the James River Squadron*. Campbell, CA: Savas Woodbury Publications, 1996.

CSS *Shenandoah* Shipping Articles. Eleanor S. Brokenbrough Library, Museum of the Confederacy, Richmond, VA.

CSS *Shenandoah* Log (1864–1865). 2 vols. MSS., mf. Wilson Library, University of North Carolina, Chapel Hill.

CSS *Shenandoah/Sea King*. Builder's Plans. National Maritime Museum, Greenwich, England.

Curry, Angus. *The Officers of the CSS* Shenandoah. Gainsville: University Press of Florida, 2006.

Dalzell, George W. *The Flight from the Flag: The Continuing Effect of the Civil War upon the American Carrying Trade*. Chapel Hill: University of North Carolina Press, 1940.

Davis, Jefferson. *Rise and Fall of the Confederate Nation*. 2 vols. 1881. Reprint, New York: Thomas Yoseloff, 1958.

Donald, David, ed. *Inside Lincoln's Cabinet: The Civil War Diaries of Salmon P. Chase*. New York: Longmans Green, 1954.

Fasano, Lawrence. *Naval Rank, Its Inception and Development: A Short History of the Evolution and Genealogy of the Naval Officer*. New York: Horizon House, 1936.

Finney, Suzanne S., and Michael W. Graves. "Site Identification and Documentation of a Civil War Shipwreck Thought to Be Sunk by the C.S.S. *Shenandoah* in April 1865." Washington, DC: Prepared for the American Battlefield Protection Program, National Park Service, 2000.

Gardiner, Robert, ed. *Steam, Steel & Shellfire: The Steam Warship 1815–1905*. London: Conway Maritime Press Ltd., 1992.

Grant, James, and Geoffrey Serle, eds. *The Melbourne Scene, 1803–1956*. Melbourne: Melbourne University Press, 1957.

Gray, Colin S. *The Leverage of Sea Power: The Strategic Advantage of Navies in War*. New York: Free Press, 1992.

Grimball, John Berkley. John Berkley Grimball Papers. David M. Rubenstein Rare Book & Manuscript Library, Duke University.

Hanlon, David. *Upon a Stone Altar: A History of the Island of Pohnpei to 1890*. Honolulu: University of Hawaii Press, 1988.

Harland, John. *Seamanship in the Age of Sail: An Account of the Shiphandling of the Sailing Man-of-War, 1600–1860, Based on Contemporary Sources*. Annapolis, MD: Naval Institute Press, 1984.

Hearn, Chester G. *Gray Raiders of the Sea: How Eight Confederate Warships Destroyed the Union's High Seas Commerce*. Camden, ME: International Marine Publishing, 1992.

———. *Naval Battles of the Civil War*. San Diego, CA: Thunder Bay Press, 2000.

Horan, James D., ed. *C.S.S.* Shenandoah: *The Memoirs of Lieutenant Commanding James I. Waddell*. New York: Crown Publishers, 1960.

Hunt, Cornelius E. *The* Shenandoah; *Or, The Last Confederate Cruiser*. New York: G. W. Carelton, 1867.

Jensen, Ann. "Rebel Captain from Annapolis, The Last Confederate Raider." *Annapolitan*, March 1990.

Jones, Howard. *Blue & Gray Diplomacy: A History of Union and Confederate Foreign Relations*. Chapel Hill: University of North Carolina Press, 2010.

Jones, Virgil Carrington. *The Civil War at Sea*. New York: Holt, Rinehart, Winston, 1960.

de Kerchove, René. *International Maritime Dictionary*. 2nd ed., privately printed.

Kinnaman, Stephen Chapin. *Captain Bulloch: The Life of James Dunwoody Bulloch, Naval Agent of the Confederacy*. Indianapolis, IN: Dog Ear Publishing, 2013.

Langley, Harold D. *Social Reform in the United States Navy, 1798–1862*. Urbana: University of Illinois Press, 1967.

Letters and Documents Relating to the Claim of the Owners, Officers, and Crew of the Ship Harvest *Captured by the* Shenandoah. Washington, DC: Committee on Foreign Relations, United States Senate, August 1, 1984.

Lining, Charles E., Journal. Eleanor S. Brokenbrough Library, Museum of the Confederacy, Richmond, VA.

Luraghi, Raimondo. *A History of the Confederate Navy*. Annapolis, MD: Naval Institute Press, 1996.

MacGregor, David R. *Fast Sailing Ships: Their Design and Construction, 1775–1875*. 2nd ed. Annapolis, MD: Naval Institute Press, 1988.

———. *The Tea Clippers: Their History and Development, 1833–1875*. 2nd ed. Annapolis, MD: Naval Institute Press, 1983.

Mahan, Captain A. T. *The Influence of Sea Power upon History, 1660–1783*. Boston: Little, Brown and Company, 1890.

Mahin, Dean B. *One War at a Time: The International Dimensions of the American Civil War*. Washington, DC: Brassey's, 1999.

Mason, John T., Journal. Eleanor S. Brokenbrough Library, Museum of the Confederacy, Richmond, VA.

Maury, M. F. *The Physical Geography of the Sea*. 2nd. ed. New York: Harper and Brothers, 1856.

McKay, Gary. *The Sea King: The Life of James Iredell Waddell*. Edinburgh: Birlinn Limited, 2009.

McKenna, Robert. *The Dictionary of Nautical Literacy*. Camden, ME: International Marine, 2001.

Melville, Herman. *White-Jacket; or, The World in a Man-of-War*. Reprint. Annapolis, MD: Naval Institute Press, 1988.

Merli, Frank J. *Great Britain and the Confederate Navy, 1861–1865*. Bloomington: Indiana University Press, 2004.

Milton, David Hepburn. *Lincoln's Spymaster: Thomas Haines Dudley and the Liverpool Network*. Mechanicsburg, PA: Stackpool Books, 2003.

Moebs, Thomas Truxtun. *Confederate States Navy Research Guide: Confederate Naval Imprints Described and Annotated, Chronology of Naval Operation and Administration, Marine Corps and Naval Officer biographies, Description and Service of Vessels, Subject Bibliography. Specifically Compiled for Collectors, Historians and Librarians*. Williamsburg, VA: Moebs, 1991.

Moran, Benjamin. *The Journal of Benjamin Moran, 1857–1865*. 2 vols. Chicago: University of Chicago Press, 1948–49.

Murphy, Dallas. *Rounding the Horn: Being the Story of Williwaws and Windjammers, Drake, Darwin, Murdered Missionaries and Naked Natives—A Deck's-Eye View of Cape Horn*. New York: Basic Books, 2004.

Murphy, John McLeod, and W. N. Jeffers Jr. *Nautical Routine and Stowage: With Short Rules in Navigation*. New York: Henry Spear, 1849.

Nagel, Paul C. *The Lees of Virginia: Seven Generations of an American Family*. Oxford: Oxford University Press, 1990.

Neff, Stephen C. *War and the Law of Nations.* Cambridge: Cambridge University Press, 2005.

Official Records of the Union and Confederate Navies in the War of the Rebellion. Series 1, vols. 1–27, Series 2, vols. 1–3. Washington, DC: U.S. Government Printing Office, 1894–1922.

Owsley, Frank Lawrence, Jr. *The C.S.S.* Florida: *Her Building and Operations.* Tuscaloosa: University of Alabama Press, 1965.

"Papers Relating to Foreign Affairs, Great Britain." In *Executive Documents Printed by Order of the House of Representatives during the First Session of the Thirty-Ninth Congress, 1865–66.* Vol. 1, No.1, Part 1. Washington, DC: U.S. Government Printing Office, 1866.

Pearl, Cyril. *Rebel Down Under: When the* Shenandoah *Shook Melbourne, 1865.* Melbourne: William Heinemann, 1970.

Perret, Geoffrey. *Lincoln's War: The Untold Story of American's Greatest President as Commander in Chief.* New York: Random House, 2004.

Petrie, Donald A. *The Prize Game: Lawful Looting on the High Seas in the Days of Fighting Sail.* Annapolis, MD: Naval Institute Press, 1999.

Phillips-Birt, Douglas. *A History of Seamanship.* Garden City, NY: Doubleday, 1971.

Pohnpei, Between Time and Tide. http://www.pohnpeiheaven.com (no longer active).

"Pohnpei (Southeast), Topographic Map of the Island of." Washington, DC: U.S. Geological Survey, 2001.

Pollard, Edward A. *The Lost Cause: A New Southern History of the War of the Confederates.* New York: E. B. Treat and Co., 1867.

Ramold, Steven J. *Slaves, Sailors, Citizens: African Americans in the Union Navy.* DeKalb, IL: Northern Illinois University Press, 2002.

Ranger, Robin. "The Anglo-French Wars 1689–1815." In Colin S. Gray and Roger W. Barnett, eds. *Seapower and Strategy.* Annapolis, MD: Naval Institute Press, 1989.

Reagan, John H. "Flight and Capture of Jefferson Davis." In *The Annals of the War, Written by Leading Participants North and South, Originally Published in the* Philadelphia Weekly Times, 147–59. Edison, NJ: Blue and Gray Press, 1996.

Riling, Ray, and Robert Halter. *Uniform and Dress, Army and Navy, of the Confederate States of America: A facsimile reproduction from the original regulation of the Confederacy and other authoritative sources.* New Hope, PA: privately printed, 1952.

Ringle, Dennis J. *Life in Mr. Lincoln's Navy.* Annapolis, MD: Naval Institute Press, 1998.

Robinson, William Morrison, Jr., *The Confederate Privateers.* Columbia: University of South Carolina Press, 1928.

Rogers, John G. *Origins of Sea Terms.* Boston: Nimrod Press, 1984.

Schooler, Lynn. *The Last Shot: The Incredible Story of the CSS* Shenandoah *and the True Conclusion of the American Civil War.* New York: Harper Collins, 2005.

Schroeder, John H. *Shaping a Maritime Empire: The Commercial and Diplomatic Role of the American Navy, 1829–1861.* Westport, CT: Greenwood Press, 1985.

Semmes, Raphael. *The Cruise of the* Alabama *and the* Sumter: *From the Private Journals and Other Papers of Commander R. Semmes, C.S.N., and Other Officers.* New York: Carleton, 1864.

———. *Memoirs of Service Afloat during the War between the States.* Baltimore, MD: Kelly, Piet and Company, 1869.

Shingleton, Royce. *High Seas Confederate: The Life and Times of John Newland Maffitt.* Columbia: University of South Carolina Press, 1994.

Silverstone, Paul H. *Warships of the Civil War Navies.* Annapolis, MD: Naval Institute Press, 1989.

Sinclair, Arthur. *Two Years on the* Alabama. Boston: Lee and Shepard, 1895.

Smyth, W. H. *The Sailor's Word-Book: An Alphabetical Digest of Nautical Terms.* Reprint, Ontario: Algrove, 2004. First published 1867 by London: Blackie and Son, Paternoster Row.

Spencer, Warren F. *The Confederate Navy in Europe.* Tuscaloosa: University of Alabama Press, 1983.

———. *Raphael Semmes: The Philosophical Mariner.* Tuscaloosa: University of Alabama Press, 1997.

Starbuck, Alexander. *History of the American Whale Fishery.* Reprint, New Jersey: Castle Books, 1989.

Still, William N., Jr., ed. *The Confederate Navy: The Ships, Men and Organization, 1861–65.* Annapolis, MD: Naval Institute Press, 1997.

Summersell, Charles G. *The Journal of George Townley Fullam, Boarding Officer of the Confederate Sea Raider* Alabama. Tuscaloosa: University of Alabama Press, 1973.

Terrill, Ross. *The Australians.* New York: Simon and Schuster, 1987.

Todorich, Charles. *The Spirited Years: A History of the Antebellum Naval Academy.* Annapolis, MD: Naval Institute Press, 1984.

Tucker, Spencer C. *Blue & Gray Navies: The Civil War Afloat.* Annapolis, MD: Naval Institute Press, 2006.

Valle, James E. *Rocks & Shoals: Naval Discipline in the Age of Fighting Sail.* Annapolis, MD: Naval Institute Press, 1980.

Vanauken, Sheldon. *The Glittering Illusion: English Sympathy for the Southern Confederacy.* Washington, DC: Regnery Gateway, 1989.

van Creveld, Martin. *Technology and War: From 2000 B.C. to the Present.* New York: Free Press, 1989.

The Visual Encyclopedia of Nautical Terms Under Sail. New York: Crown Publishers, 1978.

Waddell, James I. "Abstract log of C.S.S. *Shenandoah,* Lieutenant Commanding J. I. Waddell, C.S. Navy, commanding, October 20, 1864–November 5, 1865." In *The Official Records of the Union and Confederate Navies in the War of the Rebellion.* Vol. 1, 3:785–92. Washington, DC: U.S. Government Printing Office, 1896.

———. "Extracts from notes on the C.S.S. *Shenandoah* by her commander, James Iredell Waddell, C.S. Navy." In *The Official Records of the Union and Confederate Navies in the War of the Rebellion.* Vol. 1, 3:792–836. Washington, DC: U.S. Government Printing Office, 1896.

Welles, Gideon. *Diary of Gideon Welles: Secretary of the Navy under Lincoln and Johnson.* 3 vols. Boston: Houghton Mifflin, 1911.

Wells, Tom Henderson. *The Confederate Navy: A Study in Organization.* Tuscaloosa: University of Alabama Press, 1971.

Whittle, William C., Jr. "The Cruise of the *Shenandoah.*" *Confederate Veteran* 12 (1904): 489–90.

———. "The Cruise of the *Shenandoah.*" *Southern Historical Society Papers* 35 (1907): 235–58.

———. *The Voyage of the CSS* Shenandoah: A Memorable Cruise. Introduction and annotations by D. Alan Harris and Anne B. Harris. Tuscaloosa: University of Alabama Press, 2005. (Original journal at the Eleanor S. Brokenbrough Library, Museum of the Confederacy, Richmond, VA. A typescript copy at the Virginia Historical Society, Richmond, VA.)

Williams, Paul. *The* Shenandoah *Affair.* Rydalmere NSW, Australia: Hodder and Stoughton, 1992.

Wilson, James Harrison. "How Jefferson Davis Was Overtaken." In *Annals of the War, Written by Leading Participants North and South, Originally Published in the* Philadelphia Weekly Times, 554–89. Edison, NJ: Blue and Gray Press, 1996.

Wilson, Walter E., and Gary L. McKay. *James D. Bulloch: Secret Agent and Mastermind of the Confederate Navy.* Jefferson, NC: McFarland & Company, Inc., 2012

Index

Abigail, 161–62, 167–68

Adams, Charles Francis: on Britain and Confederate ships, 20, 22; on Britain and piracy, 206–7; on Confederate operations in England, 15; reports for, 49–50, 51; on *Sea King*, 46; on *Shenandoah*, 197, 204–5

Adelaide, 45–46, 76

Aerial, 59

Age (Melbourne newspaper), 84–85, 91–92, 93–94, 99, 103, 109–10, 117

Alabama, CSS: in British colonial ports, 84–85; as British-built, 4; building, 9–10; Bulloch and, 14–15; Cape Town visit by, 55–56; commerce raiding and, 15–16; international maritime laws and, 83; *Jamestown* on lookout for, 119; Northern newspapers on, 74; prize courts on board, 32; tribunal arbitrating claims by, 211; veterans, later work by, 2, 20, 23; *Wampanoag* and, 213

Albert Edward, 102

alcohol, 63, 102, 162, 163, 170, 191, 198. *See also* rum

Alcott, Henry, 96, 177

Aleutian Islands, 182

Alexandra, 111–12

Alina, 31–34, 43

America, 186

Amukta Pass, 182

Anna Jane, 43

Antarctic, U.S. Exploring Expedition (1838–42) to, 17, 19

Archer, William, 47

Arctic Circle, 176, 179, 180

Argus (Melbourne newspaper): on Civil War, 91–92; on Darling's cabinet meeting, 83; on Semmes, 119; on *Shenandoah* controversy, 104, 110, 113, 123; on *Shenandoah*

deserters, 118; on Union government, 95; Waddell's correspondence in, 121

Arkansas, CSS, 30

Ascension Island, 135

Ashley, E. R., 175

Atlanta, CSS, 30

Australia: belligerents' rights in, 83; colonial legislature debate on *Shenandoah*, 99–100. *See also* Melbourne, Australia

Baker, George O., 140

Barker, Frederick, 170

Barracouta, 186, 202

Barron, Samuel, 21, 22, 86–87

Bayman, Robert, 7

Behucke, Charles, 107

The Bells (Poe), 123

Benjamin, Captain, 174

Benjamin Cummings, 175

Bering Sea, 5, 169–70, 179, 181; *Shenandoah*'s prizes in, 171–78

Bill, William, 199

Black Eagle (steam tug), 111

Blacker, John C., 124–25, 127, 198

Blackstone, on fundamental principles of law, 26

Blanchard, William: on admiralty court and *Shenandoah*, 100, 101; Darling's response to, 97; Foreign Enlistment Act and, 106; group boarding after Melbourne departure and, 119–20; police court for stowaways and, 118; on *Shenandoah*, 87, 111, 118–19; *Shenandoah*'s captured seamen and, 88; as U.S. consul in Melbourne, 85–86

blockade runners, 14. *See also under* United States

Bombay, RMS, 82, 85–86, 121

Brazil, *Shenandoah* banned from, 67–68

Brooke, John Mercer, 17, 19, 21, 22, 136

Brosman, James, 148

Brown, Georgia governor, 103

Browne, Midshipman, 48, 50, 63, 75, 195

Bruce, William, 36, 42, 48

Brunswick, 176, 177

Bulloch, Irvine Stephens: *Delphine* taking and, 69; equator crossing and, 49; final destination decision and, 195, 197; French leave by, 205; head wound, 159; on ice risks, 166; illness of, 76–77; on junior officers vs. Waddell, 12; later life and career of, 210; in Melbourne, 96, 105; previous experience of, 29; as sailing master, 14; *Sea King* transfer and, 20–21; on stowaways, 111; wrestling with Lining, 57

Bulloch, James Dunwoody: *Alabama* and, 10; Civil War end and, 171; on Confederate flag on ships, 16; on further Confederate ships, 23; letter to Waddell, 193; pay for officers and crew and, 190; *Sea King* purchase and, 14, 19

Calabar, 46

Canning, George P., 125, 199

Cape Howe, Australia, 125–26

Cape Leeuwin, Australia, 75, 79

Cape of Good Hope, Africa. *See* roaring forties

Cape Otway, Australia, 80

cape pigeon, 58

Cape Town, 55–56, 85, 189–90, 192, 194, 195–97

Carter, Robert, 14, 16, 17, 19, 21, 95

Catherine, 175

Cedar Creek, Battle of, 13

Chambers, Mr., 113

channel fever, 200

Charley (cook), 107–8, 111, 113, 114, 118

Charter Oak, 37–39

Chase, Amos A., 140

Cheek, Lieutenant, 203

Chew, Francis Thornton: birthday, 192, 194–95; on crew, 71, 124; on cruise, 130–31, 166, 183–84, 195–96, 200–201; departs *Shenandoah*, 207; on Drummond Island natives, 133; equator crossing and, 48;

journal entries by, 155; later life of, 210; in Liverpool, 203; in Melbourne, 90, 96, 117, 122; navigating duties for, 77, 80; on Pohnpei, 137, 141, 148–49, 151; previous experience of, 29–30; prize ships and, 31, 32, 33–34, 43, 45, 138–39, 146–48, 178; on questions about Semmes, 84; seasickness of, 161; on *Shenandoah*'s guns, 25; on Staples, 36; storms and, 65, 158, 159; as unlucky soul, 57; on visitors on board, 89; Waddell's lack of confidence in, 61–62, 75, 129; watchstanding by, 63; on women on board, 38, 44–45, 72

Chickamauga, 104

Christmas (1864), 64, 65, 66–67

Civil War: assessing news about, 104–5; in 1864, Union concerns about, 18; end of, 149–50; *guerre de course* and, 3–4; Melbournians on, 93; news of, 102–4, 145, 167, 170–71, 186–87; progress of, 122–23, 138; Richmond retreat and, 147; uncertainty on end of, 173–74

Clarendon, Earl of, 207

Clark, James, 175

coal supplies, 118–19, 127, 129–30

Cogan, Barney, 173

Colorado, 185

Commentaries on International Law (Phillimore), 26

commerce raiding, 3–4, 15–18, 211–13

composite ships, 14, 19

Confederate States navy, 8, 17, 111–12. *See also specific ships*

Confederate States of America: Admiralty Court records, 32; international maritime laws and, 82–83; international relations and, 26–27; Melbourne and, 92, 94–95

Congress, 177

Connecticut, USS, 127

Corbett, Peter Suther, 8–9, 10, 11, 20, 21, 46

Covington, 177

Craven, Thomas T., 22, 23

crew: from *Abigail*, 167–68; added outside Melbourne, 124–25; *Alabama*'s, Semmes on, 9–10; from *Alina*, 36; from Bering Sea, 178; Civil War end and, 189; from *Delphine*, 70–71, 88; departing in civilian dress, 205; deserters from, 88, 107, 119;

diversity among, 2; duties of, 51, 79, 148, 155, 183, 198; final destination decision and, 196; full pay for, 207; from *Lizzie M. Stacey*, 47–48; in Melbourne, 90; as not British in Liverpool, 206; pay for, 199–200; from Pohnpei, 148, 152; from prize ships, 41, 106, 115; from prize ships, *Susan Abigail*, 174; return trip and, 198–99; from *Sea King*, 8–11; for *Sea King*, Whittle and, 21; from *Susan*, 44; Whittle's seamanship exercises for, 126

Criterion Hotel, Melbourne, 115–16

The Cruise of the Alabama *and the* Sumter (Semmes), 10, 153

cruising funds, 22

Cutty Sark, 59

Cyane, USS, 28, 62

D. Godfrey, 41–42, 43, 101

Dahlgren, John Adolphus Bernard, 76

Daily Alta Californian, 210

Darling, Charles H., 81, 82–83, 87, 108–9, 113, 121

David Brown, 78

Davidson, James, 118

Davis, Jefferson: anniversary of inauguration, 126; Civil War end and, 150, 174; Confederate navy under, 15; Pohnpeians on, 141, 152; retreat from Richmond and, 147, 173–74

Dea del Mare, 52

Delphine, 69–70, 82, 88, 101

Destin, George, 177

Dewey, George, 28

discipline, 40, 49, 131, 184

Donegal, HMS, 201, 202

Drummond Island, 132–33

Dudley, Thomas H., 14, 49–50, 111–12, 206

Duffett, Grant & Woolcott, 100, 101

Early, Jubal, 13, 103

East Indies, Mallory on commerce raiders and, 18

Easter (1865), 154

"easting" direction, 58–59

Edward (New Bedford bark), 52–53, 68, 76

Edward Carey, 139, 140, 147–48

Eldridge, John P., 140, 141, 213

Eldridge, Sakies, 213

Eli Whitney, 106

Elizabeth I, Queen of England, 211

Ellison, John, 11

equator, 45–49, 130, 133

Eskimos, and their boats, 174

Euphrates, 170, 172

Farragut, David, 30

Favorite, 177

"the flight from the flag," 17

Florida, CSS, 14, 15, 76, 95, 97, 104

fog, 169, 173, 178, 182

Foreign Enlistment Act, British: arrival in Liverpool and, 205; Blanchard on, 111, 112; Corbett and, 46; enforcement of, 16; Higinbotham on, 113; *Laurel* crew and, 11; non-British conflicts and, 106; *Sea King* and, 20; Waddell on, 114

Fourth of July (1865), 181–82

France, *Alabama* sinking and, 16

Francis, James G., 83, 97, 98, 108, 109, 110, 114

Fraser, Trenholm and Co., 19, 22, 117–18

freedmen, enlistment of, 42

French language, speaking or practicing, 50, 90

French leave, 204

Gage, Frank and Mrs., 38, 39

games on board, 62, 130, 156, 169

General Pike, 175, 186

General Williams, 174

German language, practicing, 50

Germany, commerce raiding by, 213

Gillman, Samuel J. and Mrs., 38, 39

Glover, Franklin, 118

goat, from *Delphine*, 70, 71, 72

gold mines, Australian, visit to, 105

Goshawk, 203, 204

Governor Troup, 175

Grant, Ulysses S., 13, 105, 138, 147

Gratitude, 178

Great Britain: *Alabama* and, 9–10; *Alexandra* and, 111–12; Civil War and, 4; Confederacy on recognition by, 26; Confederate prizes and, 34; delivers *Sea King* to Waddell, 8–9; on detaining *Shenandoah*,

192–93; newspapers of, on Civil War, 91–92; Queen's neutrality proclamation for, 82–83; sympathy for Confederacy in, 117; tribunal arbitrating claims by confederate cruisers and, 211; wartime currency exchange rate of, 92. *See also* Foreign Enlistment Act; Liverpool

Great Britain, SS, 119

Green, Peter, 55

Grimball, John: on board *Shenandoah,* 13, 25, 37, 49, 110–11, 195–96; *Alabama* and, 16; on ice risks, 166; illness of, 153; later life and career of, 210; in Melbourne, 81–82, 87, 105, 108; on Mrs. Nichols, 72; Naval Academy and, 28; previous experience of, 29; prize ships and, 33; on recruiting crew, 9, 41; storms and, 65

guerre de course, 211–12

guns: *Shenandoah's,* 25, 42–43, 85, 188; test firing of, 56, 126, 185

Gustave, 173, 174–75

Guy, John L., 25, 49, 63, 96

Gypsey, 175

H. H. Swift & Co. (New York), 76

Hae Hawaii, 173

Hall, Thomas, 40, 88

Halleck, Samuel, 41

Hansen, Captain, 43–44

Harrocke, Thomas, 137, 138, 142, 143, 153

Harvest, 139–41, 150, 152, 213

Harwood, Boatswain, 10

Hawaii, *Harvest* registered in, 140, 141

Hawes, Jonathan C., 172

Hector, 139, 140, 147–48

Helena, 101

Heppingstone, John, 173

Herald (Melbourne newspaper), 91–93, 95–96, 110, 114, 116–17

Higinbotham, George, 101, 108, 113

Hillman, 177

Hong Kong, 17

Hood, John Bell, 103–4, 145

Hopkins, Charles, 47

Hunt, Cornelius E.: on board *Shenandoah,* 34, 48, 58; on *Charter Oak,* 36; on Civil War end, 187; on Drummond Island natives,

133; in Liverpool, 205; in Melbourne, 92; Nichols and, 72, 75; on *Nimrod* captain, 77; on Pohnpei, 146; prize ships and, 41, 70; on recruiting crew, 124; on St. Paul's island, 74–75; on Waddell, 189–90

ice, 164–66, 169–70, 176, 178–79, 180–81, 194

Indian Ocean, 62–66

Industrial Revolution, 3

international maritime laws: belligerents' rights under, 83; bribes for *Shenandoah* deserters and, 88

international relations, Confederacy and, 26–27

Ireland, 200

Iroquois, USS, 57, 68, 76, 121, 138

Isaac Howland, 177

Isabella, 175

Isohkelekel, 151

Jackson, Thomas, 107

James Maury, 177

Jamestown, USS, 119, 121, 157

Jeanne Payne, 82

Jireh Swift, 172–73

John Boy, 167, 184

John Fraser, 117–18, 119

Kamchatka Peninsula, 160, 161

Kate Prince, 44–45, 51, 67–68

Kearsarge, USS, 7, 16

Kennedy, D. S., 106

Kennedy, George, 106

King, Commander, 82, 87

Kohola, 173

Kuril Islands, 160, 169. *See also* Okhotsk, Sea of

Laird rams, 14–15, 16, 112

Langland Brothers & Co. (marine engineers), 97

Laurel, HMS, 6–8, 12, 20, 21, 101

Lee, Robert E., 86, 103, 105, 138; surrender by, *Shenandoah* and, 5, 149–50, 173–74

Lee, Sidney Smith, Jr.: equator crossing and, 49; final destination decision and, 195–96;

French leave by, 205; on ice risks, 166; joking by, 57; later life of, 210; in Melbourne, 98–99, 100, 110–11; Mrs. Nichols and, 79; previous experience of, 29, 30; prize ships and, 44, 146–47, 172; storms and, 65; stowaway crew for, 124; Waddell and, 191; whalers at Pohnpei and, 139

Libby, Henry, 44, 45, 51, 67

Lincoln, Abraham: assassination of, 170; election of 1864 and, 18, 86; on international interference in Civil War, 212; on Navy in Civil War, 146; privateering vs. blockading, 15; Richmond retreat and, 147; second inauguration of, 128

Lining, Charles E., 7; blues of, 182, 184; on British mail ship, 78–79, 86; channel fever and, 200; cheerful mood of, 26; on Civil War end, 187; clothes washing and, 37; on Confederate flag on *Shenandoah*, 12–13; on cruise's first month, 42; departs *Shenandoah*, 207; on Drummond Island natives, 133; equator crossing and, 49; final destination decision and, 195, 196, 197; gifts from Ramsay to, 8; journal entries by, 51, 72, 75, 76–77, 154–55; later life and career of, 210; leisure activities of, 56, 62, 182; in Melbourne, 87, 89, 94, 98–99, 100, 105, 110–11, 119; on Melbourne visit, 80, 96, 122; Mrs. Nichols and, 79; Nichols and, 75; ocean observations, 55, 159–60; previous experience of, 30; prize ships and, 33, 45, 70, 167–68; return trip and, 191; on rolling ships, 57; on *Shenandoah*'s crew, 12; on stowaways, 124; uniforms on deck and, 49; on Waddell, 28–29, 61–62; on weather, 64–65, 161; on Whittle swallowing glass, 39–40; on women captured, 38; on Worth, 54

Liverpool: arrival in, 202–4; Confederate naval branch in, 15, 23; as final destination, 188, 189–90, 192, 195–97; *Laurel* departs from, 22; shipbuilding in, 14, 19, 20. See also Bulloch, James Dunwoody; Dudley, Thomas H.

Lizzie M. Stacey (schooner), 47, 68, 76, 101

Lloyd's of London, 6, 14

Lohd Pah Harbor, 137, 213

loose cannon, 129

Lord, Samuel, 107

Louisiana, 178

Lynch, Assistant Carpenter, 63

Lyttleton, Police Superintendent, 108, 111

Mackenzie, William, 118

Madden, Walter, 107, 108

Maguire, James, 92

Maguire, Matthew, 14

Mahan, A. T., 211

Mallory, Stephen: Bulloch and, 14–15; on Cape of Good Hope, 59; Civil War end and, 150; on commerce raiders, 15–19, 212; on Richmond retreat, 147; on safety, 23; on Union whaling fleet, 17; Waddell's report to, 87

Malvern, USS, 146

Manning, Thomas S., 168, 180

Maria Ross, 119–20

Marryat, Frederick, 6

Martha (Second), 177

Mason, James, 171

Mason, John Thomson: on cargo transfer to *Sea King*, 8; on Chew's watchstanding, 75; on deserters, 107–8; equator crossing and, 48; final destination decision and, 196; journal entries by, 7, 24, 62, 86, 155–56; later life and career of, 210; on *Laurel*'s departure, 12; leisure activities of, 50, 72, 153, 164, 184; in Melbourne, 98–101, 106–7; on Melbourne visit, 96, 117; on Pacific voyage, 132; on Pohnpei, 146, 149; prize ships and, 33, 36, 69–70, 71, 168, 178; on recruiting crew, 11; as sailor, 192; storms and, 64, 65–66, 158–59; on stowaway crew, 124; on Tristan da Cunha, 55; on Waddell, 10, 189; whalers at Pohnpei and, 139

Maury, Matthew Fontaine, 19–20

McClellan, George, 18, 104, 212

McNulty, Francis J., 48, 72, 96, 161, 191, 196, 198

Melbourne, Australia: after *Shenandoah* departure, 123; belligerents' rights in, 83; British mail ship visits to, 78–79; Civil War loyalties in, 93–94; geography and founding, 91; group boarding after departure from, 119–20; news gathering and speculation in, 84; Queen's neutrality proclamation and, 82–83; *Shenandoah* arrives in, 80–81; *Shenandoah* bombing plot in, 210–11; *Shenandoah* in, 4, 82–83, 88, 89, 92. See also *Age*; *Argus*; *Herald*; *Shenandoah*

Melbourne Club, 98–99

Memoirs of Service Afloat (Semmes), 1

Michie, Archibald, 101

Milo, 172, 173, 185

Minerva, 175

Minnesota, USS, 107

Minor, John F., 61, 63, 75, 164, 168

mosquito fleet, at Port Royal Sound, South Carolina, 29

Mother Carey's Chickens, 58

Mustang (bark), 210

Nahnmwarki of Madolenihmw, 143

Nan Madol (Pohnpei ruin), 151

Nashville, CSS, 28

Nassau, 177

Naval Academy, 2, 3, 27–28, 29, 209

naval profession, technological changes in, 3

Navy, U.S.: commerce raiding and, 3–4; enlisting freedmen and "contrabands" in, 42; notified of *Sea King*'s sale, 46; *Shenandoah*'s officers and, 2; Waddell and, 9, 28

Nearchos, 213

neutral rights, 22

neutrality proclamation, Queen's, 82–83

New Caledonia, storm off, 128–29

New England fishing industry, 17–18, 23, 172. See also whalers and whaling

New Orleans, Battle of, 30

New Year's Eve (1865), 73–74

New Zealand, pressing toward, 127

newspapers: on *Alabama*, 74; British, on Civil War, 91–92; from North and South, in Melbourne, 102–4; on *Sea King*, 23. See also *Age*; *Argus*; *Herald*

Niagara, USS, 22

Nichols, Irving, 70, 82

Nichols, Lillias: admiralty court deposition by, 101; departs *Shenandoah*, 82; as

prisoner on board *Shenandoah*, 69, 70, 71–72, 74, 75, 77–78, 79

Nichols, Phineas, 69, 70, 82

Nichols, William Green, 69–70, 72, 75, 79, 82, 85–86

Nile, 177

Nimrod, 77, 78, 110

Nimrod (whaler), 175

North British Daily Mail, 14

North Pacific Exploring Expedition, 136

Northern newspapers, 23, 74. See also newspapers

Nye, Ebenezer, 161–62, 167, 168, 173, 174

O'Brien, Eugene Matthew, 52, 55, 56, 128, 197

Ocean Rover, 175

officers: Civil War end and, 189–90; disaffection for Waddell, 127–28; eye infection among, 131, 132; French leave by, 204; junior, Waddell and, 12; Liverpool arrival and, 203–4; in Melbourne, 90, 98, 109; pay for, 199–200; previous experience of, 29–30; *Shenandoah*'s, 1–2. See also specific officers

Okhotsk, Sea of, 160, 163–68

Onekotan Island (in Kurils), 160, 161

Onward, USS, 67, 68

O'Shea, John, 24

Osprey, 102

Pacific: Bulloch on route to, 21–22; Mallory on commerce raiders and, 18; North Pacific Exploring Expedition, 136; northeast trades in, 133, 135; northern, 169; northwestern, 160–61; traveling across, 128–33, 153–56, 182–86; U.S. Exploring Expedition to, 17, 19. See also specific islands

Palmetto State, CSS, 30

Payne, Charles B., 93

Paynter, Captain, 203, 205–6

Pearl (of New London), 138–39, 140, 146–47

Pearson, Admiral, 157

Pearson, G. F., 186

Pendergrast, Mr., 45–46

Penniman, Edward, 175

Perry, Matthew C., 2, 17, 29
Petropavlovski, 170
Pfiel (trading schooner), 134
Phillimore, Robert, 26, 205
The Physical Geography of the Sea (Maury), 20
pigs, from *Delphine*, 70, 71
pilot boat, 201
plankton, in South Atlantic, 52
Pohnpei (Pacific island): castaways on, 137–38; Chew's visit to ruins on, 150–51; chiefs and society on, 143–45; conflict on, 136–37; history of, 135–36; natives pick prize whalers clean, 146; natives visit *Shenandoah*, 141–43; *Shenandoah* departs, 153; *Shenandoah* visit to, 4–5, 137–38, 148–49, 213; Waddell visits chief, 151–52; whalers at, 138–41, 146–48
Polk, Leonidas, 125
Poor, Commodore, 157
Porter, David, 145, 146, 147
Portuguese fishermen, *Shenandoah* and, 8, 13
Price, Captain, 157
Prioleau, Charles K., 19
prisoners: from *Abigail*, 162, 163–64; crew recruited from, 41; from *Delphine*, 69, 70, 71–72, 74, 75, 77–78, 79; from *General Pike*, 175; *James Maury* loaded with, 177; management of, 40–41, 53, 70–71, 125; from *Milo*, 172; parole form for, 79; put ashore in Melbourne, 82, 98; put ashore on Tristan da Cunha, 54, 55; transferred to *Milo*, 173
privateers, 15, 83, 94, 211, 212–13
prize money: for *Abigail*, 162; for Bering Sea whalers, 177; for *Charter Oak* and *D. Godfrey*, 41; crew for *Shenandoah* and, 11; as cruising funds, 22; for *Delphine*, 70; for *Kate Prince*, 45; for *Lizzie M. Stacey*, 47; Semmes on, 10; *Shenandoah*'s original cost and, 74; for *Susan* of New York, 43; for whalers at Pohnpei, 139–40
propeller, *Shenandoah*'s, 55–56, 78, 79, 97

Quinlin, Francis, 115

Ramsay, John F., 8, 10, 11, 12, 20
Rappahannock, CSS, 11
Redfield, Captain, 173
Reid, Master-at-Arms, 49, 118
Rennie, William, 59
revolutionaries: *Shenandoah*'s officers as, 2
roaring forties (below Cape of Good Horn), 58–62, 193–94
Robert Towns, 170
Rodgers, C. R., 57, 68, 76, 121, 122, 138
rum, 126, 128. *See also* alcohol
Russell, Captain, 157
Russell, Earl, 197
Russell, John, 50

Sacramento, USS, 22, 102
sails, *Shenandoah*'s: Cape of Good Hope and, 57, 59; close-hauled, 72; crew handling, 125; departing Melbourne and, 125; ice and, 165, 180; managing, 24, 25, 47–48, 51; reducing, 63–64; repairs to, 184; squalls and, 37; storms and, 64–65, 128–29, 133; wearing, 154, 158
San Francisco Bulletin, 162–63, 175, 185
Saranac, 186
Saudeleurs, on Pohnpei, 151
Scales, Dabney Minor: on Civil War end, 187; final destination decision and, 195–96; on ice risks, 166; illness of, 161; later life and career of, 210; in Melbourne, 87, 94, 98–99, 100, 106–7; near miss with bark on opposite tack and, 51; previous experience of, 29–30; Waddell and, 61, 131–32, 191; watchstanding by, 63
Scott's Hotel, Melbourne, 92
scurvy, 199, 203, 205
Sea King: Blanchard on, 112; launching of, 14; maiden voyage of, 19; Melbourne *Age* on, 84; named erased from, 30; Northern newspapers on, 23; as potential Confederate cruiser, 16, 18–19; transferring *Laurel* cargo to, 7–8; U.S. Consul and, 20–21, 22
Sears, W. Q., 210
seawater, rainwater vs., 37
Seeadler, 213
Semmes, Raphael: Adams on *Sea King* and, 46; on *Alabama*'s commissioning, 9–10;

Civil War end and, 150; on condemning a ship or cargo, 32; on *Florida* rammed in Bahia harbor, 95; on government protection for whalers, 121–22; ironclads under, 146, 147; on privateering and the Confederacy, 15; recruitment issues for, 115; sailing on *Laurel*, 22–23; as *Shenandoah*'s commander, 50, 76, 84; on ship's cruise as biography, 1, 5; on *Sumter* deserters at Cadiz, 88; on U.S. vessels' distinctiveness, 31

Seward, William H., 20, 46, 100, 104, 170, 206–7

Shenandoah, CSS: abandoned to British, 5, 208, 209; *Adelaide* and, 45–46; Arctic Circle and, 176, 179; Australia's debate on, 99–100; bickering on board, 198; British empire and, 4; as British tea clipper, 59; Civil War end and, 187–88; Confederate flag raised on, 12–13; confusion during early days on board, 24–25; deaths on board, 199; engine problem, 25; equator crossing by, 48–49, 130, 133; guerilla warfare mission of, 3–4; heritage of, 2–3; *Laurel* rendezvous and, 6–8; in Liverpool, 201–8; in Melbourne, 109, 116–23; Melbourne visitors on board, 82–83, 88, 89; obfuscating name of, 50, 52; officers on board, 1–2; orders to desist offensive operations sent to, 171; personnel list with places of origin, 206–7; Pohnpei visit, 137–41; prize ships and, 31–34, 37–39, 41, 53; relationships on board, 30; repairs to, 97, 98, 101, 102; speed, 30–31, 193; supplies for, 97–98; warlike elements removed from, 188–89; watchstanding lieutenants on board, 29–30. *See also* crew; ice; officers; propeller; sails; Waddell, James Iredell

Shenandoah Valley, Virginia, burning of, 13
Sheridan, Philip, 13, 103, 105
Sherman, William Tecumseh, 103, 145, 212
ships, sinking of, sailors on, 34
Siberia, 176
Silvester, George, 101
Sinclair, Arthur, 96, 167
smallpox, 175

Smith, Breedlove, 31–32, 98–99, 100, 105, 192, 195, 197
Smith, F. C., 170
Sophia Thornton, 172, 173
St. George's Channel, 200
St. Mary's, USS, 162–63
St. Paul (volcanic island), 74–75
Staples, Everett, 31–33, 34, 35, 36, 43
steam gunboats, 29–30
Stephens, Alexander, 104
Stevenson, Joseph, 148
Stonewall (ironclad), 102, 127
storms: Indian Ocean, 64–67; Mason on tiresomeness of, 192; off New Caledonia, 128–29; in Pacific, 156, 158–59, 184–85; in Sea of Okhotsk, 164–65. *See also* roaring forties
stowaways, 111, 114–15, 118
Sumter, 15, 32, 88
Susan, 43, 101
Susan Abigail, 173–74
Suwanee (gunboat), 76, 121, 186
Swasey, J. B., 101
Sylvester, George, 40

Tallahassee, 104
Tausk Bay, near Siberia, 166
Thermopylae, 59
Thomson, Edwin P., 140
Trent, 97
Tristan da Cunha, South Atlantic, 52–55
Tuft, Francis, 53
Tuscaloosa, CSS, 17

Uncle Tom's Cabin, 82
United States: blockade of Southern ports, 15, 34, 212; Exploring Expedition (1838–42), 17; wartime currency exchange rate of, 92
United States Consul: secret ship inspection system of, 20; on taking *Laurel*, 23

Vaulpré, Captain, 173, 174–75
venereal disease, 199
Victoria (Australia's first warship), 110, 117
Victoria, queen of England, 82–83

Wachusett, USS, 95, 119

Waddell, Ann Sellman Inglehart, 27, 60, 209

Waddell, Annie, 27

Waddell, James Iredell: arrests Guy, 96; Articles of War read by, 39, 74, 130, 181; birthday, 184; Blacker and, 124–25; British empire and, 4; on Chew, 61–62, 75, 80; Civil War end and, 5, 171, 187–89; crew issues for, 8–9, 10–11, 41–42, 108–9, 205–6; equator crossing and, 49; final report of, 207–8; later life and career of, 209; leisure activities, 72; in Melbourne, 87, 97–99, 110–11, 113–14, 120; Melbourne newspapers and, 84, 85, 86; Melbourne visit and, 81–82; on midshipmen's training journals, 50; on morale after *Alina* capture, 36; Mrs. Nichols and, 71–72; paying officers and crew, 199–200; on Pohnpei, 141–42, 146, 149, 151–52; previous wartime experience, 29–30; prisoners to *Anna Jane*, 43; prize ships and, 31–33, 34, 70, 77, 140–41, 175–76, 177–78; report to Mallory by, 87; return trip and, 191, 195–96, 198; on Scales, 61–62; *Sea King* purchase and, 8, 21, 22; as *Shenandoah*'s captain, 6–7, 9, 11–12, 25–27, 202–5; at St. Paul's island, 74; storms and, 67, 158, 159; watchkeeping and, 161; Whittle and, 27–28, 126–27

Waddell, USS, 213

Walke, Henry, 102

Walmsley, Arthur, 118

Wampanoag, USS, 212–13

Warwick, Mr. (paymaster), 205, 206

Washington, George, 126

water issues, 198

Wateree, USS, 157

Watie, Stand, 174

Waverly, 176–77

Webb, Minister, 68

Welles, Gideon, 57, 60, 76, 119, 121, 157, 212

Welsh, James, 148

West, William, 66

West Australian, 193

West Indies, Mallory on commerce raiders and, 18

West Point, 27

Weymouth, of Melbourne, 96, 102

whalers and whaling: American, at Strong Island, 134; in Bering Sea, 171–78; decline in, 212; Mallory on, 18; Maury charts and, 19–20; Minor and, 164; in Pacific, 157; at Pohnpei, 138–40; in Sea of Okhotsk, 161–62; Semmes on, 121–22; *Shenandoah* and, 5; South Atlantic and, 52–53; U.S. Exploring Expedition (1838–42) and, 17; Waddell hunting for, 131

White, Francis Maloney, 100

Whittle, Pattie, 46, 56

Whittle, William Conway, Jr.: on action for *Shenandoah*, 11–12; *Alabama* and, 16; on British mail ship in Melbourne, 78–79; Bulloch on hiding *Sea King* until transfer, 21; on Cape of Good Hope, 59; on cheerful mood on board *Shenandoah*, 26; on Civil War, 145, 170–71; on Civil War end, 86, 186–87; on converting *Sea King* to *Shenandoah*, 8, 36–37; on crew, 47–48, 130; departs *Shenandoah*, 207; on discipline, 40; early life and training, 28; *Favorite*'s master's threats and, 177; gun spaces and, 42–43; on ice risks, 166; illness of, 49; Indian Ocean storm and, 65–66; inebriated, 102; journal of, 24; later life and career of, 209; leisure activities of, 155; in Melbourne, 87–88, 90, 110–11; Mrs. Nichols and, 77–78; on New Year's dinner 1865, 74; optimism on *Shenandoah*'s condition by, 51; previous wartime experience, 30; prize ships and, 31–32, 35, 44, 45, 70, 71, 127–28, 178; return trip and, 192, 195–97; on *Shenandoah* as symbol, 13; Sunday inspections by, 50; Sundays for, 184; swallows glass bottle neck, 39–40; on Tristan da Cunha, 54–55; *Uncle Tom's Cabin* and, 82; on visitors on board, 89; Waddell and, 27, 28, 29, 61, 126–27, 131; watchstanding, 63; on wind rolling the ship about, 57; on women captured, 39

Wicker, Hermann, 107

William C. Nye, 175

William Gifford, 173
William Thompson, 170, 172
Williams, Captain, 172–73
Williams, James P., 45, 46
Williams, John, 41–42, 47, 106, 107
Williamstown battery, Melbourne, 109–10
women: prize ships and, 37, 38, 44–45, 72.
    See also Nichols, Lillias

Worth, Charles, 53, 54, 55
Wright, Richard, 19, 21
Wyoming, USS, 121

Young, Thomas G., 177

About the Author

Dwight Hughes graduated from the U.S. Naval Academy in 1967 and served twenty years as a surface warfare officer in ship types from destroyer to aircraft carrier and with river forces in Vietnam. Applying a lifetime of study in naval history, he seeks to translate a love of the sea and ships into a better understanding of our naval heritage.